1/in Center Point 37 oo

born
bright

Center Point
Large Print

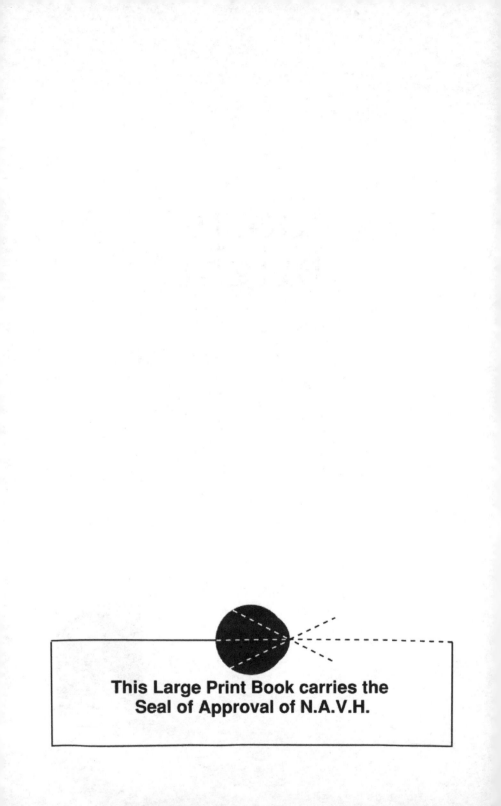

**This Large Print Book carries the
Seal of Approval of N.A.V.H.**

born bright

······················

a young girl's
journey
from nothing
to something
in america

······················

C. NICOLE
MASON

CENTER POINT LARGE PRINT
THORNDIKE, MAINE

This Center Point Large Print edition is published
in the year 2017 by arrangement with St. Martin's Press.

The text of this Large Print edition is unabridged.
In other aspects, this book may vary
from the original edition.
Printed in the United States of America
on permanent paper.
Set in 16-point Times New Roman type.

ISBN: 978-1-68324-234-5

Library of Congress Cataloging-in-Publication Data

Names: Mason, C. Nicole, 1976– author.
Title: Born bright : a young girl's journey from nothing to something
in America / C. Nicole Mason.
Description: Large print edition. | Thorndike, Maine : Center Point
Large Print, 2017. | "Unabridged"—Title page verso. | Originally
published: New York : St. Martin's Press, 2016.
Identifiers: LCCN 2016043682 | ISBN 9781683242345
    (hardcover : alkaline paper : large print)
Subjects: LCSH: Mason, C. Nicole, 1976– | Mason, C. Nicole, 1976–
—Childhood and youth. | African American women—Biography. |
African Americans—Biography. | African American women
educators—Biography. | Gifted women—United States—Biography. |
Successful people—United States—Biography. | Poor children—
United States—Biography. | Homeless persons—United States—
Biography. | Large type books.
Classification: LCC E185.97.M374 A3 2017 | DDC 370.92 [B] —dc23
LC record available at https://lccn.loc.gov/2016043682

dedication

To Ms. Slaughter, Blythe Anderson,
Lillie Motley, Joanne Parker,
Roylestine Bowman, Clarence Lee,
Joseph P. McCormick, Bonnie Thornton Dill,
Seung-kyung Kim, Linda Faye Williams,
Fred Alford, Ronald Walters, Ana Oliviera,
and the elementary school teacher
who told me I was a beautiful writer.
Thank you for seeing my light.

For Charli and Parker

contents

We are all born bright. The difference between you and me is small. From the start, we all have the same potential for greatness and reach for the same things. However, our experiences and interactions in the world and the denial of humanity in very subtle but meaningful ways threaten the light. And then it is gone.

After going dark, some of us learn to reignite ourselves.

With the exception of immediate family, the names of most people have been changed. Much of the book is based on the oral histories of my family, interviews, and my direct recollection of events. The dialogue is an approximation of what was actually said or relayed to me.

what do you want to be?

The author, age 7

I got to school early and found Ms. Ward in our empty classroom erasing the chalkboard and shuffling papers at her desk. I had never had a conversation with her that was not related to an assignment, so I crept to my desk, pulled out a book, and began to read silently, hoping she would not notice me.

Ms. Ward, a brawny woman with silver wires in her mouth, was my second-grade teacher at Abbott Elementary, a predominantly Black and Latino school in Lynwood, California. Whenever we misbehaved, her voice rolled like thunder and bounced off the walls. My sole purpose in class, besides trying to impress her with my reading

11

skills, was to keep from getting my ear twisted and my arm pinched or from being told to stand next to her desk while she continued to teach as if I were a lamppost. In horror, I watched the other kids squirm as she grabbed hold of their body parts and lectured them about the need to follow directions, stay in their seats, or not talk out of turn. It looked painful.

"Chataquoa, come here," she said.

Oh no, I thought. This was it. She was going to twist my ear for coming to school early. I knew I should have waited for the bell to ring. Now, it was too late. I pushed my chair from underneath the desk and carried the book with me to the front of the classroom.

"Where do you live?" she asked.

"Down the street," I said, exhaling. Our little pink house at the foot of a cul-de-sac was not far from the school. I walked the short distance alone.

"With who?"

"My mother, my brother, and grandfather."

She continued to write in her grade book as I stood fully prepared to answer any question she threw my way. To keep from getting pinched, I would tell her anything she wanted to know. She dropped her pen and looked up at me.

"You're smart. Do you know that? What do you want to be when you grow up?" Her unblinking eyes were trained on mine. She wanted me to understand what she was saying.

I shrugged. No one had ever asked me that quesion before and I did not have an answer.

"It doesn't matter if you don't know now. You're a smart little girl and you can go far, just keep it up."

I stood there, feet glued to the floor, waiting for her to say more, but she did not. She returned to her grade book. After a few moments, I retreated back to my desk. What did she mean by "keep it up" or that I could "go far," I wondered. Go where?

I remembered my conversation with Ms. Ward decades later, when I came across a study revealing that when inner-city kids were asked to draw the world, they drew their immediate neighborhoods—the corner stores, the local carryouts, and their houses. Conversely, when middle-class and affluent kids were asked to do the same, they drew countries such as China or those in Europe. I believe if I had been given the task of drawing the world as a young child, I would have drawn my neighborhood, too. That was my world, and I could not see beyond it.

day of reckoning

The chandelier with its dangling diamond-shaped cut glass seemed brighter than usual as I looked up at it from the stage. I surveyed the audience, consisting of the usual lot of do-gooders, social workers, politicians, and policy advocates. I jotted "SYSTEMS" down in all caps and underlined it twice. The oversized room was elegant, the tables dressed in white linens, and it had good chairs, the ones with cushiony, carpet-like bottoms.

I was there to talk about poverty. I had delivered some version of the same speech nearly a dozen times in the past year. I barely had to prepare. Each time I gave a talk, polite applause circled the room and I was flooded with invitations to speak at the next event. I knew just what to say to not ruffle any feathers—stronger programs, more money, stricter rules, and the development of life skills for the impoverished. However, I was growing uneasy with the lie. What we were saying worked, did not.

When my turn came, rather than give my usual spiel, I wondered aloud whether or not it was the systems that were broken rather than the people. I spoke about the need to examine the institutions and structures in society and in the communities that impede rather than support self-sufficiency

14

and economic mobility for individuals and families.

Standing behind the podium in my nicely tailored suit, I felt safe saying what I had been thinking for so long. I was the director of a research center at New York University's Robert F. Wagner Graduate School of Public Service. I felt comforted by the position and believed perhaps I would be heard. I was an authority.

During the question-and-answer segment of the program, a woman stood and identified herself as a social worker employed at one of the many agencies scattered throughout the city that supported poor and low-income individuals. "This comment is for you, Dr. Mason," she said. While she agreed that the systems did need some tinkering, she opined that what was really missing from the equation was individual responsibility and that people needed to help themselves.

A flash of heat washed over my body as I realized she was talking about me. In that moment, I was transported back to the countless hours I spent as a child waiting with my mother for social services in oversized rooms in unmarked city buildings. At the break of dawn, we rose to catch several buses only to be told to come back on another day because we were missing some document or that our application was still under review. For their part, the social workers seemed contemptuous and treated us as if they were doing

15

us a favor by allowing us to receive ration-sized aid. Undeterred, we would repeat the trip the following day.

"That's not true," is all I could muster before a skinny White man with wiry glasses began to speak.

"I agree with the woman over there," he said, pointing in the direction of the woman who had challenged me. "There are programs out there, and the women—I mean families—are not doing their part to better their situations. I see it every day."

As I scanned the room, the sea of White faces, with specks of color here and there, seemed to agree with them. There was no dissent, only stillness. My stomach churned as I shuffled my papers. My eyes darted across the panel for help. Was anyone else going to say something? Why hadn't I just stuck to my notes? When I did, everything went well, and the narrative remained intact, cohesive, and unquestioned.

By "narrative," I mean the stories we all have in our heads about the lives of poor people, their behavior, and the reasons for their circumstances. In this forum, I was not only disrupting that narrative, but also challenging the financial investments, institutions, and structures predicated upon an understanding of the poor as lazy, infantile, morally corrupt, and in need of direction and supervision. It was the narrative

16

that, consciously or subconsciously, most of us in the room were responsible for perpetuating in some form or another through our work as advocates, practitioners, and legislators.

I swallowed hard.

"I did the right thing. I am the beneficiary of many of the programs that we are talking about here today. I attended Head Start. I was involved in afterschool programs. I'm the first person in my family to graduate from high school, to attend college, and to receive a PhD."

By now, my voice was shaking, but I could not stop. I was having in public the private conversation I reserved for my first-generation Black and Latino colleagues who had also successfully navigated their way out of poverty and into the middle class and who have a deep understanding of the journey from there to here. These people, in this room, were strangers.

"But, I'm only *one* person," I continued. "Growing up, I knew many kids in my neighborhood who were smarter and more capable than me, and they didn't make it out. Many have been killed, gone to prison, are living hand to mouth or otherwise on the margins of society. Should I blame them or the system that only allows a few of us at a time to escape?"

The room was pregnant with silence. I couldn't take it back.

I felt like an intruder and exposed. In these

types of professional settings, my personal experiences with hunger, poverty, and episodic homelessness often go undetected. It is assumed that I am just like everyone else, an advocate, a policy expert, or an academic.

Typically, when a woman is invited to tell her story during these panels or meetings, it feels voyeuristic and slimy, like a performance. Her story has a perfect, predictable arc—she was lost then found by one of the many social service agencies in the city. She changed her behavior, became a better mother, and, although she still struggles to make ends meet, is on her way to economic prosperity—Hallelujah, THE END. Her story is meant to inspire, to whip up emotion, and to make the people in the audience feel good about their work and themselves. It is not meant to challenge or change how we make policies or to shift how poor people in our communities, our cities, or the larger society are perceived.

There is also a clear separation between her and the experts on the stage. They, not she, are deciding what should be done. Here I was, blurring that line. I was both the subject and the authority on the matter. I had firsthand knowledge of the messiness of poverty and the feelings the poor internalize from birth—like the belief that our very existence is a burden on society. The collapse of this boundary made me uncomfortable. I had worked hard to disguise my beginning in life—from the decision to change my name during my first week of college to the effort of erasing words and phrases like "cain't" and "finsta go" from my vocabulary. I had succeeded in creating the perfect, impenetrable middle-class mask. Now, it was off.

a crack
in the foundation

In the United States there is no shortage of belief in the possible or, in the case of the nearly forty-seven million people living in poverty, the seemingly *impossible*. The idea is that through hard work, ambition, and dogged persistence, all people can overcome where they began in life to enjoy middle-class success—a home, steady income, a healthy family, and a comfortable retirement. According to this narrative, when individuals fail to attain this level of success, it is because they did not try hard enough.

The truth is that only about 4 percent of those born into poverty, or in the bottom 20 percent of Americans economically, will ever make it to the top fifth of income earners in the U.S. For most, regardless of race, escaping poverty is akin to winning the lottery.

Why is this? Why, in a nation overflowing with riches and teeming with opportunity, are the odds of escaping poverty on par with the odds of being struck by lightning?

Over the years, I have turned this question over and over in my mind even as I have safely navigated my way to a comfortable middle-class existence where the poor are mostly out of sight. I now live in a neighborhood with great public schools, low levels of crime and unemployment, and high levels of civic engagement. My children, twins, have been enrolled in a Mandarin immersion program since they were eighteen months old and have tested years beyond their age intellectually. My son plays soccer and my daughter takes ballet lessons. All signs read: "You're doing the right thing. Your children will go on to college and become successful, productive members of society."

When President Barack Obama said in his historic second-term inaugural speech that we all believe in the same promise that says, "[America] is a place where you can make it if you try regardless of who you are or where you start," he was speaking about himself—he was also talking about me and others who started out with very little and ended up winning big in the game of life. Similarly, I suppose that when conservatives speak of hardworking Americans and the *givers* supporting the *takers* who are draining our collective pockets, they are also talking about me. For Democrats, I am proof that as a society, we have achieved some modicum of equality. For Republicans, my formative years support their claims that racial and ethnic minorities are poor because of bad choices, laziness, and intergenerational pathologies such as out-of-wedlock births, crime, and high rates of single motherhood. I am a winner no matter which side of the aisle you occupy.

Yet, I do not feel like a winner.

Since I left my childhood community, more than two decades ago, very little has changed about the way it looks and feels and the individuals and families who still live there. In fact, I would argue that things have gotten progressively worse. The inequality gap, measured not only by income but by access to opportunity and resources as well, has become a chasm far too wide to cross for most people living in poverty, including many in my old neighborhoods.

Ironically, the emergence of a solid middle class, beginning in the 1930s, expanding in the 1960s to include some African-Americans, and created through employment, education, housing, and tax policies, allowed some individuals and families to obtain higher wages, buy homes, and access a solid post-secondary education—while hurting poor people and communities. This upward mobility created a new class of citizens as well as a new set of policy priorities and concerns for this group, which were no longer connected to the concerns of those who were considered poor. These developments continued to create and build suspicion in the minds of the American public regarding poor people and their personal failure to reach the middle class.

Today, the public schools in poor neighborhoods are in far worse condition than before the passage of *Brown v. the Board of Education*, and the growth and privatization of U.S. prisons have robbed many communities of vital human and economic resources. Double-digit unemployment continues to threaten the day-to-day survival of families, and entire neighborhoods have been ripped apart by neglect, decay, and the predatory lending practices of large banks and lending institutions.

Many of the cities and neighborhoods that I called home during my childhood in San Bernardino, Compton, and Inglewood, California, are bankrupt or do not have the resources, either institutionally or structurally, that are necessary to ensure that everyone has a fair shot at the American Dream. These are facts, not conjectures or postulations.

In public conversations about poverty, very little consideration is given to the preconditions for success or the maximization of opportunity in society. These preconditions include quality schools and institutions in neighborhoods, sufficient food, safety, access to adequate health care, stable housing, and the resources and critical information needed to negotiate complex social and political institutions. When these necessities are absent from communities, individuals and families are rightfully preoccupied with basic survival. And those who are able to succeed despite the lack of these foundational conditions are likely to be perceived as extraordinary or exceptional—superhumans of a sort.

Poverty cannot be defined solely by the lack of income or material wealth. It is also characterized by a severe lack of access to opportunities, resources, and vital networks, which, taken together, make it nearly impossible for individuals and entire generations of families to escape. Over time, individuals living in poverty learn to negotiate these systems. They adapt, make do, go without, rationalize, or internalize the attitudes of the structures that are failing them in bulk. They, too, have come to believe that *they* are the problem.

Middle-class and upper-income individuals and families have a different set of rules that govern their lives and that speak to their capabilities and aspirations. They feel a sense of entitlement and assume systems will respond to their needs. Their daily engagement with groups, institutions, and communities is very different from that of families living in poverty.

By "rules," I mean the practices that allow individuals to succeed in any given society. For the most part, the institutional, social, and political rules that govern our many systems— from the education system to the criminal legal system—are invisible to most poor people. These systems and structures are connected, and a particular disadvantage in one system is sometimes compounded by another disadvantage reflecting a separate system or structure.

These rules can be as simple as knowing that you must take the SAT to apply to a four-year institution, knowing how to prepare a résumé and dress for a job interview, or knowing where to go to access information that can help one gain citizenship status or obtain a loan for the purchase of a new home. Without knowledge of or experience with negotiating these codes or rules, most poor people will remain impoverished, or their incremental gains will be diminished by losses reflected in a separate but connected system.

Born Bright is about how, through keen observation and what at times felt like peeping through an opaque window of someone else's home, I learned the systemic and structural rules of the game, the often complex and unfamiliar rules of engagement. It is also about how others in my life did *not*. Along the way, I make the case that success and opportunity in the United States are shaped much less by hard work, intelligence, or aspirational drive than by the conditions under which individuals are able to pursue success and opportunity, the social capital gained through personal connections, and the mastery of the institutional and structural rules of engagement in our society. Individual effort, determination, and possibilities are only a part of the equation.

To write this book, I went back to visit the places I remember and to talk to the people who helped me exit poverty. These teachers, family members, and friends, these schools, buildings, and neighborhoods, are those I hold close to my heart, the ones I have in mind when I am speaking about the kinds of policies and solutions that we will need to ensure that in the new economy, no individuals—regardless of where they start in life—are left behind.

This is a true story. My objective is to offer a fresh perspective on the dynamics of poverty that have long been concealed by grandiose narratives of American exceptionalism promoted by liberals and conservatives alike.

In his poignant and insightful book, *The Working Poor: Invisible in America*, David Shipler observes that "an exit from poverty is not like showing your passport and crossing a frontier. There is a broad strip of contested territory between destitution and comfort, and the passage is not the same distance for everyone."

Born Bright takes place in that contested territory and seeks to illuminate the sheer fortitude it takes to navigate systems and structures designed for the success of a few rather than the many. Stated differently, the poor girl in me wants to explain why everyone does not make it out.

origins

The expectations for my life were carved out before I could have ever begun to imagine what I might want for myself. I suppose this is true for all children, including those born into privilege. Our environment—our homes, schools, and communities, along with our primary caregivers and daily interactions with the outside world— signals to us what we can expect to become or how far we can go.

For those of us born at the bottom of the economic and social ladder, messages of success, opportunity, and fairness in the larger society are often in conflict with the harsh and uneven realities of our daily lives. From the beginning, we internalize the idea that we are less than others are and that to strive for more is to chase an out-of-reach dream, like the one-in-a-million chance of becoming a world-class basketball player or famous politician. And we believe there is very little we can do about it.

As a brown-skinned girl born to a teenaged mother, I had a low bar of success. No one in my family had finished high school, and because we were poor, I did not expect much more than what I had, which was very little. It was assumed that I would become a domestic worker or maid in one of the mega-hotels in Las Vegas, Nevada, like my grandmother, a school bus driver like my mother, a hairdresser, or a certified nursing assistant. And while these were all considered "good" jobs in my neighborhood and by my family, it is safe to say that none of them would lead to a solid middle-class existence with a comfortable retirement package and enough to pay for college tuition for my children.

I was born on April 27, 1976, twelve years after President Lyndon B. Johnson declared a "War on Poverty," at the end of the Civil Rights movement and in the middle of the Feminist movement. It was a time of change, of political upheaval and social activism. Women and Blacks were organizing, in their respective movements, and demanding a seat at the table, access to better jobs, and an end to racial and sex discrimination. For those women, mostly White, educated, and middle-class, and well-positioned Blacks, doors opened; they were offered access to education and employment opportunities that had previously been denied to them.

For working-class and poor Blacks with limited access to quality schools and social capital, however, this was not the case. Their opportunities continued to be limited, their prospects bleak. They were corralled into specific neighborhoods through housing discrimination and low-income housing programs and deprived of the most basic access to quality services, institutions, and resources, including hospitals, schools, banks, and food.

At the time of the declaration of a War on Poverty, there was national recognition that poverty was less of an individual problem and more of a structural and systemic one that could be solved or alleviated through sound programs designed to raise incomes and provide opportunities for quality education, job training, and community development. There was the public will to invest in, or at least a willingness to experiment with, programs at both the federal and state levels that could move families toward full economic security and participation in society. From 1961 to 1968, spending on poverty-related programs rose more than 300 percent, from $9.1 billion to $30 billion.

The infusion of cash, however, was not enough to contend with the cumulative effects of discrimination against Blacks, Latinos, and other ethnic groups across time in the labor market and housing and lending practices, the criminal legal system, and other systems and structures present in society. By the time programs and money arrived, it was already too late. The inequality gap manifested in disparate social conditions and entrenched in our structures and institutions had already taken hold of lives and communities.

By the late 1960s, the appeal of a national War

on Poverty had begun to wane. In an effort to assuage Republican constituencies in his 1968 presidential bid, Richard Nixon attacked many of the Great Society policies, including the War on Poverty. During his first term, he maintained many of the programs initiated by Johnson, but soon after his reelection in 1972, he made vicious cuts. After Nixon's resignation in 1974, and the 1976 election, now Democratic president Jimmy Carter distanced himself from the War on Poverty and conceded that the government alone could not eliminate poverty. This concession, in conjunction with other woes facing the national economy, including inflation and high unemployment, provided an opening for conservatives to frame poverty as an individual and moral problem and federal efforts to alleviate it as a waste.

The individual responsibility frame was supported by leading scholars and legislators of the time, including well-known Black sociologists such as William Julius Wilson, who had begun to describe poverty as a cultural pathology rooted in individual and community behavior. In 1965, then–U.S. assistant secretary of labor Daniel Patrick Moynihan released his now-infamous report, *The Negro Family: The Case for National Action*, which argued that poverty experienced by Blacks was due to a "tangle of pathology" caused by households headed by single mothers. Never mind that rural Whites had poverty rates similar to those of Blacks in inner cities; the frame created by Moynihan and others was meant to undermine structural and systemic explanations focused on historic practices of discrimination that denied Blacks, Latinos, and other marginalized groups access to economic, educational, and political power and opportunity.

From the 1960s on, Blacks were routinely and negatively associated with poverty by the media and others. Outlier examples of Black welfare abuse or fraud were used to explain impoverished conditions. Conversely, when stories on poverty took on a more sympathetic tone (as they tend to do during economic downturns), images of poor Blacks were replaced with images of poor Whites.[1]

As a consequence, there was very little sympathy in the public sphere for poor people or assistance programs. In fact, there was outright hostility and anger toward the poor. This period also marked the beginning of the racialization and genderization of programs and policies. African-American women, depicted as welfare queens, were identified primarily with antipoverty policies and became a symbol of public waste through expenditures on such programs. By the mid-1980s, with the help of President Ronald Reagan, most discussions related to antipoverty programs were mapped to race.[2]

In his 1986 presidential radio address on

welfare, Reagan referred to welfare recipients as permanent scars on the American promise of hope and opportunity and as people who lived in a separate America of lost dreams and stunted lives. As a high school dropout on welfare with two small children by the age of seventeen, my mother was a walking billboard for Reagan's other world in the forgotten streets of the inner city,[3] and so, too, were my brother and I.

In my world, when I was a child, there was no one more powerful and more beautiful than my mother. I had witnessed her topple men double her size and leave them huddled in corners nursing open wounds. She also fought off women who on occasion would show up to our home unannounced, looking for my father. She learned to fight from her uncle Toot. With her good looks, she could also talk her way into anything—a house, a new car, or money.

She was scrappy and knew how to take care of herself. My maternal grandmother Willie Mae had passed away when my mother was just twelve years old, leaving her and her siblings to fend for themselves. They moved to a tiny top-floor apartment in Houston, Texas. Rather than continuing to care for the children, Mr. White, my grandmother's lover, dropped groceries off once a week. Before leaving, he would visit my mother's bedroom and lay hands on her body. When her

Ainee, a southern term of endearment for aunt, learned what was happening, she called the Department of Children's Services and arranged to have the four siblings sent to Lynwood, California, to live with their biological father, my *PaPa.* The oldest, my mother's brother Junior, refused to leave, but with no anchor, my mother decided to go. Her other two siblings followed.

When she arrived on her father's doorsteps, my twelve-year-old mother was set on not needing anyone or anything. Her father had made it clear that he would offer nothing more than a roof over her head and food. He did not question how she spent her days. For his part, he spent his evenings in dark bars and with different women in and out of his bed.

Perhaps that is why he and my grandmother Willie Mae originally separated. They could not tame one another or agree on who would raise their children while the other had unencumbered good times. He left her, and in his absence she refused to stay at home. She often went straight from her job as a registered nurse to carouse without regard for the four little ones waiting for her to walk through the front door.

My grandmother's death was shrouded in unknowns. "What happened to your mother?" I would ask my mother, curious about the woman with the wide, gold-toothed smile and neatly coifed hair in my mother's lone picture of her. In that picture, her legs were crossed and she was squeezed between two men. Her dress was lilac with billowy frills. In one hand a lit cigarette hung lazily between her index and middle fingers; the other held a short glass of brown liquor on ice. She looked like she was having a good time.

According to my mother, there are two versions of her death. In one, Grandma Willie Mae fell, hit her head on the edge of a sharp coffee table, and died. In the other, she stopped at a local bar on her way home from work, and a fellow patron slipped poison into her drink. She made it home but collapsed in the bathroom, where her eyes rolled to the back of her head. My mother believed the latter. Since then, she has avoided nightclubs, and she warns anyone who will listen of the killing power of jealousy. I always thought there was more to the story, but knew enough not to ask for more than I was prepared to receive.

This was also the case when I asked about my twin sister, who had died during birth. Over the years I had attempted to broach the subject with my mother by asking mundane questions such as "What time was I born?" or "Do you think we would have gotten along, my twin and me?" Her answers were always vacant and inconsequential. I'd retreat, waiting months, sometimes years before inquiring again. Recently, I asked once more.

"Mom, I need to ask you about something. Do you have time to talk?"

"Yes," she said, her voice cracking. I could feel her tensing up.

"I need you to tell me about my sister, the one that died. I really never understood what happened to her."

"Let me try to remember," she said.

I could hear the bedsprings squeak as she positioned herself close to the edge. "I was so young, my body was not developed," she explained. She cleared her throat to hold back the tears I was sure were forming in her lower eyelids.

"Did you know you were pregnant with twins?"

"No, I did not know," she said in her most perfect interview voice. "All along, I thought it was one baby."

"When did you find out it was twins?" I asked disbelievingly.

"The three of us were there in the delivery room; your father, me, and your uncle Poochie," she said. "He was the first one from the family to arrive. It was Poochie who noticed two heart-beats on the fetal monitor. He pointed to the lines on the screen. Both were jumping up and down. I thought he was kidding. He then raced down the hallway to alert the doctor."

"Why didn't you believe him?"

"Because I had gone to my prenatal appoint-ments faithfully and no one ever told me I was having twins. I took my vitamins and did every-thing else they told me to do."

"Then what happened?" I pressed.

"I don't know. I woke up and there was only one baby," she said, sounding distant and confused.

I knew this confusion and tone well. She used it when she should have known the answer to a question but didn't. It was only a matter of time before she would try to switch the subject or derail the conversation. I had to force her to stay in the moment.

"You didn't ask what happened," I prodded. "Did the doctor give you any explanation?"

"No, I never saw the baby and they didn't tell me anything. They just said it died. I was in shock, but didn't question it because it was only supposed to be one and I'm not sure we could have taken care of two."

To her, our conversation was over. What more could she say about the daughter she birthed, but never knew? As consolation, she offered up my father, who she claimed might be able to fill in the gaps. I could not let it go.

"Did you and my daddy ever discuss it?" I inquired.

"No, we never talked about it. I just . . . I just . . ."

Her voice trailed off. By now, I was certain her eyes were fire red and her yellow skin flushed.

"I just never thought about it, the baby. I never had anyone to guide or help me. I was so young."

I knew she was telling the truth.

"Do you think they treated you that way because you were young and poor?" I asked pointedly. "You were just fifteen."

"No, I don't think that had anything to do with it. I wasn't poor," she shot back.

"Were you on welfare? Were you on Medicaid? Did you receive food stamps?"

"Yes, but we never thought of ourselves as poor. It wasn't like that," she explained. "It was what it was."

"We were obviously poor. There were times we didn't have a home," I said, my voice raised and shaking.

Later in the conversation, after the emotion had subsided, as she took a long drag of her Newport cigarette, she conceded that we might have been a little poor.

My mother told me that I lived in an incubator for the first several weeks of my life and that I was the length of my father's forearm from head to toe. My progress, she said, was monitored by a social worker who visited every month to make sure I was developing properly. The woman stopped coming after I began to exceed the developmental milestones, a clear sign that I had indeed survived. I found it odd that the doctor who had not cared enough to explain to my mother what had happened to her dead child was the same one who had ordered monthly visits from the social worker to ensure I was healthy and thriving.

If we hadn't been poor, would my twin sister still be alive? As futile and dark as the question may seem, I can't help asking it. To the doctors at Brookdale Memorial Hospital, my mother was just another unwed, pregnant Black teenager on Medicaid, and they treated her as such. She had no recourse and very little power. Who would she have complained to? And what would they have done to help her?

To be sure, my current perspective on my childhood is shaded by what I have learned about poverty through my work and research over the years. Growing up, I too never believed we were poor. We had systems and networks that worked. If the electricity got turned off for nonpayment, we went to a neighbor's house or burned candles until it was turned back on. If we ran out of milk or money, we borrowed a couple of bucks from a relative or friend.

We lived with little regard for what others had that we did not. There were no rich people in our lives to show us the deep divide or to make us wish for more. As a result, I did not resent my lack or understand the depths of my deprivation because I had nothing to measure it against. I lived in a cocoon of familiarity and geographic isolation, segregated by invisible but known boundaries that I knew never to cross. There was also no roadmap to a life or destination other than where I lived at any given time.

For the first twenty years of my life, I had never been to a solidly middle-class or White neighborhood, grocery store, or school. There was no need.

The only White people I had ever seen on a consistent basis were my teachers, all of whom were young women. They seemed so naïve and soft. How they got to our neighborhood, I never knew. They did not understand our lives or us. Our problems were not their problems, at least not permanently. If they became overwhelmed, they could leave or decide not to come back. We did not have this option. As a child, I always imagined that they lived far away, perhaps on another planet. And they would drop in just in time to line us up after the first bell rang for school to start.

They also never pronounced my name correctly. CHA-TA-QUOA, I would say, rolling my eyes at the obvious fumble. What was so hard about it, I wondered. Everyone in my family said it with ease.

I was named after a street in Malibu, California —Chautauqua Boulevard—by my aunt Linda Rose, a fiery and brilliant woman whose early losses in life had hardened her. The street, lined with multimillion-dollar homes, met the Pacific Ocean and reeked of success and of having made it. The name was aspirational and represented her hopes for me.

Early on, I learned to apologize for my name's being so hard to say, and I even let some of my teachers get away with calling me Chiquita, like the banana, or Shaniqua. It was all the same to them. In kindergarten, my teacher said my name was too long to practice writing and allowed me to use my middle name instead—Nicole. It was short and manageable. I did not mind because in my loopy handwriting, my first name took up the entire sheet.

The teachers I favored, however, were allowed to call me Pumpkin, the nickname bestowed upon me by my father shortly after my birth. He called me that, he said, because my big head, with the wee patch of hair, the stem, in the center of it, had a difficult time navigating its way through the tiny hole of my pint-sized *onesies*. I loved the name so much that it was even emblazoned on the back of my high school cheerleading uniform.

The teachers always mistook my mother for my sister. The morning following parent-teacher conference night or an open house, they would ask why my sister instead of my mother had come to the meeting. She should really come, they would say admonishingly.

"She did," I would reply, bursting into a fit of laughter, thinking this was the most absurd thing I had ever heard. "That *was* my mom."

"Oh," is the only response I remember.

At home when I questioned my mother about the mix-up, she would chalk it up to her beauty. She was way too beautiful to be a mom of two, she would say. I wholeheartedly believed this explanation.

Looking back, I can see that my mother did her best to shield my brother and me from the things that would make us question her, our circumstances, or our lives. She never talked about politics, race, or what was going on outside our neighborhood. She convinced us that our world was right and that the things we did not understand were of no consequence. She, and she alone, was the master interpreter.

the end of things

My mother was off-putting and prickly. Her large doe eyes, long, flowing hair, and sun-kissed skin belied her hardened core. She met my father in the fall of 1974, a little more than two weeks after her arrival in California. They were introduced through her newest best friend, Sabrina, a curveless busybody with a heart-shaped face, while hanging out on the corner of McMillan Street in Lynwood, watching the cars zoom past. Sabrina was a motherless girl as well.

In the beginning, my mother was not interested. Sure, he was cute, but since she'd just touched down in the city, she had nearly a dozen suitors. He was just one of many vying for her attention. She let him know as much when he asked her name. "Don't worry about it ugly," she snarked. Taken aback by her response, he decided she was not worth his time, at least not until he figured out a strategy.

For the next few months, my father managed to make his way to her house nearly every afternoon for a game of Ping-Pong with her youngest brother, Calvin. To tease him, my mother would poke her head into the garage where they played, talk a little trash about his serve, then disappear. He had believed he was getting closer, but his hopes were dashed when on one occasion he arrived early for his daily match and found her kissing a neighborhood boy on the stairs of the front porch. Crushed, he was done—for now.

My father was born in Milan, Tennessee, a small military town about one hundred miles northeast of Memphis. His father was in the army, and he and my grandmother Josephine, JoJo for short, a dutiful and sturdy woman, crisscrossed the country with three children in tow.

Neither of my father's parents had much more than a third-grade education. My grandfather was from Oklahoma and my grandmother from New Orleans, Louisiana. Her mother, my great grandmother, *My Dear,* as she was affectionately known, had buttery skin, piercing green eyes, and long, straight hair. My grandmother did not possess these things. She was deep chocolate with high cheekbones and kinky hair. Because of this she was an outcast, made to sleep outside on the porch and taunted by her sisters. To compensate, she learned to take care of others and to be needed. This, she thought, was a way around the burden imposed upon her by her looks.

My paternal grandfather, Henry, was violent to all of *his* women, my father said, including *my* mama. He was filled with rage and unforgiving; not the loving type. My grandmother had endured his fists and irascible temper from the very start of their courtship. Everyone knew about it, and the children bore witness to it.

When they returned to New Orleans from Tennessee, the beatings became grisly. After a brutal whipping that left her holed up in bed for a week, my grandmother stole away with few possessions and little money to Los Angeles, California. On her way out, she warned him to not come looking for her or the children; she wasn't ever coming back.

The family settled in the Jordan Down housing projects in Watts, an impoverished, predominantly Black neighborhood in South Los Angeles ravaged economically and socially by racially fueled riots in 1965, one year after the passage of the Civil Rights Act. The riots were sparked by the overpolicing and harassment of residents by the Los Angeles Police Department (LAPD) under the direction of Police Chief William H. Parker and by the mounting feelings of hope-lessness on the part of Blacks in the isolated community. Residents there experienced high rates of unemployment, poor-quality housing and schools, and unprecedented levels of violence.

At the time, in the mid-1960s, the LAPD treated Black men and women as enemies of the city. One of the primary responsibilities of the police was to make certain that Blacks did not cross the invisible line into White neighborhoods—with the line in Los Angeles, at the time, being Alameda

44

Boulevard. Those who dared venture past the barrier were harassed, beaten, or threatened with arrest.

In a very real way, for those living in poverty, the rules associated with boundaries and belonging are internalized from a very early age. Certain neighborhoods—the houses, the schools, the grocery stores, the banks, the hospitals, even the people in them—are off-limits.

The unrest in Watts lasted six days and resulted in thirty-four fatalities, thousands of injuries, and more than $40 million in irreparable damages to businesses, homes, and other property. This was my father's new home.

My most vivid memory of visiting my grand-mother's house as a child is of the stories my cousins would tell my brother and me on the way to the dilapidated, graffiti-laced playground in the center of the complex. We didn't play as much as we sat around talking about what we had seen or heard.

"We heard gunshots the other night," they would report to us. "You've got to be careful—someone can just grab you, like they did that little girl. They did *it* to her."

By *it*, they meant rape. At the time, we did not have the language for the word "rape." My brother and I did our best not to appear afraid or other-wise affected by what we heard. Showing fear, crying, or pleading to go back home with the adults meant that you were a *punk* or a *mark*. And I did not want to be either of those. It also meant you were weak and could be taken advantage of easily. I wanted to be tough.

My cousins also told us the rules about the colors we were allowed to wear. On certain blocks, you could get chased home, beaten up, or killed for wearing the wrong color. My brother and I quickly scanned our clothes and shoes to make sure we were not wearing any potentially offending colors.

"You can wear white or black. No blue, purple, or red," they instructed us. "Don't worry, if they stop you, you can just tell them that you're not from around here and they'll leave you alone." The city blocks—Piru Street, Grape Street, Crenshaw, and many more—marked a new gang territory. Walking in that neighborhood felt like crossing a minefield.

This was no way to live, I thought. Making a simple mistake or turning down the wrong neighborhood block could cost you your life. I was only six years old, and I did not want to die.

Once, a young boy no more than thirteen years old stopped us on our way from the candy house, a makeshift storefront operated out of a lady's apartment, which sold candy, ices, and chips to the local kids. He approached Kenny, the oldest in the group and the son of my grandfather's new girlfriend, who also lived in Jordan Downs.

"What set you from?" The boy demanded to know. His undeveloped face looked so serious.

I was afraid for Kenny and for us. What would happen if he gave the wrong answer, I wondered. Would we be shot right there on the spot? Should we run? My six-year-old brain raced.

"My mama's *pussy*," he answered.

The answer was so direct; it was like he had been saving it for just this moment. And it rang. I was impressed. The boy, startled by his response, waved his hand in the air as if to say we weren't worth his trouble and walked away. Kenny had saved us. In that moment, he was my hero.

Kenny was the middle of five children and the second boy. His older brother Gino was a Crip, a member of a predominantly African-American gang in Los Angeles, and in and out of jail. And although Kenny kept to himself, by default and by association he was also a Crip. I suppose I was too. Gino wore blue at all times and spent hours ironing creases into the long narrow legs of his dark Levi 501s before he left the apartment to roam the streets from the early afternoon into the wee hours of the night. We never asked Gino questions about why he went to jail or what it was like in there. We knew better. It was considered rude and intrusive. There was always a celebration and a big dinner when he returned home. We were happy to see him.

In retrospect, although I considered Gino an

adult, he could not have been more than seventeen years old. However, because he seemed so hard and untouchable and was considered the man of the house, we treated him as such. The same was true for his sister Lena, an auburn-colored girl with a round scar on the side of her face from a street fight. At sixteen she was pregnant with her first child. In conversations, she spoke knowingly about the kind of mother she hoped to be: she wasn't going to let her baby curse or act too grown for her age. Her baby was going to be smart and not eat too much candy. All good things, I thought.

Lena watched cartoons with us and sucked her thumb just like I did. Her too-small T-shirt no longer reached the waist of her unbuttoned jeans. When she walked she braced her back and rubbed her belly. At times she winced and at others she smiled.

Now, I wonder if it was all just an act—Gino's toughness and the armor that he had built up in order to survive and Lena's mix of naiveté and hubris about her ability to mother a child. Was it real? Seeing them now as children, rather than as adults, I know that it wasn't. The toughness and the hubris were a cover for their fear and vulnerability.

My father was having a house party and although my mother was not officially invited, she made up her mind that she had to be there. She had not seen him in weeks and had begun to miss his daily visits to play Ping-Pong with her brother, Calvin. To the party, she wore tight, flared-leg jeans and her favorite T-shirt, which hugged her tiny breasts. Her hair was twisted into two neat French braids along the sides of her head.

She watched him throughout the night and waited until the party was over to speak with him. Then she asked if he would walk her home. On the way to the house on McMillan Street, they talked and held hands. From that day forward, they were inseparable.

My father was macho and street-smart and seemed to know his way around the world in a way that my mother simply did not. He came and went as he pleased. He also never had anywhere to be in particular. When she would head to school on most mornings, he would be off on his next adventure. Later in the afternoon, he would meet her at the entrance of the school gates to walk her home, recounting his day.

My mother had never met anyone like him before. He had class. He made this pronouncement one afternoon while primping in the bathroom mirror as she sat on the toilet seat next to the steel bathtub. She watched intently as he picked his hair while simultaneously spraying Afro Sheen and patting methodically until his Afro was perfectly round. He was handsome with a somewhat muscular build and dimples on both cheeks. He was red-clay brown. According to him, she did not have class. "Don't worry," he said. "Just stick with me. I got enough for both of us." She did not know what it meant to have class but vowed to stay close so that some of it might rub off on her.

Following my birth, the three of us moved into a tiny one-bedroom duplex in the Pine Terrace apartments in Compton, California, that cost $100 per month. My grandfather, *PaPa,* managed the building and allowed my parents, both under the age of eighteen, to set up a home there.

South of Los Angeles, Compton, California, was founded in 1867 by White settlers from Northern California who came south to eke out a living once the gold rush had ended. Although portions of the land had been deeded in 1784 to Juan Jose Dominguez, a Spanish soldier, the lands were ceded in 1848, after the Mexican-American War, and turned over to Whites. The first Blacks moved to Compton in the late 1950s. Prior to this, the city was exclusively White, with racially restrictive covenants and aggressive policing strategies that sought to keep Blacks out.

For a short period, from the late 1950s and until the 1965 riots, which ravaged many parts of the area, Whites and Blacks co-existed in Compton. Following the riots, however, Whites fled the area for other parts of the city, stripping the fledgling metropolis of a vital tax base. From the 1970s and well into the late '80s, Compton was pre-dominantly African-American and home to many working- to middle-class Blacks. Shortly there-after, due to high crime rates and the infiltration of neighborhood gangs, many middle-class Blacks with the means to do so left for other areas, such as Ladera Heights and Baldwin Hills. Today, Compton is predominantly Latino, and about 1 percent of its population is White.

My father worked construction with several guys in the neighborhood. These were all word-of-mouth gigs that you had to know someone to get. The work was consistent and allowed him to provide for the three of us with relative ease.

My mother's friend Sabrina was a regular visitor to the apartment. Months after my mother became pregnant, Sabrina's stomach began to bulge as well. They were best friends, and as with most of the experiences they would go on to share, such as experimenting with drugs, they looked forward to becoming mothers.

The apartment complex was always busy with people coming and going. At night it would come alive with music and the sound of dice hitting the concrete walkway. Young boys crouched in tight circles, clutching dollar bills, yelling at the dice to come up *right*. A halo of marijuana smoke hung above their ring of Afros. Cans of Schlitz malt liquor and bottles of Thunderbird were lined up neatly just outside the circle, waiting for a fumbling hand to reach back for a swig. After a long day's work, my father would join the group to blow off some steam before dinner.

My mother resented his freedom and missed her carefree life on McMillan Street desperately. She could smell the marijuana in the air and wanted a puff and some *Schlitz*. On McMillan Street, she and Sabrina had sat for hours in her father's brown Cadillac, listening to his eight-track player, talking about boys and their lives. The windows were rolled airtight so that the marijuana smoke would envelop them. Now, she had responsibilities. She was a mother, someone's steady girlfriend, and pregnant with a second child within three months of having given birth.

My brother was named after my father, Lanny Charles Mason. He burst into the world on June 15, 1977. We were a little more than a year apart in age. My father was proud of his growing family and the birth of his namesake. Outgrowing the shoebox-sized apartment on Pine Street, three years later we moved to a two-bedroom top-floor apartment on Hill and Lewis in Long Beach, California, a port city twenty miles south of downtown Los Angeles. I was five years old, and this is the first home I remember.

At the back of the complex was a long, cavernous ditch. There was a slight opening in the fence that separated the building from the trench that we kids crawled through in search of sweet sugarcane or to get to the other side of the neighborhood without taking the long way around. We stepped cautiously over broken glass with liquor labels still attached, oversized boulders, and pieces of old railroad-track steel for our treat, the sugarcane, which was sometimes hidden between tall weeds.

The complex was a six-unit, split-level building with black wrought-iron security gates as doors and a crumbling white exterior. Throughout the building, ropes were draped from window to window and filled with socks, shirts, and pants held in place by wooden pins. In place of blinds, white sheets on some of the windows kept outside eyes from prying. In the adjacent building, rippled tin roofs kept both the rain and sun out. There were flowerbeds, but no blooms, only soft chocolate dirt and weeds.

All the people in my life were Black. When I played outside on the block, the men and women who sat watching the action in the neighborhood greeted me with laughter and care. They watched out for us. The only White people I saw in our neighborhood, on an irregular basis, were police officers or social workers who paced the streets looking for addresses, pounding on doors that almost always refused to open. They were outsiders to me and not to be trusted. They were a part of the systems that hurt us. When I saw them coming, I knew it was trouble—a kid could be taken away, benefits cut, or a loved one hauled off to jail. I had seen it before or heard stories whispered between the adults in my life.

I am not sure what it looked like to people on the outside, but to me this was my home.

This is the place where I rode my first skateboard, owned my first dog, and learned to snap my fingers to the beat of the music that often wafted through the paper-thin walls of my neighbor's home. It is also where I tumbled headfirst down a flight of pebbled stairs as I attempted to ride my tricycle after watching an older boy do it with ease on two wheels weeks earlier. Although my body throbbed and tears streamed down my face, I was too embarrassed to tell my mother what had happened or why the skin on the side of my head was all of a sudden missing.

"Get up, it's time to get ready for school," my mother said as she tousled the sheets and pulled on my limp arm.

"Already?" I asked groggily, rubbing my eyes and bending my back toward the sky.

She did not answer and was on to the next bed to awaken my brother.

"We're late, the bus will be here soon and you haven't eaten breakfast."

She was already dressed for the day in her crisp white nurse's uniform as she dashed back to the kitchen to check on the sausage that was crackling in the skillet.

Her voice was urgent, and I knew that I needed to kick into gear. I climbed down the wooden ladder that led to my top bunk and reached for my shirt and pants that were now draped over the dresser drawer. I zombie-walked to the bathroom and began to brush my teeth. Before I could spit the toothpaste out, my mother had come from behind and grabbed a fistful of my hair with one hand and a brown brush with the other. She put the brush in her mouth as she dipped two fingers into the Blue Magic hair grease and applied it to the edges of my hair just above my chestnut-colored forehead. My head jerked back and forth as she worked out the kinks. When she was done, I had one perfectly plaited ponytail that touched the nape of my neck. I was officially awake.

"Here, just take it," she said, shoving the sausage sandwich wrapped in a white paper towel in my hand. "The bus is here."

I grabbed the sandwich, threw on my shoes, and raced down the stairs to meet the small yellow bus that would shuttle me to the local Head Start program at the Community Improvement League a few blocks from our home. The League, as my mother called it, was established in 1964 as an antipoverty agency and ran several programs, job training and tutoring among them. It also housed the first Head Start program in the region. My mother had heard about the program through friends in the neighborhood and enrolled me as soon as I was of age.

The Community Improvement League, with its teachers plucked from our neighborhood, worked hard to counter the many strikes against us, from poverty to hunger. The teachers knew our families and where we came from. They were insiders, as opposed to people sent in from other neighbor-hoods to tell us how to be, live, or act.

The Community Improvement League nurtured my curiosity by allowing a few other students and me to participate in a program at a school across town for gifted learners. I remember feeling satisfaction after mastering a new skill and thoroughly enjoying the praise stingily doled out by the teacher with her clipboard firmly in hand. I was a pleaser and a good girl.

I loved school and learning from the very start. To my parents, I was an alien, not their child. I asked a lot of questions and was content spending my spare time reading, neatly organizing my school worksheets from the day in my purple Rubik's Cube tote bag, and teaching myself how to write in cursive.

On weekends, I would beg them to take me to the library so that I could check out books. Not now, was their standard reply. When I was old enough, around eight or nine years old, I began riding my skateboard alone to the library in my neighborhood. For hours I would sit crammed in a hidden corner absorbed in far-off tales. On the way home, I would sandwich the books I had checked out between my knee and the skateboard, pushing myself all the way home.

In my neighborhood, the library was mostly empty, with few people and a limited selection of titles and activities such as story time or reading circles. This stands in sharp contrast to the palatial libraries in my current neighborhood. They are hubs of learning and activity, with thousands of titles, including the latest releases.

Today, as I am certain was the case then, libraries in poor and low-income communities are open fewer hours and have staggeringly fewer books than those in middle- and upper-income neighborhoods—ninety thousand books in Compton compared with two hundred thousand in Beverly Hills. In the classroom, it is worse. In Beverly Hills there are eight times as many books in classroom libraries as in Watts or Compton. Now, as it was during my childhood, it is hard to believe that the difference between the libraries is based solely on neighborhood and income. As a child, I was none the wiser.

After I was out the door, my mother turned her attention to getting my brother ready. She packed a bag complete with bottles and diapers and dropped him off next-door for our neighbor, another single mother with two teenaged daughters, to babysit until she returned from work. The other mothers in our apartment complex were her support system. Whenever we needed something, she turned to one of them. And they relied on us as well. We were a community.

My mother found a job at a convalescent home taking care of the elderly. Because she lacked a high school diploma and formal training, she was relegated to lowly tasks such as changing bedpans, cleaning laundry, mopping floors, and serving food to the patients. For his part, my father had begun to drive charter buses at Disney Land in Anaheim, California. At the time, I thought he had the coolest job on the planet. He soon lost that job to a licensed operator, and the construction work was sporadic. It was not enough to support us.

My desire to please was matched only by my curiosity about things and circumstances that seemed out of reach or out of sorts. I watched and observed. As a result, I knew everything that went on inside our house and in our neighbor-hood. I listened intently to the conversations around me. I took mental notes without appearing to do so and stashed the information for a later date.

If a fight broke out between my mother and father, I saw it coming days ahead of time because I would have overheard her talking about the problem, whatever it happened to be, with her friends as they sat huddled in our living room smoking Kool cigarettes and drinking malt liquor. The fights, volatile and uncontained, usually centered on other women or money spent carelessly on my father's new and growing drug habit. To make ends meet, he had begun to sell crack cocaine and Sherm, a street name for PCP mixed with embalming fluid, known for the quick high and hallucinations it caused.

As a petty drug dealer, he was a part of a new underground economy that was emerging in the 1980s: the open-air drug market. With his new income, he convinced himself that he no longer needed to look for a steady job. He was making hundreds of dollars by standing on the corner in the comfort of his own neighborhood. He did not have to answer to anyone; he had become his own boss.

The adoration I felt for him was beginning to wane. Up to that point, I had considered myself a daddy's girl. My name, Chataquoa, was tattooed across his muscular chest, and I loved to rest my head on it as I listened to the beat of his heart. The rhythmic thud was comforting and lulled me to sleep. In those moments, I could not imagine being anywhere else. He was my protector.

Now, things were different. He had a new set of friends and was becoming someone I did not recognize, cold and unfeeling. He moved too fast for a hug or for me to tell him what I had learned in school that day. He was simply not interested. We, his family, once the only thing he lived for, had become insignificant. The pain and the longing were unbearable. Our lives were unraveling, and there was nothing I could do about it.

"My daddy's not home," I would say, breathing like fire through the iron gate, trying to persuade the charcoal-colored man on the other side to retreat back into the hole I was certain he had come from.

"Go get him for me, Pumpkin," he pleaded. "Tell him I'm here."

I didn't budge. Instead, I perched on the corner of the couch sucking my thumb, refusing to look at the door. He continued to pound. The reverberations from his knuckles hitting the metal gate made the window shake. Bam. Bam. Bam.

Just then, my mother rushed from the back of the apartment, apologizing for the delay in answering the door.

"He's in the back," she explained. "He'll be right out." She cut her eyes in my direction and pulled her robe closed.

He leaned over to me, grimacing, "Why didn't you let me in? You always do that to me." He chuckled uncomfortably into my ear. "What's the matter, don't you like me?" he inquired.

I didn't, but could not say as much. His name was Jeff and he was the man I held responsible for my father's downward spiral. Whenever he came around, my father changed. I needed someone to blame, and he was the perfect scapegoat.

In the beginning my mother complained when my father left for days or returned home hollow-eyed. The fights between the two of them grew intense and bloody.

"How could you do this to me?" she would yell. "Don't leave me by myself." She would often throw herself in front of the door, blocking his exit. "Stay here," she demanded.

Her pleas only angered him, and he would hit her until she moved out of his way. It was not long until she was partying alongside him and in a deep haze herself.

I tried my best to hold us all together, but my mother and father were both out of reach. The only person I could grip was my brother. He was now my charge, and nothing was going to happen to him or us if I could help it.

"What the fuck," is all my mother said as she surveyed the empty apartment. It was as if we had never moved in. Panicked, she dropped her keys and bags to the floor and raced toward the bed-rooms. We followed like two baby geese on a mother's tail. I hoped that we would find all of our furniture stacked neatly inside of one of the bedrooms. We didn't. We had been robbed.

I had heard stories about people being robbed and houses broken into, but this was different. In those instances, I always imagined a masked man in dark clothes tiptoeing through a house filled with valuables, dropping them into an oversized bag. Here, at the crime scene, there was no broken glass on the floor or cracked window left open to allow intruders access.

The only things left as we surveyed the apartment were a few pots and pans, a velvet painting that hung in the hallway of a man with an Afro who had a joint hanging out of the corner of his mouth, our bunk beds, and toys. I was upset that the painting hadn't been stolen; it spooked me out every time I passed it, no matter the time of day.

Why hadn't the thieves taken our beds and toys, I wondered. Everything else was gone—the couch, the coffee table, the wicker dinette set, the lamps, my mother's bed and dresser—vanished.

"This motherfucker done came up in here and cleaned us out. He took everything!" she yelled through the phone. "I can't believe he did this to me."

She pulled a cigarette out of a half-smoked pack, lit it, and continued to talk. My brother and I turned cartwheels and played tag in the empty room. As I played, seemingly without a care, my heart was sinking. Did my father really take our stuff? Was he gone for good? My head was swirling with the idea of losing him. As I flipped, my feet over my head, the floor beneath me was once again shifting.

"Mama, was Daddy the person who took our stuff?" I asked. "Why did he do that?"

She did not answer. She knew how I felt about my father, and answering would change how I saw him. She refused to look me in the eye and waved me out of sight. I retreated, not sure of what to make of our missing furniture, my screaming mother, and absent father. My head was heavy.

I had a feeling something big was going to happen; I just did not know what or when. Days earlier, a big burly woman with bulging eyes had visited us. She had two friends with her who were just as frightening.

"*Bitch,* open up the door. I know you're in there." She pounded on the door, all the while assuring the women with her that they were not leaving until they got inside.

"Who the fuck are you?" my mother spat out as she flung the entry door open, still separated from the other women by the iron gate. She had her back arched, like an angry cat ready to pounce. She looked back at us. We were watching, hidden behind the doorframe of the bathroom. I held the sleeve of my brother's shirt, my fingernails cutting through his skin. I knew if I let go, he would run and hide.

We had grown accustomed to these visits from these "hussies," as my mother called them, who were bent on letting her know that my father belonged to them, not her.

"Why don't y'all just get the hell on," she advised. "I'm not opening the door. My kids are here. I ain't got time for this bullshit."

My stomach leapt and I closed my eyes, hoping they would disappear. They did not.

"*Bitch*, I don't give a fuck about yo' kids. You betta open this door or I'ma knock it down. You just don't want to get yo' ass kicked."

My mother, seeing us out of the corner of her eye, rushed over and prodded us into our bedroom. "No matter what, don't open this door until I tell you to," she said. "No matter what, you hear me." We nodded. I did not want to leave her alone with those women. I left the door ajar so that I could listen. I peeked through the cracked door. She might need my help, and I needed to be ready if she called for me.

"You think I care about you?" my mother asked cynically when she returned to the gate. "I don't. You're just another one of his bitches that feel the need to come here telling me about him fucking you."

The burly one chortled, "This *bitch* thinks I care, I get more pussy than her man. I'm here 'cause I'm pregnant, and I just thought you should know."

I heard the squeak of the iron gate swing open. Why did she do that? The three women swarmed into our home. By then, my brother and I had eased our way out of the room and back into the bathroom. We had front row seats.

She was fighting for her life. My mother's tiny frame bobbed and weaved around onto the couch, then off, onto the coffee table then off, all while they were in hot pursuit. She was like a target, the punches and kicks coming in rapid succession. My mother and the women slammed into the walls, tumbled onto the carpets, and pushed into the kitchen cabinets. Blinded by anger and betrayal, my mother kicked, punched, and clawed at the air until it connected with a body part. No way was she going to lose this battle *and* be humiliated by this woman who moments earlier announced that she was carrying my father's child. She was ferocious.

I am not sure what happened, but after about twenty minutes or so, the fighting came to an end. The three women stood in the middle of the living room, panting, thinking of what to do next. They had not anticipated my mom's being such a strong fighter.

"Now, get the fuck out!" my mother screamed.

"Come on, let's go," the burly one directed the others. They talked loudly as they walked down the breezy corridor. They would not return.

Moments later, there was another knock at the

gate. It was Sabrina. My mother had called her after the women left. With her were Amber and Chantelle, her two children, my age and my brother's age, respectively.

"Girl, look at your face," she said, touching my mother's swollen, tomato-red lip. "Does that hurt?" Seeing the four of us watching, she shooed us to the back.

"I'm getting tired of this shit. I can't take it no more," I heard my mother say through the cracked door. "He sent me to the clinic the other day. I had to get some pills."

Sabrina shook her head in disbelief although she knew just what my father was capable of, as she had known since he had moved into the neighborhood.

Now Sabrina was back. She had been the first person my mother called after discovering the near empty apartment.

"At least he left the kid's beds," she said. "What are you going to do?"

"I don't know. I don't want to go back to my daddy's house," my mother said. "He's got that woman and her kids living there, and it'll be too much."

They sat in silence, hatching a plan of revenge and for tomorrow.

"I know, I can move in here with you. We can split the rent and help one another out with the kids. I have a couch, a table and some other stuff that we can put in here," Sabrina offered as she surveyed the vacant apartment.

Saying yes to her meant abandoning any hope of reconciliation with my father. What if he wanted to come home? There would be no place for him. My mother wasn't quite sure she was ready. Certainly, he had treated her badly, but she still cared for him deeply and was hopeful that we could all be a family again soon.

Sabrina could sense my mother's hesitance. "Just think about it. You don't have to answer right now. I think it would be fun. We do everything else together," she rationalized.

A few weeks after the epic throw down, there was a new couch in our living room and a dining table in our kitchen. The six of us were crammed into our small apartment, and I did not like it one bit. There was an extra body sleeping at the foot of my bed and new hands on my toys.

"No, you can't play with her. She's mine," I admonished as I snatched my favorite doll out of Amber's clutch. "Get your own."

"Let her play with it," my mother chided from the other room. "You can play with something else."

It wasn't fair, I thought. Why were they here? Why didn't they have any toys of their own? How long were they staying? Where was my daddy? I wanted to know, but was too afraid to ask. These were the kind of questions that could get misconstrued as disrespectful and land me a whipping.

Our lives had become unpredictable and volatile. From day to day, there was always a crisis or problem to be solved. Inside, I felt unsettled and out of control. Externally, I could look around and see that there was no one to tell or to confide in. As a result, I learned to see but not absorb and to feel but not cry. I buried what I had seen, heard, or been told in the deepest, most hidden place within my soul.

I believe this is true for most children who live in poverty. They deny, conceal, and stuff down the pain and violence they experience in order to make it to the next day. If and when they do let it out, it is an emotional explosion that too often falls on deaf ears or leads to punishment.

My father visited us once every couple of weeks. We had begun to craft a life without him. My mother had applied for cash assistance and food stamps from the local county office and was waiting for approval.

I tried my hardest to make his visits as pleasant as possible so that he might consider coming home. I convinced my brother that if we showed we weren't mad at him for leaving, maybe he would stay. My brother agreed. As a part of our plan, we would be as loving and accepting of him as possible. We would also be on our best behavior, no bickering or asking for things. Deep down, though, that is not how I felt. I was angry with him and well aware of his many transgressions against us. If my mother would not punish him for leaving us, I would do so secretly and on my own terms.

"You better be careful," my mother warned during one of his visits. "They are looking for you."

"Who is they?" he sneered.

"The police. They were rummaging through our garbage can outside of the window the other night with flashlights," she said matter-of-factly.

"What for? They ain't gon' find nothing," he said defiantly.

Before my father moved out the last time, my mother told him that she thought he was under surveillance. The police had set up camp in the apartment across from our building. Through the back windows, they had an unobstructed view of all of the happenings at our building. They also had cameras, she said. My father dismissed her as paranoid and her claims as another feeble attempt to persuade him to come home.

The last time he paid us a visit, he never made it up the stairs. As he walked toward the gate, a pack of police officers leapt from the bushes and wrestled him to the ground. Before they could handcuff him, he managed to reach into his pocket, pull out the unlabeled Gerber baby food jar filled with apple-juice-colored liquid, and throw it onto the concrete. Whatever was inside evaporated when it hit the air.

We could hear him yelling up to our apartment, "They got me. They got me. Call my mama and tell her what happened."

My mother made it down the stairs just in time to see the door to the cop car slam closed. He was gone; not just to the streets, but to jail. There was a difference. In jail, he belonged to the system, and there were rules about when we could see him.

My father was sentenced to one year in the Wayside Honor Rancho of the Los Angeles County Jail system for possession of a controlled substance with the intent to distribute. Wayside was built in 1938 as a minimum-security prison for low-level offenders; inmates worked on a farm. In 1983, the prison was renamed the Peter J. Pitchess, after a Los Angeles County sheriff, and all farming and ranching operations were eventually terminated. By 1998 the prison had grown to accommodate almost nine thousand inmates. Today it is the largest and oldest correctional complex in the county.

We visited my father weekly. On Sundays, along with other families, we would board the bus to Castaic, California, a small, unincorporated dairy town an hour outside Los Angeles. On the way there, the bus would be filled with laughter and familiar talk across the aisles.

On one visit, when we arrived, the women and children were all escorted single file into a large, generic room with scary Health Department posters on the wall warning about the dangers of drugs and alcohol abuse. While some of the other children played games and ran around the room, I clung to my mother. Jail was no place for children. It was made for punishment. There were few smiles, no crayons or toys. It was cold and hard, sterile. I tried to pretend I was at ease, but I wasn't.

Looking around, I recognized the thick brick walls. They were the same as the ones in the subsidized housing apartments in my neighborhood. They were even the same color and as hard to penetrate. Both the prison and the apartments were government-issued and controlled.

After what seemed like hours, my mother's name was finally called. Anxiously, we stood up and walked over to the female guard. She worked her fingers down my little body. Her face lacked expression. I could not tell if she liked her job or not. For me, it had become routine and before she could ask, I stretched my arms out like airplane wings so that she would not have to lift them herself. It was a time-saving gesture.

I could see him from the door. His smile was wide and his eyes bright. He was happy to see us.

His Afro looked dull, not as shiny as I remembered. We scurried up to the low wooden partition and took our seats.

"You look good." Compliments always softened my mother, and he knew it. "I like your hair like that."

"Thank you," she replied sheepishly.

As they continued with small talk, my mother reached inside her bag and pulled out a small jewelry box made of old cigarette wrappings weaved together into intricate designs without glue or nails. She handed it to him. He then reached to his side and returned the gesture. I did not understand this ritualistic exchange until much later. My father continued to sell drugs while incarcerated. The boxes hid both marijuana and their proceeds, which were exchanged during each visit. To the guards, the seemingly empty boxes looked like prison craft projects undertaken to pass the time. My mother used the money to supplement her income while he was away.

"Daddy, do you want to see what I can do?" I asked. I still craved his attention. Each visit, I came with a new fact or trick, something I believed was sure to impress him. Clearing my throat, I stood on the stool, steadying myself on the way up. I was too fast for my mother to snatch down. I began to beat my chest like Tarzan and to make the loud *Ohhhowowhooh* sound I had

72

seen in a commercial for the movie *The Adventures of Tarzan* that past week. "Look, I'm Tarzan," I exclaimed. I believed it was a spot-on impersonation.

His smile quickly faded. "Girls don't do that," he chided. He was embarrassed; everyone in our row had turned to look at us. I slinked back down into my chair. They talked for a few minutes more before a stern voice over the speaker system announced that visiting hours were over. Everyone stood up and collected their things. Although it was against the rules to touch, I extended my arms for a hug, hoping he would reach back. He did. He was still my father.

On the way home, the mood on the bus was somber and reflective. We missed the men whom we had left behind in that big box in the middle of nowhere. All we could do was wait until days turned into weeks, months, and sometimes years and they were released.

starved

Our cupboards were bare. I hoisted myself onto the kitchen counter in search of sustenance for the four of us—Lanny, Amber, Chantelle, and me—but there was none. The most I could find was a stale box of taco shells on the back shelf and a lone bottle of ketchup in the refrigerator. At the start of the month, the refrigerator and shelves overflowed with milk, cereal, chicken, grits, Oreo cookies, and fresh fruit. However, by the end of the month, we ate rice and butter at nearly every meal and drank sugar water.

"Mama, we're hungry," I said, no longer able to ignore the persistent gnawing at the pit of my stomach. She was still asleep, but it was well into morning and tipping into the afternoon. I stood by her bedside awaiting a response. I refused to leave.

"Okay, I'll be up in a minute," she said as she rolled away from me to face the wall. I tugged on her shirt. "I'm hungry." This time my voice was raised and strained.

Although I knew my mother considered this kind of behavior defiant, a residual of her own strict southern upbringing, I persisted. If I was going to get a whipping, it would be for a good reason. As the oldest, I was the self-appointed spokesperson for the group, and we were hungry. She turned over onto her back and looked at me through slit eyes. I did not flinch.

She sighed, "I need to go borrow some money from Harrison so I can buy some food."

With that, she got up and slipped on her clothes, the same ones she had worn the day before. On the way out the door, she made a call to Harrison to let him know she was on her way. In the top bunk, Sabrina was snoring, her skinny legs entangled in the bedsheets, oblivious to all that had just transpired and to the fact that my mother had gone.

Harrison, a longtime friend of my grandfather's, worked for the city of Long Beach. He was the person who climbed the thick wooden poles when there was a problem with the electricity or a power outage. He had a good job. When she was strapped for cash, my mother called him. He would pick us up in his wide black car and take us to Church's Chicken or some other local restaurant. My brother and I ate while they made small talk. At the end of our visit, he would hand her a crisp twenty-dollar bill, a little more if he could spare it. "You be careful," he would say as we exited the car. This time, she went alone.

While she was away, we pretended to clean the apartment. I say "pretended" because the most we did was smear dust and dirt around on the coffee table and windows. It gave us something to do while we listened for the turn of the keys in the door. It also assuaged our hunger pangs.

Hours later, when she returned, she had a bag full of groceries—chicken, flour, a pint of milk, bread, bologna, Del Monte corn in the can, and a box of Jiffy cornbread. She made us bologna sandwiches for lunch. For dinner that night, we had fried chicken and corn, one of my favorite meals.

Amber and I were in kindergarten and attended the same elementary school. It was up the block and around the corner from our apartment. We learned to wake ourselves up on time in the mornings and get dressed on our own. On rare occasions, one of our mothers would wake to see us off, but mostly we let ourselves out the door.

My mother had long since quit her job at the convalescent home because the next-door neighbor could no longer take care of my brother. I believed her inability to get to work on time might also have been a contributing factor. Either way, her main source of income was "The County," as she called public assistance, and the money my father sent home in the origami-like jewelry boxes.

One morning, we were about ready to leave for school when Sabrina managed to drag herself out of bed to see us off. The hair on her head stood straight up, and her bones poked through the skin. She walked into the kitchen scratching her head while opening and closing the cabinets. She was looking for something for us to eat, I assumed. There was nothing there. She opened the refrigerator and pulled out two pieces of leftover chicken wrapped in aluminum foil. We were relieved at her find. We were hungry. We waited for her to hand the drumsticks over to us. She didn't.

"Y'all don't need this," she said as she bit into the chicken. "Y'all gone eat when you get to school."

She gobbled both pieces while we watched in disbelief. She was supposed to be the mom. She didn't care if we were hungry. She avoided our tear-filled eyes as she ushered us out the door.

On the way to school, we stopped halfway down the block to pick up a little girl who lived on the opposite side of the street from us. We arrived early and stood in the doorway as she ate Trix cereal and giggled at cartoons. The slurp of the milk and the crunch of the cereal were so familiar. My eyes tracked the motion of the spoon in her hand, from the bowl to her mouth. I desperately wanted some.

"Do y'all want a bowl?" the girl's mother asked. I had been caught staring.

Before Amber could open her mouth to say yes, I answered no for the both of us. I did not want the woman to know we had not eaten before we left home. I thought it would make our mothers look bad and us needy. I felt ashamed and did not want her to pity us. She did not offer again.

A few years ago, I was reminded of this childhood bout with hunger when I stumbled across a speech given by Representative Jack Kingston, a veteran Republican congressman from Georgia, to the Department of Agriculture. He proposed that in exchange for lunch, poor students should sweep floors. Rather than retreat in response to the public outcry, he doubled down and insisted that working for food would instill a strong work ethic in the next generation of Americans. He stated,

> Why don't you have the kids pay a dime, pay a nickel to instill in them that there is, in fact, no such thing as a free lunch? Or maybe sweep the floor of the cafeteria . . . We would gain as a society in getting people—getting the myth out of their head that there is such a thing as a free lunch.

He was talking about me—specifically, my five-year-old self whose first meal of the day was often eaten in the school cafeteria. Despite labor laws that prohibit such work for minors during the school day, Kingston would have expected me to pick up a broom to sweep floors in order to earn my keep.

What I find so disturbing about Kingston's comments is that they are more in alignment than not with our society's attitudes and beliefs about poor people, even children. As a country, we have bought into the idea that the reason people fail to realize their potential or achieve success is that they lack a strong work ethic. Further, we believe that if we deprive poor people of basic necessities such as food, housing, quality education, and health care, they will pick up a broom and work.

Growing up, I believed our family was the only one in our neighborhood that suffered a food shortage at some point during the month. I did not know until recently that more than likely, behind every three doors in many of the neighborhoods I lived in, there was a child wondering where his next meal would come from or feeling too embarrassed to ask for something to eat.

putting out the fire

My father had been gone for close to six months, and I could not decide if we were better or worse off. Our weekly trips to visit him had become an inconvenience to my mother and they began to taper off. His calls home were too expensive. Our phone service was interrupted for non-payment on a few occasions because of the cost of the collect calls. My mother decided to write instead and to see him when she could. Sometimes I would pen a letter, mostly drawings and hearts, to stuff inside the envelope alongside her notes. He was a smaller part of her life now. Partying with Sabrina and entertaining new men, some of whom had been put on the back burner for my father, consumed the lion's share of her time. She was still young.

My brother and I had also become smaller parts of her life. She fed and clothed us and kept us out of true harm's way. By "out of harm's way," I mean that she made sure we didn't drink poison from underneath the kitchen sink or get run over by a semi truck. This was the extent of her care. She made a promise to herself that no matter how much fun she wanted to have or how bad it got, she would never give us away to a relative to raise. This imaginary litmus test of motherhood came about because she had known young girls who had lost their children to the state because of neglect or left them with family members to care for. She vowed not to become one of those mothers.

But she was not far off. She dropped us off almost nightly in our pajamas at my grandma JoJo's house so that she could run the streets. She also left us for days at the homes of people we had only met once or twice. She would tell them she'd return in a couple of hours, but I knew better and tried not be a burden to the host family. We were always on our best behavior. My brother followed my lead. We asked for very little, ate only what was given to us, and sat quietly next to one another until she came back for us.

Sickened by her wild ways, my grandmother asked my mother to let us stay with her.

"Why don't you just leave Pumpkin and Lanny here with me," my grandmother pleaded. "I'll take care of them. You're young. Go live your life. You can come back for them later."

Even I could see that this was a tempting offer. Why should my mother be saddled with two children while everyone else her age was partying and having fun? My father was gone and of no help. Why should she have to bear this burden alone? It wasn't fair.

"I can take care of them. I just need a break every once in a while. It's hard," my mother said. "My kids belong with me. If I don't have a place to stay, they don't have a place to stay. If I'm hungry, they're hungry. At least we're together."

She was proud of this answer, and whenever my brother or I stepped out of line, she reminded us that she could have left us with Grandma JoJo, but she had chosen not to because she was a good mother. We believed her.

I did not want to stay at my grandmother's house. We belonged with our mother. She needed us as much as we needed her. I wanted to watch over and take care of her. I also wanted her to see us as more than an obligation. We were her family.

There were also too many people—adults, children, and babies—crammed into too small a space at my grandmother's house. She let anyone who needed a place to stay live there, regardless of whether there was room. Once in a while a stray dog or cat would also take up residence.

It was chaotic, and there was never any food in the cupboards or the refrigerator besides government-issued block cheese and powdered milk. No one had an assigned bed. At night, it was a task to find a corner or a piece of the floor to rest on until the morning. The floors were blackened with dirt, and the walls were covered in a hard-to-clean combination of fingerprints, food, and scum. This was normal there.

When my mother left us, my brother and I would watch the door, anxiously awaiting her return. If a new day turned into another night, we'd ask my grandmother, "When is my mama coming to get us?"

"Soon," was her standard reply. However, I knew she didn't know. I learned to be patient and not to miss my mother while she was away.

My grandmother had not always been so tolerant and accommodating to my mother. When they were first introduced, around the time my mother was five months pregnant, my grandmother refused to acknowledge that her son was the father of the unborn child.

"That's not Lanny's baby," she said stone-faced and staring deeply into my mother's eyes. "She's just trying to pin it on him. It looks like she gets around." She was talking through my mother, not to her.

My mother was frightened of my grandmother and ashamed of the insinuation that she had been sleeping around with other boys. This was not the case; my father was her first. The air between the two of them softened when my grandmother learned that my mother had no mother. For her, it explained my mother's poor choices and inability to parent. She attempted to fill the role by offering my mother advice on relationships, how to raise her children, and how to conduct herself as a woman in public. For the most part, my mother absorbed the teachings, but whenever the new information clashed with her current reality, she tucked it away for another day and time.

"I ain't worried about it," I heard her say. "If he gets out early, we'll just have to see. He wants to start all over again, but he got a lot of proving to do to me."

She was on the phone with my aunt Linda Rose. I knew because my mother was downplaying her love for my father. She always did that when she talked to Linda Rose. My aunt despised my father. She thought he was a low-down, scraggier version of my *PaPa*.

Although my aunt had moved to California with my mother, they barely spoke on account of my mother's affection for my grandfather. Linda Rose believed that my mother had forgiven him far too easily for leaving them in Texas, and because of that she kept her distance.

Linda Rose was smart, driven, beautiful, and a little off her rocker. Her wide hips, teardrop-shaped breasts, and pristine, white teeth were all inherited from her father's side of the family. She wore her hair straightened, just below her chin. Physically, she was the opposite of my mother. Over the years, she had shot or stabbed at least three people, two men and one woman I knew of for sure. When angered or slighted, she erupted; you never knew what she would do, how much damage she would cause, or what she would reach for in order to avenge herself.

At the time, she was enrolled in Compton

Community College, a chronically struggling, predominantly Black and Latino junior college in Los Angeles. The institution was a bridge to nowhere in particular—very few students ever graduated or mastered the skills needed to move on to a traditional four-year institution. Compton Community College was where students in the community enrolled when they had aspirations for college but lacked the grades or the experience of navigating larger systems outside their comfort zones or neighborhoods.

As my mother and my aunt yammered on, I eyed a book of matches in the ashtray on the coffee table. They were hidden underneath a feathered roach clip, a tweezer-like contraption that smokers used to grasp the last bit of a marijuana joint. It was the day after the Fourth of July, and I still had a lone firework, a ground bloom flower I had pocketed and hid underneath my bed. Now, it was next to me on the couch. All I needed were those matches.

A few weeks earlier, I had gotten a spanking for luring the other kids into the bedroom closet as I attempted to light matches while they looked on in fascination. The flame from the match lit up the closet as we set cross-legged in a circle under dangling clothes. At once and without warning, the door jerked open, and my mother looked with horror as she pulled us out one by one. She must have smelled the scent of a freshly lit match wafting from underneath the door. As I was spanked with a thin woven belt, she went on about how I could have burned down the entire apartment. This time, I would be more careful.

I made my move on the ashtray as she continued to talk about the possibility of my father's returning home. The matches were in my hands, hidden by my tight fist. I inched over to the iron gate, turned the knob, and slipped out of the door. I was free.

I galloped down the pebbled stairs and to the back of our apartment building. The sun had sucked the life out of the grass and left in its place yellow, hay-like weeds that crunched under my feet as I walked to the center of the brick wall. I looked through the holes in the fence that separated our apartment from the ditch. The fence was not very useful, I thought. People scaled it all of the time to gain access to our building or crawled through the opening on the other side. Why was it there?

I was bubbling over with excitement and anticipation. I loved fireworks—the colors, the sparkles, and the noises they made as they spun uncontrollably until sputtering out. Now, it was my turn to ignite the stem and watch it break out into a display of bright colors, a job that was otherwise reserved for grown-ups.

I pulled the cover of the matches back, pulled out a red-tipped match, and wedged it between the covers. Then I snatched it out, causing a flame to erupt. I shook my hand, my index finger throbbing. I dropped the lit match to the ground. The flame ignited the hay. Suddenly, there was a line of fire at my feet, blocking my view of both the fence and the ditch. I was pinned to the wall, as the flames became full-bodied, fanned by the hot Santa Ana like winds.

"I am going to get a whipping" is all I could think, as I stood against the fence, unable to move. After what felt like hours, but was probably no more than a few minutes, a boy on a BMX bike rolled up along the side of the ditch and stopped in front of me. He could see me through the flames.

"Hey girl," he said.

I heard him but didn't answer. I was too afraid to speak. He dropped his bike and walked closer to the fence. I was amazed by how calm he appeared.

He surveyed the situation. "What I want you to do," he said as he began to give me instructions, "is to press your back against the wall, like this." He demonstrated what looked like a slow and stiff slide along the wall toward the parking lot.

I could feel the heat of the fire on my face and arms. My nose felt like it was melting. There was only a sliver of space between my sneakers and the fire. Mimicking his movement, I shimmied my way to the end of the building. Once I got out, I looked around for the boy, but he was gone. All I could see in the distance was the back of his white T-shirt and his brown elbows flapping like wings in the wind.

I turned the sharp corner of the building and raced back up the stairs. With my heart pounding and legs quaking, I banged on the door to be let inside. My mother twisted the handle, pushed the door open with one hand, and continued her conversation. If she had looked into my face, she would have seen that it was soaked with guilt. She did not. I returned to the edge of the couch and began to suck my thumb with a combination of vigor and worry. Had it not been attached to my hand, I probably would have swallowed it whole. Through the windows, I could hear the fire engines drawing near.

"There's a fire in the building," someone yelled down the corridor. "Everybody out and downstairs." The voice was authoritative and sounded like the White manager of our building. We never saw him unless there was a problem or someone was moving in or out.

"A fire," my mother repeated frantically. "Pumpkin, there's a fire. Help me get the other kids together." The others, usually my partners in crime, had been playing some version of house or school in the back room while I was off on my adventure. They, too, were clueless about what I had done.

I feigned ignorance and began to run around the apartment with my mother shouting "Fire, fire, we have to get out of here." Within minutes we were at the front of the building alongside other residents watching the firemen work to extinguish the flames.

Everyone wondered aloud what or who had caused the fire. Was it the summer heat? Was it a teenager sneaking a smoke behind the building? As they tossed around theories, I remained silent. As long as the boy on the BMX bike did not emerge from the crowd of onlookers and finger me as the culprit, I was free to speculate alongside the others. To my surprise and relief, nothing was damaged, except that poor crabgrass.

My father had won release from jail after serving eight months and twenty days of his one-year sentence. With no place to go, he returned to our apartment on Hill and Lewis. I was happy to see him but did not trust his presence or his smile, both of which seemed temporary. My mother did everything within her power to keep him there, including severing ties with the men she had met while he was away.

"We can start over. You can go to trucking school and I can go back to school for my GED," she said, outlining her plan for their future together. "We can move out of here and get our own place again; too many bad memories in this apartment."

My father agreed. He also could not chance

staying too long in the apartment building he had been arrested in just several months prior, lest the same cops discover he was back and began tracking him again. He wanted to remain a free man.

Sabrina understood my mother's desire to make things work with my father and did not stand in the way of our moving out and on with our lives. She was slipping further into addiction and could not manage her half of the bills. It was better this way. She moved her children in with her mother and disappeared into the local trap houses for days on end.

We moved to a one-bedroom duplex a few miles from our old neighborhood. With the exception of the mattresses from the bunk beds, blankets, a few pots and pans, and cooking utensils, the apartment was bare. I did not mind not having a couch or television, as long as we were a family again.

My father, using some of the money he had stashed away before he went to jail, enrolled in trucking school to obtain his commercial driver's license. Given his limited education and training, this was one of the better jobs he could get that paid enough to support our family. He had grown tired of the unpredictability of day-laborer construction jobs that paid poorly and offered little stability. He needed something more permanent that did not require a lot of reading or book smarts.

My mother, seeing his desire to make good on his promise to provide for us, helped him study for his exams and shuttled him to and from driving school each day in our tiny blue Ford Pinto. Late into the night, she would read the dense practice exam book to him because he said the words jumped lines or appeared jumbled when he tried. She saw it as an investment that would pay off handsomely when he was finished. She wanted the four of us to be a family again.

"How did you do?" she asked as he walked through the door. My father had taken his first written exam earlier that day. We were waiting for his answer with smiles of anticipation smeared across our faces.

"I failed it," he mumbled.

"You failed," my mother repeated. They had studied continuously for the last week, and he had answered all of the questions correctly when she posed them to him in a call-and-response practice test.

"I don't know what happened," he said. "I knew the answers, but I was only halfway through the test when they called time."

I could hear the frustration and disappointment in his voice. It was like school all over again, he said. There, too, he couldn't figure out why he never seemed to finish assignments on time or understand the lesson of the day. Then, no one seemed to care enough to help him figure it out.

His mother, an overworked housekeeper, never inquired about his failing grades or missed days of school. She also had very little time to spend talking to White people about how badly behaved her son was or how he was disruptive in class. She hoped he would figure it out on his own. He did not and continued to fall behind. Eventually, he was labeled a delinquent and dropped out of school soon after. Those feelings of inadequacy had resurfaced.

"I don't know if I can do it," he said. "It's too hard."

"You've already passed the driving part of the test. This is the only thing left. You're almost there," my mother said, trying to convince him.

There was no consoling him. He stood against the kitchen counter clearing the dirt from underneath his fingernails with a pocketknife, avoiding my mother's sympathetic eyes.

"I'll be back," he said as he pushed past us and grabbed his jacket from the floor.

"Where are you going?" my mother asked, desperately.

"Down the street to Booty's house." (Booty was my mother's friend that she met when we moved to the apartment; she also partied with my father.)

"When are you coming back," she wanted to know. "I'm cooking dinner."

"Soon, don't worry about it."

When the door slammed, it rocked the apartment. There was nothing she could do except wait for his return. She cooked dinner and put us to bed. I could smell the Kool cigarettes in my sleep and knew that things wcrc shifting again.

For the next several weeks, my father came and went as he pleased, offering no explanation for his whereabouts. When he returned, he would harass my mother for the rent or food money that she kept hidden in the house in an empty Crisco can, in aluminum foil in the freezer, or tucked away on a shelf. On occasion, if she refused, he would beat her until she complied. She would try to resist, but seeing the determination in his eyes and feeling it in his fists, she relented. She never cried.

"Give it to me."

"No, it's the money I need to buy the kids' clothes for school. It's all I have left."

"I'll give it back. I just need it for a little while."

She knew he was not telling the truth. He never gave it back and only asked for more once it was all spent.

"No, I'm not giving it to you. I can't."

I could hear him stalking around the living room begging her for the money. She turned a deaf ear and hoped he would just leave.

"Be quiet. You're going to wake the kids up," she pleaded through gritted teeth, trying to remind him of the obligations he had outside of himself.

It was too late. I had already rolled off the

mattress and was at the threshold of the living room watching the scene unfold. I wiped the sleep from my eyes and focused. This man was unbelievable, I thought. He was weak and selfish, not a father at all.

He was on top of her, his long back curved and his sweaty forehead dripping beads of perspiration onto her face. He was alternating between punching her and demanding the money. She refused to give it to him. I walked over and stood to the left of them. I began to cry.

Seeing me, my mother yelled, "Pumpkin, go get me the knife."

I turned toward the kitchen and walked slowly toward the wooden drawer. I pulled it open and grabbed the black handle of the longest knife I could find. I walked toward the fight. I was not afraid; I was going to give it to her.

"No, give it to me," he said. "Give it to daddy."

"No, to me. I'm the one who told you to go get it," my mother begged, her free arm reaching for the butcher knife.

I stood in the middle of the room, with tears streaming down my cheeks, confused by their claims to the weapon.

"The money's at Booty's house," my mother shouted. "It's not here. I have to go get it." He got off of her.

"Pumpkin, go get Lanny and tell him we're going down the street," she instructed.

When I entered the bedroom, my brother was rolled up into a tight ball with the sheet pulled over his head. He was not asleep. When fights broke out, he stayed away. He also never spoke about what he saw, the next day or ever. And I never asked him to.

"Let's go." I did not say more or make eye contact.

He threw the sheets back, rolled onto the floor, and followed me out of the room. He was still in his pajamas. I too was in what I had worn to bed the night before—a white cotton camisole with a small pink flower in the center, underwear, and socks. My ponytails were askew.

The cold morning air sent a sharp chill down my backside as soon as the door closed behind the four of us. My brother and I were without jackets or shoes. The street was quiet and the grass was dewy as we walked the long stretch of pavement to Booty's house. My mother reached the door first and began to bang on it. There was no answer, so she went around to Booty's bedroom window and hit it with her fist. The curtain twisted open. The woman's face was sour and unwelcoming.

"Open the door," my mother said. "I need to get something. Hurry."

"What's up? What y'all doing here?" Booty asked as she reluctantly opened the door. We poured in.

"I left my money over here the other day. I hid it in your room. I need to get it."

She didn't wait for a response or permission. She made a beeline to the bedroom. I was in hot pursuit. She closed the door behind us. She needed room to breathe. Believing the money was under the mattress or in a shoe in the closet, I waited for her to reach into her secret hiding place. She did not. Instead, she hiked her leg onto the dresser drawer, rolled down her knee-high socks, and pulled out a sweaty one hundred dollar bill.

"I had it the whole time," she said. "But I'm not giving it to him. I need this money to buy y'all's school clothes." She put the bill back in her sock and rolled the sock back up to her knee.

My eyes grew wide as I realized she was buying time to prepare for the fight. I was afraid for her. However, when I looked at her, I knew she was ready. She jerked the door open and stormed down the hallway. "I got it, but I ain't giving it to you, motherfucker," she yelled out.

His eyes were bulging as he wrapped his fist around her long, thick black hair and dragged her outside. I stood on the cliff of the porch watching the scene unfold. My mother's body was twisted as she swung and kicked at the air. I rushed to the door behind them. He kicked and punched; with each blow, he demanded the money.

She fell to the ground and wrapped her arms

around her face for protection. He pushed her onto her back with one foot and got on top of her. I could see her hands grasping for his T-shirt and her feet thrusting upward in her attempt to dislodge him. His body was too heavy. In all of the fights between them that I had witnessed, she was a rag doll, never fighting back. Before I could digest all that was happening, things changed.

"Why did you hit me?" I heard him say as he was knocked off balance and rolled over onto his knees. She jumped up and ran back inside the house. I followed, leaving my father on the ground in agony.

"I hit him in the head. I hit him in the head," she repeated. "There was a brick on the ground and I picked it up and hit him with it." Her breath was heavy and there was a tinge of elation in her voice. The brick was one of a pile that had fallen from the wall separating the houses. I had played on or stepped over those bricks hundreds of times. Not once had I imagined they would win my mother her freedom.

Booty called the police. She did not appreciate being woken up and was afraid my mother might be killed this time. She had seen them tussle many times, but this felt different, more dangerous to her. By the time my father made it down the driveway, there were two squad cars posted alongside the house.

The officers questioned the two of them

separately. While they spoke with my mother, I walked over to my father, who was nursing his wound as blood spilled out between his fingers. He picked me up.

"Do you see what your mother did to me?" he asked. "She hit me in the head with a brick." I nodded. I was proud of my mother for finally fighting back. He had it coming for all of the lies and broken promises, and the way he had terrorized us; he deserved that and much more.

When we returned to the apartment, my mother packed up our clothing, and we moved back to my grandfather's house on McMillan Street. That was the last time the four of us—my mother, father, brother and me—lived together as a family.

"Everyone's entitled to make mistakes, but why keep making the same mistakes over and over again?" my grandfather asked as my mother unpacked our things and settled into the back room of the house.

She did not respond but knew exactly what he meant. She had been living recklessly, and her face and body bore the scars. He could not offer comfort, but he could provide temporary cover while she sorted out her life.

free today

The mark of a good childhood is freedom—the freedom from worry, stress, and burdens coupled with the freedom to explore, grow, and learn without consequence or incident. These freedoms are often denied to children living in poverty, whose minds are consumed daily with thoughts of survival and questions about their next meal, safety, or housing, concerns they may never speak aloud.

My grandfather's house was a welcome respite from the chaos and unpredictability in the Hill and Lewis duplex. There were no fights, arrests, or out-of-control women banging on our door at odd hours of the night. For the first time, my brother and I had the space to be children. We played jacks, marbles, and Barbies and listened to New Edition, Michael Jackson, and Stevie Wonder on my grandfather's record player in the living room. I even joined the Girl Scouts as a Brownie.

Once a week, a hippie-looking woman with long blonde hair picked me up in a rusty flatbed truck and took me to the Brownie meetings held in an old church across town. I am not sure if it was my mother's idea or mine that I become a member, but I never quite understood what was going on or what we were supposed to be doing there—collecting badges, making pledges, selling cookies, I just did not get it. I was one of two Black girls in the large troop and felt out of place.

To make matters worse, while we played jump rope during one of the meetings, the other Black girl punched me out for not allowing her to have two turns in a row. It was my first fight, and I had lost. I did not understand how she could be so angry with me, when we were the only two there who looked like us. In my young mind, I had already made peace with the White girls' not wanting to play with me. I was different from them—my hair was spongy, not blonde or stringy. I did not live in their neighborhoods or listen to the same music. They were strange to me too.

However, I could not figure her, the Black one, out. Why didn't she want to be my friend? When I hopped out of the side of the truck that evening after the meeting, I decided that I had had enough and was never going back. A couple of weeks prior, I had suffered through a slumber party where no one talked to me, asked me to brush their hair, or offered to brush mine. This was not my type of sisterhood.

My mother did not question my decision or ask why I had decided to quit. The following week, when the hippie honked her horn outside our home for me to come out, my mother waved her off and told her I would not be back.

At my grandfather's house, there was plenty of room to roam and a huge backyard with apricot and peach trees that I climbed to pluck the fruit from the heavy branches. My brother and I foraged between the bushes and trees pretending to be pirates unearthing gold and other hidden treasures. There was so much fun to be had between the two of us, thinking up new games to play or forts to build.

My brother was my first best friend. We were inseparable and I adored him. I loved his soft reddish-brown Afro, Chiclet-white teeth, and scrawny frame. He was bright, athletic, and full of energy. He played chess and could do double back handsprings, neither of which I could do, although he tried his best to teach me both. He was also quite sensitive, a trait that I found annoying. When it was just the two of us, he cried a lot and showed too much concern for the things we could not control, like whether or not my father showed up for a promised visit. I believed his tears to be wasteful and hoped over time he would learn not to cry over the things he could not change.

For the most part, my mother left us alone; she spent her days watching soap operas—*All My Children*, *One Life to Live*, and *General Hospital*, in that order—and her nights on the front porch smoking cigarettes and drinking beer. She decided that she needed a break to figure out her plan for the future and for us. So far, she had nothing. At twenty-two years old with two children, she had given up on the idea of going back to school for her GED. With the exception of Linda Rose, she had not known anyone else who had attempted postsecondary education and succeeded. Everyone she knew worked at nursing homes, in retail, or in construction, or else hung out in the streets. And any job she thought about getting, like at another old folks' home, as she called it, she could get without a high school diploma.

She was a high school dropout who had made seemingly bad choices—not respectable at all. As such, she was absent from the middle-class feminist narratives circulating during the late 1970s and early '80s. So were the women she ran with.

We survived on the once-monthly checks that arrived in the mail and on food stamps. If it had not been for my grandfather, we would have bounced from house to house as we had done previously, when my mother and father were separated. I learned that accepting the checks meant that we were open to scrutiny by the state and social workers. On occasion, they would conduct a welfare check to make sure my mother was telling the truth about her circumstances. They were suspicious and scribbled notes on their writing pads as they walked through surveying our house and belongings. Did the television belong to us? Was that our car in the driveway? What was in the refrigerator?

We walked behind the social worker on edge. It was understood that one bad review could result in the loss of income, no matter if it was accurate or not. My brother and I were on our best behavior.

During one visit, the social worker questioned my mother about dark, circular marks on our bodies. Was she burning us with cigarettes? the social worker wanted to know. Were we being abused? The marks were fleabites, my mother explained, from the neighborhood dogs that occasionally wandered into our backyard. It was true. The woman did not believe her. My mother turned to us for help. We confirmed her story. I was puzzled and thought the social worker's zealousness was bizarre. Was she looking for a reason to cut us off? Was she trained to see my mother as a criminal, trying to get over on the system? I believed she was.

In the lives of most poor people, three systems are omnipresent: the criminal legal system, the social service system, and the educational system. On a daily basis, poor people interact, in mostly negative or dehumanizing ways, with these systems. In a very real way, their lives are regulated by these systems, which historically have caused them more harm than good.

My grandfather was a big, chocolate man with bowed legs and a thick Texas accent. When he was home, he cooked big southern dinners of chicken and dumplings, collard greens, neck bones, cornbread, smothered chicken and gravy, and liver and onions.

He had lots of women. I remember many of them, young and old, beautiful and less so. Many of them were single mothers who depended on him to supplement their meager incomes or to help make ends meet. He knew he had the power and could dictate the terms of the relationships. Some affairs lasted longer than others. The smart ones would figure out quickly that he was not the settling kind and would move on, cursing his name. He would stand coolly in the frame of the pink house as they screeched their way out of the cul-de-sac and into the distance. Sometimes, he would whistle as he walked away.

He adored me, his first grandchild. The feeling was mutual. He listened to my stories without interruption and gave me fifty cents whenever I asked so that I could buy a Twix candy bar from the corner store. Every morning at about five o'clock, I would ease into his bedroom to watch the news with him while he sipped sweet coffee, read the newspaper, and prepared for his day. He called me his early bird.

My new school, Abbott Elementary, was about

a mile away from our house. It was my third elementary school in less than two years. I was becoming accustomed to the constant changing of teachers, friends, and playgrounds. I learned not to become too attached to any one thing, lest it be gone the next day.

Somewhere between the Community Improvement League and Abbott Elementary, I figured out that I was bright and that school could be one of the few things in my life that I could control. It was a place, both physically and mentally, away from the chaos, where I could create myself anew. When I parachuted into a new school, I would do my best not only to catch up to the lesson, but to exceed it with bonus assignments. And I was rewarded for my performance. My teachers, seeing my eagerness, created independent learning circles away from the others so that I could continue to excel without distraction.

My teachers were not the only ones who believed I was smart; my mother did too. One of her favorite things to do in front of company was to pull out the *TV Guide* or the Yellow Pages and have me read it to them. She would also ask them to pick a word, any word, and make me spell it. I loved this game because it gave me a chance to show off what I had learned and to make my mother proud.

The big difference between my mother and my teachers was that she did not know how to nurture my curiosity or love of learning. Once, Ms. Ward, my second-grade teacher, called to inquire about my advancing one grade level. She had already spoken to the principal and had gotten his approval. My mother, not sure how to respond or what it would mean for me in the long run, declined her offer, reasoning that she wanted me to understand what second grade was all about. She also said that I would not have any friends if I moved grades because the third-graders would bc too mature. Ms. Ward accepted her answer and never called our home again.

When my mother told me about the conversation between her and Ms. Ward, I was crestfallen. For me, being invited to skip a grade was proof that I was smart and that all of my hard work had not been in vain. From her tone, I could tell my mother was conflicted and still trying to make sense of the seemingly out-of-the-blue call. I assured her it was the right decision and that it was indeed best that I stayed in second grade with all of my friends.

My mother began dating a man named Rick, one of my grandfather's friends. He was a certified jerk and only tolerated my brother and me so that he could gain access to my mother. My father had faded away, and she had become restless, in need of attention. My grandfather had also moved a woman along with her two kids into the house on

McMillan Street. As a result, there was less space, and Rick's house became our new de facto home.

I hated it there at Rick's place. In the entire house, he had only a small sofa, a dining room table, a king-sized bed, and a lamp in the spare room where my brother and I slept on the floor with sheets. It was a true bachelor's pad, not made for children. When Rick came home from work in the evenings, my brother and I would take the lamp into the bedroom closet and tell jokes and laugh until the sides of our stomachs ached. We were out of sight, protected by the closed door and in our own world. We did not care if we were ever found, as long as we had one another and our stories.

When it came time for dinner, we ate quietly while Rick looked at us with contempt. "Look at them, they're heathens," he declared as we scooped chicken-flavored Rice-a-Roni and green beans into our mouths. I did not know what a heathen was, but I was certain he was wrong. We were good, well-behaved kids. Where did this dude, who barely knew us, get off calling us names? If anyone was a heathen, it was most certainly him; he was the ugliest man I had seen in a good while. My mother just stared, not saying a word. I was angry with her for not defending us or packing up our belongings and moving us back to my grandfather's house, where we belonged.

It would not be long before I got my wish. One evening, while we slept in the next room, my mother and Rick got into an argument over the other women he had been seeing, and he hit her. She hit him back and they tumbled through the house.

"Don't hit my mama," I screamed, begging him to stop as I followed the brawl from room to room.

Hearing my voice, my mother began to fight back harder and used all of her strength to not only beat him back, but to whip him. Her punches pushed him out of the door and into the driveway. She chased him around his car, where he jangled his keys until he managed to unlock the door. Once in the car, he called her a crazy bitch, revved the engine, and sped off down the street.

I was happy to be back at my grandfather's house. Although there was less space than there had been, I had missed the peach tree, my walks to school, and Ms. Ward. When we lived with Rick, we barely made it to school. Rather than having us switch schools again, my mother was tasked with waking up early enough to get us back across town to Abbott. Some mornings, she would announce, "Surprise, you get to stay home from school today." "I don't want to stay home, I want to go to school," I would plead. I liked school, and staying home to watch Erica Kane's antics on *All My Children* was not how I wanted to spend my day. Exasperated by my persistence, she would often relent and drop us off late. To me, late was better than not going at all. The teachers never complained or wondered why we were late or absent.

My mother had convinced my brother and me that my father was no good, a deadbeat.

"Your daddy doesn't give a *fuck* about you, us," she would say. "Where is he? He ain't *shit*. He's not here. Ask him for some money the next time you see him, I bet he doesn't have it," she would challenge us.

Though his absence more than confirmed her venomous words, I did not want to believe her. Some days, my brother and I sat perched for hours in the window of the living room, the heavy curtains at our backs, waiting for him to ring the doorbell. I was looking for his Afro, first smaller in the distance, then larger, as he barreled toward our house. It rarely happened. My mother would try to coax us from the windowsill, but we would not budge until it became painfully obvious that he wasn't coming. The next time I saw him, I declared to myself, I would prove her wrong.

My father had long ago stopped announcing his visits in advance. I suppose he grew tired of making appointments, blowing them off, and subsequently having to explain why he did not make it. He figured that if he just showed up on our doorstep, it would feel like a treat, a surprise. It worked. After not seeing him for weeks, we showered him with hugs and kisses and forgot about the gap between then and the last time we had seen him. It no longer mattered. Rushing through the house filled with the anticipation of spending time with him, we packed our overnight bags and a few toys.

"Daddy," I asked as we stood in the driveway of my grandfather's house, my eyes pointed down toward the concrete, "Do you have any money?" The sun beamed down on my bulbous forehead and into my eyes, making it hard for me to see his face. I put my hand up in a salute to block its brightness.

"Why? Why do you need money?" he asked, seemingly annoyed.

I shrugged. I had not thought that far in advance. He tapped on the pockets of his corduroy pants, then slid his hand inside the right-hand pocket. He pulled out a quarter.

"Here, you can have this. This is all I have," he said as he handed it over to me. I was embarrassed for him and for us.

I asked, "Can we come to your house?"

"Not today." He avoided my eyes and straightened his back.

"Why? We never get to go to your house," I pleaded. Whenever we went with him, he would drop us over at my grandmother's house and disappear, not to be seen again until it was time for us to go home.

"Next time."

Just as tears started to well up in the corners of my eyes, my mother wedged herself between the two of us. I sucked them back in as I prepared for her to unleash on him.

"You can't keep doing this to them. You keep disappointing them. If you keep on, I'm not going to let you see them anymore."

"You can't do that. They're my kids too."

"Watch and see."

I knew she meant it. She did not flinch, but took a drag of the last of her cigarette and tossed the butt on the ground, crushing it with the point of her sneaker.

"Y'all come on and get in this house," she commanded as she turned to the door. We followed. I did not look back to see if he was still there.

Between 1982 and 1994, a little more than a decade, I had seen my father no more than a handful of times. He was gone, not to anywhere in particular, just out of sight and unavailable to us.

He had begun seeing a woman named Laurie, a beautiful but broken woman he had met through mutual friends in the neighborhood. She had three children, Antonio, Monica, and Duke, and they all lived pillar to post as a family as Laurie and my father continued to struggle with addiction. I liked Laurie well enough. She spoke her mind without regard for what others thought of her or her decisions. My brother, however, despised her and my father's new family.

I pictured my father's life, when he was away from me, as being incomplete and without purpose. This was comforting as I worked daily to convince myself that we, my brother and I, were better off without him. After a while, he became a distant stranger, not my father at all. That was how I preferred it.

a home of our own

"Do you like it?" my mother asked as she stroked the furry sleeves of her new gift. Her face was lit, and I could tell she was satisfied with herself. The coat enveloped her entire body and made the back of her hair sit up high.

"Yeah, it's nice," my brother replied, saucer-eyed, as he reached out to pet it with the tips of his fingers.

"Who is that man outside?" I asked, pointing out of the window.

My eyes were trained on the metallic pink Cadillac parked toward the end of our cul-de-sac. A husky man stood near the hood of the car with one foot resting on the passenger's-side rim. My mother continued to chatter on about her new coat as she waved her hands up and down its sides and walked in small circles as if she were a model on *The Price Is Right*.

"He said he wanted me to have it. He said a woman as *fine* as me deserves a coat like this."

When she turned away, I rolled my eyes. She could sense I wasn't impressed. "Come over here and touch it. It's so soft, expensive."

I did not move. She looked ridiculous, I thought. Who needs a fur coat in Los Angeles? It is too hot; even on cold days the most you need

113

is a heavy sweater. I wanted her to answer my question and she was stalling. I continued to look out of the window.

"Let's go outside so that you guys can meet him," she said as she flung open the front door and teetered down the stairs. From behind she looked like a stuffed brown bear.

"Stevie, these are my kids—Pumpkin and Lanny. You guys say hello," she directed us. Her voice was full and expectant. She needed us to like him and for him to like us, right away. "Hello," we chimed in unison. I fidgeted and looked toward the sky. She put her hand on my shoulder to quell my movement.

He looked at us through his dark, snake-skinned Gazelle sunglasses. He had a toothpick hanging from one side of his mouth. "How y'all doing," he asked coolly. "Do you like your mother's new fur coat?" He said it with the flair of a fat peacock.

I remained silent. He reminded me of the pictures I had seen in school of Dr. Martin Luther King, Jr., during Black History Month. He was the same shade of brown as Reverend King, and his lips were just as round. That is no doubt where the similarities ended.

"Your mama tells me you're real smart and like school." He stooped to my level and removed his sunglasses.

"Yes, I do. I'm in the second grade," I replied trying to keep my answers as concise as possible.

"That's real good, keep it up."

They continued to make small talk as my brother and I raced around in the grass. I wanted to not care about what was unfolding just a few feet away, but I could not. My ears were bent as I tried to eavesdrop on their conversation. From what I could glean, they had met a few weeks ago at a block party and she planned on seeing him again later that evening. She was also smiling, fake laughing, and caressing his arm— the trifecta she used when she was attempting to decouple someone from his or her money or possessions. It usually worked.

"I'll see you later. I have to take care of some business." He leaned in and gave my mother a kiss on the mouth. She reciprocated. My stomach lurched. I knew this was the beginning of a new love affair, one that I did not trust. The music from his car filled both sides of the street as he turned the corner away from our block.

"I like him. He's got money," she told us as she grabbed a wire hanger from the closet to hang her new coat. The weight of the coat was no match for the cheap hanger. It collapsed, causing the lifeless mink to fall to the floor. She swept it up and carried it to our bedroom. She was floating.

For the next several weeks, she continued to see Stevie. She made herself available to him, no matter the time of day. On occasion, my brother and I tagged along on their dates to Venice Beach, the Santa Monica pier, or the Hollywood Walk of Fame.

Although many of these places were only about a thirty-minute drive from our home, these were the only few times during my childhood that I remember going to the beach or Hollywood. These places were for White people and others without cares, I believed.

Stevie wanted us to like him and tried hard to impress us with his cars, jewelry, and stories of growing up on the tough streets of the South Side of Chicago. He said he had left Chicago to follow his older sister to California because his mother could no longer afford to take care of him. He was on his own, and in California he had learned how to fend for himself.

My brother, now six years old, took the bait. He was smitten and hoped that he and Stevie could do manly things together, like play football, watch boxing matches, or talk about girls. With my father out of the picture, he was thirsty for male attention. It was an easy void to fill.

I, on the other hand, was skeptical and kept a watchful eye. I wanted my mother to be happy, but I could not get past Stevie's slickness and boastful talk. Where did he work? Where did he live? Where did all of these things come from? There were too many unanswered questions for me.

While riding along in the backseat of his car

listening to the song "Midas Touch" by Midnight Star, my brother wedged himself on the armrest between the front seats to ask if Stevie had ever seen a million dollars. Without skipping a beat, Stevie replied that he had probably had more than a million dollars pass through his hands since he began dating my mother. My mother nodded, adding credibility to his claim. *What a load of crap,* I thought.

When my mother went out alone with Stevie, she left us a few doors down with our neighbor Marta, a Mexican woman with long, black hair past her waist. My mother paid her to babysit us with money from her new suitor—he seemed to have an endless supply. As a result, Marta did not care how long we stayed.

Marta's house was filled with people. Her grandmother, father, and brothers all lived there. One of her brothers, Poncho, was wheelchair-bound due to a car accident that occurred at the end of our cul-de-sac following a night of heavy drinking and partying. Everyone took turns feeding and caring for him. There was no talk of his condition or paralysis. We just knew that he would not get better or ever walk again.

When we visited, Marta's grandmother made us hand-rolled tortillas on the stove and set us out on the back porch to play. There is where we stayed until my mother came to fetch us.

"Come see it," she exclaimed as she rushed back

out of the door. From the backyard of Marta's house we had heard a horn honking, but assumed it was not meant for us. It was. By the time we met her, she was behind the wheel of the blue Pontiac Thunderbird.

"Get in," she motioned to my brother and me as she reached over to unlock the passenger's-side door. "This is our new car." Stevie had purchased it for her. No woman of his, he said, would be catching the bus or begging others for a ride across town.

We piled into the backseat as she fired up the engine. "Do you like it?" she asked as she peered at us in the rearview mirror. We both nodded. "Let's go for a ride." There was no denying its beauty and our need for a car. We walked or took the bus everywhere, even at night. If we had a doctor's appointment or needed to visit the county office, we would have to rise early to catch several buses and walk long city blocks before we got to our destination. My legs were usually tired upon our arrival. The car was a welcome relief.

I was excelling in school, and Ms. Ward continued to dote on my performance, without appearing to do so. Another girl joined our learning circle, and I secretly enjoyed competing with her to finish the books or assignments first. I wanted to be number one, and I craved the affirmation that usually came upon the completion of a task. At home, in addition to playing with my brother, I spent hours poring over returned worksheets with the letter *A* circled in red marker or "good job" scribbled across the top, preparing for the next day.

"I have something to tell you guys," my mother said as she stepped in front of the television, blocking our view of the Pac-Man game. This almost never happened unless we were fighting over the console or about whose turn it was next.

"I'm pregnant." Her face was taut, and I could not tell if this was a good or bad thing. I waited for a cue. "Aren't you all excited, you're going to have a little brother or sister?" Suddenly, I could see in her eyes that she wanted us to be happy. She needed our approval and to accept not only the new baby, but also the changes that were happening in our lives.

"We're moving," she added. "At the end of the month, we're moving into our own apartment."

"What about school?" I couldn't think of anything else to say in that moment.

"You can still go to Abbott. I'll just take you there in the morning and pick you up after school," she explained.

I did not like this at all. Moving away to Rick's house had been a disaster; I barely made it to school. How would this be any different?

"Is Stevie going to live with us?" I mustered the courage to ask. I was not ready for a new father

and had grown quite comfortable with our trio—
my mother, my brother, and me. We did not need
anyone else.

"No, not right now, but he'll visit. It's only a
one-bedroom. He did give me the money for
the security deposit and the first month's rent.
This is what we wanted, right, a place of our
own?"

"Yes," I replied flatly. I was numb. The decision
had already been made, and there was nothing
I could say or do that would change the fact
that she was pregnant and we were leaving my
grandfather's house for good. I was going to miss
the peach tree, the early mornings with my *PaPa,*
and the backyard. I took comfort in knowing
that my brother was coming with me. In this
moment, that is all that mattered to me.

I counted down the days until our move. We
did not have much to pack, only our clothes,
toiletries, and a few odds and ends. We would
buy most of what we needed, including new beds,
my mother said, when we were settled.

With the exception of special visits to Kmart, we
did most of our shopping at the Compton Swap
Meet, a big open warehouse with tiny, makeshift
stalls divided by black curtains or metal walls
with hooks on them to hang merchandise. It was
one of the few places in the city where we could
afford to shop and that was accessible by bus.

At the Swap Meet, you could buy almost anything, from a piñata to a Turkish gold chain to socks with the little small cotton balls on the back to laundry detergent, sneakers, and jeans. On weekends the parking lot was filled with souped-up cars and low-riders with music blaring out of the windows. The wide aisles of the warehouse were packed with browsing teenagers and families. In many ways, it was much like malls in suburbia, where young people flocked to hang out with friends, spend their allowances, and test out their adolescent prowess.

The stalls at the Swap Meet were rented mostly by fresh-off-the-boat Korean and Chinese immigrants who, with limited English proficiency and little capital or access to traditional business loans, saw an opportunity to import goods and sell them cheaply to us low-income African-Americans, who had few, if any, stores in our neighborhoods. Wan Joon Kim, a Korean immigrant, for example, referred to as the merchant godfather of gangsta rap by some, escaped North Korea on a fishing boat, landing in California in 1976. To support his family, he rented a stall at the Compton Swap Meet, where he sold a random assortment of household and clothing items, until he found a niche selling gangsta rap by Ice Cube and Eazy-E, long before either had a national or global audience.

Kim had a great and long-lasting relationship with Black patrons until his death in 2014, at the age of seventy-nine. However, this was not the case for most of the stall owners. Most of them were rude and treated us with disdain. In broken English, they rushed us to make purchases, watched us suspiciously if we touched items to feel their fabric or texture, or ignored us if they did not like the way we looked. I found these encounters humiliating and believed they thought we were beneath them. But we had no place to shop where owners would treat us differently.

I imagine this is how Blacks felt during Reconstruction when visiting stores owned by Whites who permitted them to shop but treated us as if they were doing us a favor. Everything we purchased from the Swap Meet was cheaply made and imported from China and usually fell apart within the first few weeks of wear. There was a no-return policy, and within a few weeks, we would go back to buy more stuff. It was a never-ending cycle.

"Mama, can I get this?" I was holding the new Michael Jackson *Thriller* album, the one showing him in a white suit lying on his side. Her hands were full with shower curtains, soap, and a dish rack. A few weeks earlier, we had witnessed Jackson's performance on the Motown 25 television special. He had performed the moonwalk for the first time. He was electrifying. I had to have the album. "Please, we'll listen to it all of the time," I begged. She huffed, but figured it might help to ease our transition to the new apartment. She tossed the album on the register along with the other items.

Our new home, on Caldwell Street, was a ten-minute drive from the Compton Swap Meet and in walking distance of Dale Donuts, home of the thirty-foot concrete donut seemingly suspended above a quaint hamburger-stand-like edifice. We lived in a three-apartment duplex on the corner, diagonal from a huge apartment complex and with single-family homes across the street.

As was the practice in our neighborhood, we waited until the middle of the night before we moved our belongings into the apartment. When I inquired about why, since it seemed silly to move when most people were asleep and the streets were pitch black, I was told matter-of-factly that it was so no one would break in or rob us after seeing what we had moved in.

"Who?" I wanted to know. "Who would steal our things and why would they do such a thing?" My mother ignored my questions, as she did most of the time when the answers pointed to a version of reality that she was not prepared for me to face just yet.

In the small hours of the morning, Stevie pulled up to the curb in front of our apartment in a giant U-Haul with two of his buddies in the long seat of the truck. They quickly unloaded the boxes along with a new bunk bed set for my brother and me. My mother's car, filled with household knick-knacks, was emptied as well. Once inside, they assembled the beds and placed them next to one another, rather than stacked.

Our tiny color television was set on a makeshift stand at the head of the room between the beds. With the beds and television, the room had reached its capacity. We had no living room furniture. My mother made both of the beds; she slept in one and we in the other.

It was the weekend. While my mother continued to unpack, we played on the steps of the duplex. In sunlight, it was modest and just enough for us. To the right of us was a family headed by a single mother, Glenda, who had three children, two girls and one boy. On the other side was a man who lived alone.

Glenda seemed smart and determined. She wore big, round glasses and had slightly bucked teeth. Each morning, she packed her children in her car and drove them across town to attend a better elementary school—as she referred to it in a conversation with my mother—near her mother's house. She said the schools in the neighborhood where we lived weren't teaching what she needed her kids to learn, and that the kids who attended them were hoodlums. My mother agreed, as she continued to chauffeur us back and forth to Abbott.

Glenda was making a distinction, albeit a small one, between us and the people in our neighborhood she viewed as hoodlums. They were the gang-bangers, the drug dealers, and the local kids who were allowed to wander the streets aimlessly. She felt that she was better than them. In her view, she lived in the neighborhood because she had no other choice. She could not afford to live anywhere else.

On occasion, I rode with Glenda to pick up her kids from school. We'd wait at the entrance of the school for the doors to open and for the three of them to race toward the car, pulling at the door handle with eagerness to be let in. All of the other kids who left the building and piled into waiting cars were White. I could not see any brown faces.

One of the girls, Tracey, was around my age and wore her hair in two twisted ponytails with plastic barrettes at the end. On Friday and Saturday nights, we had sleepovers that consisted mostly of watching late-night videos of Madonna on MTV, listening to my Michael Jackson album on my record player, and eating popcorn.

Madonna, with her pale skin, blonde hair, and blue eyes, seemed so far away from me—her looks, her freedom, and especially her geographic location. Where did she live? I had never seen anyone like her in my neighborhood. I watched her move her body, rolling on the floor in one scene and doing high kicks in another in the

125

"Lucky Star" video. Could I do that with my body? Better yet, could I make my hair do that? In the end, I surmised that if I really wanted to look like that, I could. All she had done was tease her hair, throw on some bangles, and put on black tights—I could do that if I wanted to, easily, I thought to myself as I studied her dance moves.

Although we played between our two apartments, Tracey's mother refused to allow her to leave the front porch of our duplex. It was like an island, and she was stranded on it. Even though they lived in the neighborhood, they did not have to be of it, her mother preached on an almost daily basis.

Word spread quickly throughout the neighborhood that there were new kids on the block. Soon, our front yard was filled with children who looked like they'd come straight from the set of the Little Rascals, only all Black. It was on those steps that my first birthday party was held, consisting of bobbing for apples from a large mop bucket, eating cake and ice cream, and having a nonstop Michael Jackson dance party. It was awesome.

My mother, needing her free time, allowed us to wander around the neighborhood and visit the apartments of our newfound friends. I had started to hang with a mix of older girls and ones my age, although they all seemed a little more advanced than me. They didn't play with Barbies or talk about school. They cursed when they talked, using words like "fuck" and "shit" as if they were "please" and "thank you." They also danced like grown women, gyrating and moving their hips wildly to music that boomed out of passing cars and open apartment windows. Where did they learn to do that, I wondered.

They were developed, with breasts and butts. I was not, but believed I should be. No boy would look at me or want to give me things if I did not have a big butt, I thought. I was skinny and average height. My saving grace was my hair. It was beautiful and thick. The neighborhood girls took turns combing and styling it.

The boys on the streets in our neighborhood were not boys at all; they were men. At least I thought so at the time. They shot dice on the side of our duplex in plain sight, looking up at us briefly as we sauntered by, trying to catch their eye. Tameka, the loudest and oldest among us, would often be called back to talk to one of them and be given a couple of dollars for doing so. Sometimes after the guys finished rolling, we would find cash on the ground left behind after a forced dispersal by the police.

Early on I learned not to trust or like the police; they caused us nothing but trouble. When they came into our neighborhood, someone was always taken away in handcuffs—a mother, a father, or a cousin. Sometimes, they disappeared for months or years. Whenever the police came around, everyone scattered and knew not to give up any information or to answer any questions. We could solve our own problems. Justice was dealt on the streets, not in the courtroom or in a jail cell.

In one instance in particular, I remember the police being called because a woman had been sexually assaulted at knifepoint by an intruder who entered through an open bedroom window. The following day, she saw the perpetrator talking to some dudes in the apartment complex. Upon seeing him, she screamed and ranted until he, the perpetrator, was surrounded by neighbors and onlookers who would not let him escape. When the police arrived, with tears streaming down her face and foam in the corners of her mouth, she described for all of us to hear what had happened to her the night before. She was not ashamed. It was gruesome. The police asked the man if what the woman was claiming was true. He denied her accusations, and as a result, they refused to arrest him. Instead, he was held by the police, hands behind his back, while she punched, kicked, and clawed at him until she collapsed to the ground in exhaustion. Once released, he fled, never to be seen again.

My mother thought Tameka was fast. "Fast" meant that she was behaving sexually or being overtly flirtatious with boys or men. And although my mother allowed me to hang out with Tameka, she cautioned me about picking up any of her ways. I wasn't sure if Tameka was having sex— we were all still so young. I thought my mother was being too hasty in her judgment. Tameka craved attention and would do just about anything to get it. Like most young girls, I believe, she was attempting to work through the physical and hormonal changes that were happening to her body. And because she did not have a healthy or safe outlet to talk about the changes, her angst was directed toward the boys on the corner.

Tameka's mother was never home. For the most part, she had the place to herself. At the time, I thought it was cool. There was no adult around to nag her to clean up, tell her to behave, or dictate when to take a bath. Pure heaven. We held lip-sync contests to Prince's *Purple Rain* album for hours on end without interruption. "When Doves Cry" was my favorite; I pretended to fly and everything. I never won. Tameka was the judge, and she said I could not dance and had no rhythm. When we weren't pretending to be Prince or the girl group Vanity Six, we listened to the radio and talked about boys.

"Look what I found." Tameka was holding a loose cigarette in her hand. Despite her claims of having "found" it, I knew it was more like, "Look what I took from my mother's pack while she was sleeping."

"I'm going to smoke it." She rushed over to the

stove, turned it on, put the cigarette in her mouth, leaned her face toward the gas pilot, and inhaled until it was lit.

"I want to see how I look." She walked to the bathroom. We followed. "I look cool," she said. She took another puff as she sat on the lid of the toilet seat with one leg folded and the other pulled close to her thigh. "Here, have a puff," she said, hitting my arm as a signal to take the cigarette from her. I sucked hard.

"Dummy, that's not how you're supposed to do it." She snatched it back. "It's like this," she said before taking a long drag. I was coughing and my eyes watered. She looked like one of those commercials I had seen during afterschool specials, warning kids to stay away from drugs.

"I'm going home," I mumbled.

"Why, are you scared you're going to get in trouble?"

I was, but I made up an excuse. "My mother told me to be home soon because we're going to visit my grandfather."

"She's lying. Get the fuck on," Tameka snarked, waving her hand dismissively toward the door and rolling her eyes. With that, I slipped out the front door and ran the few paces to my house.

When I was out by myself, I ran or skipped. I did not want to get stopped, kidnapped, or worse. The group of us had talked frequently about girls our age who had been raped, had sex, or gone

130

missing, and I did not want to take any chances. I am unsure if what we had heard were urban legends or the truth, but as a result of those stories, I did not feel safe.

Despite our move in the middle of the night, our house was broken into several times. The first time it happened, my mother's prized fur coat was stolen, and the thief left bologna from the refrigerator and a cup of Kool-Aid on the windowsill on his way out. We figured it was a kid. After a few more times, there was not much else to take. These episodes caused me to have nightmares and to awaken in the night to ensure that the windows were secured.

I continued to hang out with the band of "fast" girls but made a promise to myself to never smoke again. For their part, whenever they wanted to get me to do something like shoplift candy from the corner store or sneak a swig of beer left on the coffee table from an adult party the night before, they would call me Smokey the Bear, the mascot for the prevention of forest fires, and threaten to tell my mother that I had smoked a cigarette. The mere thought of them telling my mom sent chills down my spine. It was enough to keep me in line.

Observing the men rolling dice and smoking weed on the corner of my duplex, Tameka vowed that if they dropped a joint after their game had broken up, we would smoke that too. The others nodded and imagined out loud how much fun that would be. I was silent. In my head, that is where I drew a line. Tameka and the crew had gone too far. I did not care if she told my mother that I had smoked the cigarette; a joint was a legitimate drug, and from the Drug Abuse Resistance Education (D.A.R.E.) lectures in class, I knew better.

Between the break-ins and the impending birth of the new baby, Stevie decided to move us to a new home on 110th and Lemoli in Inglewood, about a forty-five-minute drive from my grand-father's house. Although I had to change schools, I was happy to be away from those girls and the secret they held over my head. I had a clean slate and could make new friends.

Our house, a two-bedroom with a deep front yard and wide porch, was located in a residential neighborhood next door to my aunt Linda Rose. She had given birth to a daughter, Thalia, my first cousin, who was now five years old and in kindergarten. Her father, Nicholas, a pie-faced, mixed-race man, had taken off, leaving her mother to raise their daughter alone. Linda Rose did not seem to care and supported the two of them on her secretary's salary.

Behind our house, there was also a small studio apartment where a mother, grandmother, and child lived—Shirley, Miss Bessie, and Clearlie, respec-tively. Clearlie was a year younger than me and was talkative in a know-it-all kind of way. In our first meeting, she challenged me to a spelling contest. I could tell I was going to like her and we were going to be good friends. She was full of life and generous, and she liked to hula hoop and taught me how to play Chinese jump rope.

"Are you sick? Are you all right?" I asked as Clearlie struggled for breath. I had never heard anyone cough like that before, with so much phlegm and mucus lodged in their throat. Her skinny arm grabbed the side of the wall of the house to contain her convulsions.

"I have cystic fibrosis," she said between breaths. "I'll be back, I have to get on my breathing machine." She returned about twenty minutes later, eager to finish our hula hooping contest. I could tell she did not want to talk about it.

"What's cystic fibrosis?" I queried.

"It's a disease that makes it hard for me to breathe and I cough a lot. Sometimes I have to use a machine to help me breathe." I had never met anyone with a disease before. Besides being super skinny, she looked normal, like me, not sick at all.

Shirley, Clearlie's mother, was round with smoky gray eyes and tiny, black freckles sprinkled along her cheekbones. Similar to my mother now, Shirley did not work. Her job was taking care of her child. The two of them became fast friends.

In our new neighborhood, much to his relief

and my chagrin, my brother found a group of boys to hang with. He was no longer subject to my bossiness or requests to play Barbies or house for the umpteenth time. He and the other boys rode bikes, talked smack, and perfected their back handsprings in our front yard. To earn spending money for candy and soda, they also pumped gas at the local station. I was envious of my brother's heavy pockets, weighed down with loose quarters, dimes, and nickels. I wanted in on the business, but he told me only boys could pump gas. I believed him.

"When Ms. Yaguchi is talking, everyone listens. We do what Ms. Yaguchi says."

"Yes, we do what Ms. Yaguchi says," the class sang out in union.

I was in the third grade, it was the second day in my new school, and I was confused. I sat at my desk anxiously looking around for a clue. I thought *she* was Ms. Yaguchi, but now it seemed like somebody else was. This was the worst part of switching schools so often. Once I arrived, I had to learn an entirely new set of rules and start from scratch impressing my teachers and peers. After a few more exchanges, I figured out she was indeed Ms. Yaguchi; she liked to speak of herself in the third person. Weird, I thought. It didn't matter; my only task was to make her like me.

To do so, I did my work and stayed out of

trouble. There were a lot of troublemakers and class clowns, and I did my best to create space between them and me. I rushed through my assignments and was always the first in line at her desk to turn them in for review. It worked. Within a month of being there, I received the student of the week award for my class. The manila certificate handed out during the weekly class assembly had a tear-off certificate for a free McDonald's cheeseburger and french fries. I also came in second place in our class spelling bee, misspelling the word "sandwich." I added an *h* after the *w*, narrowly missing my chance to represent our class in the schoolwide bee. To this day, I have a tiny panic attack every time I write the word sandwich—I still second-guess the exclusion of the *h*.

On our way to school each morning, we stopped next-door to pick up our cousin Thalia. She was home alone with strict instructions from her mother to not leave the house before 8:00 a.m. If we arrived five minutes early, she would not budge until the little hand was on the eight and the big hand was on the twelve. After school, she stayed with a babysitter down the street from our school until her mother got home from work.

Thalia was a beautiful and precocious little girl. Her imagination was wild, and she felt most comfortable with animals. In family pictures, she posed as if she were in a movie or waiting to make her big debut. Linda Rose bragged about her intelligence and her oratory skills. At the school assembly, she had recited the Martin Luther King "I Have a Dream" speech perfectly.

We did not see Thalia as much as we should have, given our proximity to one another. Despite my mother's decision to move one house over from my aunt, their relationship remained strained. When the two of them fought, they kept us apart and did not allow us to play together. Their fights were always over old childhood stuff, disputes that were never settled and wounds that never healed. They were tied by blood and fate it seemed.

"Elaine, I shot that motherfucker." Elaine was my mother's middle name; only family called her that. The house rattled as Linda Rose slammed the back door and locked it behind her. Thalia was with us, waiting for her to return from an errand she said she had to run.

"Who, you shot who?" my mother asked frantically, panicked that the police would arrive to our house any minute. Linda Rose was shaking, but there was no blood on her hands or clothes.

"That Mexican motherfucker. He was *fucking* with Thalia," she said as her knees began to buckle underneath the weight of her words. My mother pushed the wicker dining room chair beneath her bottom. By now, she was sobbing uncontrollably.

"How did you find out?"

"I heard Thalia screaming while she was asleep and I went in to check on her. I thought it was just a nightmare. I woke her up and asked what she had dreamt. She told me that Fredo, the husband of the woman who keeps her after school, had been touching her private parts."

"Did Fredo or his wife call the police?"

"No."

"What did he say when you confronted him?"

"He denied it, pretended he didn't understand what I was saying. So, I shot him."

"Did you kill him?"

"No, the bullet hit him in the arm."

I listened, wide-eyed and ears perked. There were so many questions swirling around in my head. Where did she get the gun? Did she always have it? In my eyes, she was a bona fide badass. She had avenged her daughter. There was no doubt the bullet also carried with it the force of the transgressions of her stepfather against her and my mother. I believed he deserved it.

The police never came to take Linda Rose away, and Thalia never went back to that house or that babysitter again. Case closed. We never spoke about the incident anymore.

School was officially out. Summer had come, and every morning we gathered up the neighborhood kids and walked the four miles to Lenox Park, where the community pool was located, with towels draped around our necks. My mother did not like going to the pool because, she said, there were too many Mexicans. The Mexicans, I believe, felt the same way about our presence. However, these feelings were not enough to keep parents from sending us to the park day after day during the summer.

Although we all swam in the same pool, we were still very much segregated and kept to ourselves. We did not talk to the other swimmers, who did not look like us. An invisible line, like a buoyed rope, separated us.

The irony was that we were not really separated at all. Our lives intersected in so many ways through our foods, neighborhoods, grocery stores, schools, and the disdain we collectively elicited from White people. In their eyes, we were tiny criminals, soon-to-be welfare recipients or teenaged mothers, not like their kids at all.

Without knowing it, I had internalized these feelings of inferiority and of being less than. From a very early age, I worked hard to not be seen as a stereotype. I wanted to be respectable, not a burden. To my disappointment, I realized soon enough that it did not matter how much I tried to fit in, I was still Black. As early as elementary school, I had been called a monkey, a nigger, an Oreo cookie, and a *wannabe*.

I had also called other kids "wetbacks,"

"Mexican jumping beans," and "chinks," all without knowing or understanding why. The only word I had for White people was "honky," which did not seem to have the same effect on them as "nigger" had on me. There was never an explanation of the history or the development of the contentious relationships or distrust among Blacks, Asians, and Mexicans. Or why Whites seemed to be on the top and everyone else was on the bottom. It was the way it was, and I did not think to question it.

In my family, we never talked about politics or watched the news. My mother never cast a ballot in a local or national election. When I was a kid, the only politician I could recognize with any degree of confidence was Tom Bradley, the first Black mayor of Los Angeles. He was a source of pride, and teachers used him as an example that we could be anything we wanted to be if we worked hard enough.

To be sure, the things we cared about most were right in front of us, not out there in some distant and unfamiliar place. We understood what was happening in our community and not much more. I learned to understand racism, racial hierarchy, and class through my interactions on the play-ground, from casual conversations between my mother and her friends, and from watching television.

only one rule

"Mama, can I ask you something?" My mother was in the kitchen, chopping vegetables for dinner. There were pots bubbling on the stove and the baby, my sister, Kamilah, was fast asleep in her swing.

"Yes," she said, wiping her hand on a damp towel.

"Is Stevie a drug dealer?" he asked.

"What? Where did you hear that?" she demanded. Her openness shriveled. My brother rarely asked questions, and this one was his biggest yet. He didn't like confrontation and had learned early on that he fared better when he just went along with the program, whatever it happened to be. My mother was not prepared for his questions.

"Why do you want to know?" She whipped around to face him, hoping that her directness would cause him to retreat. It did not.

"I was just wondering. He has a lot of nice things."

"He does. He works hard to take care of us and to buy all of us nice things." By this time, all of her fingers sparkled with expensive diamond rings, and her neck was adorned with gold. My brother was not satisfied with her answer. He stood fidgeting, waiting for her to tell the truth. His silence was unsettling.

"He is and he isn't," she said. "He's the main drug dealer. He gives the drugs to other people to sell for him. He just collects the money."

What a *bullshit* answer, I thought as I lay on my bed listening to their conversation. I knew it. The only people in our neighborhood who had money and fancy cars were drug dealers. Everyone else walked or took the bus. Previously, I had tried to tell my brother this, but he refused to believe me. He wanted Stevie to be more than, different from, the other men who lived in our neighborhood. Now, he knew the truth.

"We have a rule though. I told him that he can't sell drugs from our house and to keep all of that activity away from us," she said. "Do you understand what I'm saying?" She was proud of the boundary she had set. It was to keep us out of harm's way.

"Yes."

"If anybody asks you what he does for a living, you tell them he's a plumber. He owns his own plumbing company—J and J Plumbing. It's none of their business."

She walked over to our bedroom door and repeated the information to me. She knew I had been listening. Her face was serious and her voice was heavy. Without her having to spell it out to us, we knew there would be consequences if we did not follow the script. We could be taken away. He could go to jail and we would have nothing again. She returned to the kitchen and her cooking.

"I told you," is all I could say as Lanny flopped on the bed across from me. His world was shaken. I sensed that in his head he was trying to put in some type of order the things that he had just heard, but couldn't. I had no words of comfort. I could not tell him that we were going to be okay or that we would not be taken away. We would just have to wait and see.

Being asked to keep such a big secret at such an early age weighed heavily on me, emotionally. It also interfered with my sense of right and wrong. In school, I was taught that drugs were bad and drug dealers were criminals. The cops were the good guys whose job it was to keep both drugs and criminals off of the streets. They were heroes. At home, it was the opposite. Drugs were a means to an end. They provided my mother with the money she needed to take care of us. The men who passed through our house were not criminals, but friends and family members who came to holiday dinners. It was difficult to reconcile, to make sense of these two realities.

My life had changed dramatically, seemingly overnight. I had gone from sharing a tiny room in my grandfather's house with my mother and brother to living in a one-bedroom flat to now residing in the local drug house. It was surreal. We had Doberman pinschers and pit bulls as pets. They barked viciously at strangers, sometimes chasing the neighborhood kids who visited us up the chain-linked fence. There were men, not addicts, moving freely throughout our house, refilling their stock to sell on the streets. There was also a safe filled with thousands of dollars of cash, marijuana, and cocaine stashed in my mother's bedroom.

When I arrived home from school on most days, there were often mountains of marijuana, different kinds—skunk and sess—and snow-white powder spread out on the smoke-colored glass table in the kitchen, waiting to be weighed and bagged for sale. There were empty baby bottles and baking soda on the counter next to the stove, used to turn powder cocaine into crack. Although my eyes clocked all that was on display and I had all but memorized the alchemy for turning one substance into another, I pretended to be oblivious to all that was happening as I walked briskly past the table and into my bedroom.

This is where I stayed until I was called to dinner or into the kitchen by my mother. When I was called, usually to answer a question about school or my brother or to say hello to the group of people around the table, I looked right through my mother and ignored the heavy stench of weed that enveloped the room. I knew better than to wave the smoke out of my face, cough, or complain. I answered the question politely and returned to my room to do my homework or play a game made up with my brother to pass the time.

My brother and I ate alone at a rickety card table on the back porch. At the table, we laughed and talked about our day and the friends we had in common. There was no conversation about how our lives had changed, the distance between us and our mother, or the new man in our lives. We had an unspoken pact, an agreement to step inside and to never question this new world. Who was I to know what was right? I was no longer hungry. I had a home. I was safe, so I believed. This was my life, and I had to make it make sense.

My mother was right. Stevie *was* the main dude —the highest dealer in a low-level street game. Apparently what he lacked in looks, he more than made up for in street smarts. The other guys listened to him and followed his lead. When they did not, he beat them mercilessly. There were frequent stories of bloody lips and blackened eyes as Stevie shadowboxed in the middle of the living room to demonstrate what he had done. To the men, he was a strict father. He showed them the ropes, protected them, and disciplined them whenever they got out of line. Unlike my father, he was never arrested and always managed to remain one step ahead of the police or the detectives often in hot pursuit. I could not make up my mind if Stevie was a diabolical genius or a monster. Time would tell.

54 out of 54

I missed Clearlie, the skinny girl with cystic fibrosis, and Ms. Roberts, my fourth-grade teacher with the petal-soft blonde hair and porcelain features. Ms. Roberts had become my friend, I believed, allowing me to hug her whenever I chose. She also did not mind that I talked too much or moved around the class when I finished with my work. She asked me questions and wanted to know what I thought. I often stayed after school to help her straighten up and prepare for the next day. Among the teachers, I had garnered a reputation as an incessant talker. In the comment section of all of my report cards from first grade on, this was always noted. I wanted to be seen and heard. At school, between the students and teacher, I had a captive audience.

After two years in Inglewood, California, we packed up the items in our two-bedroom starter home and moved to La Puente, a working-class, predominantly Latino suburb about twenty miles east of downtown Los Angeles. There was never any specific explanation given or discussion as to why we had to leave our neighborhood. We just said our goodbyes and left. Although I rationalized that we could not stay in any one place for too long lest we be found out, I was growing sick and tired of moving and the now-familiar routine of starting over.

Moving from Inglewood felt different to me. My time there was the first I could remember in which I'd had attachments, obligations, and an identity. I was seen and understood by people other than my immediate family. I had a best friend and a community of people, old and young, who lived up and down our block who cared about me and whether or not I was safe. I had sleepovers and birthday parties and spent hours riding my bike throughout the hilly streets of our neighbor-hood. I was a child again, enjoying childish things.

After we moved away, I saw Thalia, my cousin, sporadically. She and her mother moved into a local motel after Linda Rose refused the advances of her landlord. She was tired of his shit, she said. Eventually, she met and married a Black aerospace engineer named John. He was nearly double her age. In him, she saw security and a way out of her daily struggles and economic insecurity. They divorced a few short years later, though, leaving her in nearly the same position as before.

Thalia was smarter than me. Her intelligence was natural, innate. Mine was earned, sharpened by my curiosity and tenacity. I had grit and was determined to not take no for an answer. In her eleventh-grade year, Thalia had already taken several classes at the local state college. I was proud of her. By all measures, she was a high-performing student. When I received word while in college myself that she had dropped out of school, I was rocked to the core. I wondered what was the big difference between her and me. How come I was able to make it and she wasn't?

From the outside looking in, we appeared to be a normal family—a mother, a father, three children, and a dog. My mother was friendly with the neighbors and presented like a manicured stay-at-home mom. She made mundane small talk across the fence about the scorching temperatures that plagued the San Gabriel Valley, cooking, or the upcoming holiday. She also bragged about Stevie's successful plumbing business, which afforded us multiple cars, including a Cadillac, Pontiac Trans-Am, and a van for family trips. If the people living beside or across the street from us were suspicious, I was none the wiser.

Truthfully, I really did not want to know what they thought of us. I could not bear the thought of being judged or looked down upon. When the neighborhood kids or their parents asked me questions, I repeated my mother's story word for word. I was determined not to be the reason that Stevie was sent to prison and that we were taken away to live in a foster home or were not accepted by the community.

Our house in La Puente was larger than our last home, with three bedrooms and a huge backyard. A heavy metal gate in the front that screeched when it was forced open and a wooden fence in the back surrounded the fawn-colored rambler. There was also a tire swing that hung from a tall tree in the neighbor's backyard, whether or not they were home. I let myself in by moving a loose wooden slat in the fence. As I spun around with my feet above the ground, the sky was expansive and the sun was warm against my face. On the swing, I felt unburdened and as if my life were my own, disconnected from everything that had become my truth.

In the new house, we were surrounded by things: televisions and VCRs in every room, a microwave, a Nintendo gaming system, a state-of-the-art stereo system with oversized speakers, and a fish tank that stretched across the living room wall. We had all of the latest records—Will Smith and DJ Jazzy Jeff, Keith Sweat and Al B. Sure—and they were played on rotation throughout the day. My mother's fingers, even the pinky, were weighed down with gold and diamond rings. The jewelry that she did not want or could not rotate on and off her fingers, ears, or neck was passed down to my sister, Kamilah, or to me. She had hit the jackpot.

Within a couple of weeks, I always lost or misplaced whatever trinket she had given me.

Each time, she scolded me and warned that if I kept losing things, she would not give me any more. I nodded my head in understanding and pretended to be distressed by my carelessness. I was not. My failure to keep up with the things that held value to my mother was one of my first real acts of defiance and a way of saying I would not be bought.

The house was boisterous and buzzed with activity. The metal fence opened and closed until the wee hours of the morning with people, mostly men, coming and going. My mother enjoyed the attention showered upon her by the men who ate her rich southern cooking of fried chicken, collard greens, and cornbread, doled out compliments about her hair and figure, and hung on her every word. She was flirtatious but knew never to cross the line. That would mean trouble for all involved. The women who visited, usually the girlfriends of the men, looked up to my mother and sought out her advice. She was the Queen Bee, a status she relished.

My brother and I stayed out of her line of sight, and that is how she preferred it. We had been edged out in favor of Stevie, the new baby, and her fast life. Although we had the things we needed—housing, food, clothing, Easter baskets on Easter, Christmas presents on Christmas, and occasional trips to the local amusement parks—I felt like an attachment, something easily removable or disposable, rather than a permanent fixture in the family. We were raising ourselves, my brother and I, emotionally and intellectually, figuring out our places in the world on our own. I was his moral compass and he was mine.

"Sit here," the poufy-red-haired woman said as she pointed to the first desk near the head of the class. Behind me were four other desks divided by a wide strip of Berber carpet that separated us from the rest of the class. We were the fifth-graders in the sixth-grade classroom. It was a special arrangement made just for the few of us. The girl behind me, Karen, a Filipina girl, did calligraphy after she finished her work. The girl behind her, LaShawnda, was Black with long skinny legs and French braids. During the week, she lived with her grandmother so that she could go to our school. I wanted desperately to ask them what the deal was with the seating and the teacher. Mrs. McCabe seemed scary, worse than Ms. Ward and Ms. Yaguchi combined. The two of them were of no help.

"Here are your books. You are expected to cover them with book covers by the end of the week. And do not write in them; they do not belong to you," she said. I did not speak, only nodded in acceptance.

I could see she was going to be tough to win over. Mrs. McCabe was a veteran teacher and crotchety, not like Ms. Roberts at all. She had a low tolerance for misbehavior and did not coddle anyone. She explained things once and that was it; either you got it or you didn't. And if you didn't, it was your fault, not hers.

Her drawl was unrecognizable. It belonged in a Western movie or in *The Dukes of Hazzard*, not here. It certainly was not from the Valley. Where was she from? If I knew a little bit more about her, I convinced myself, I could get on her good side.

At recess, I played with Karen and LaShawnda because no one else seemed to want to be bothered with us. The other kids in the regular fifth-grade class called us nerds and Oreo cookies—Black on the outside, white on the inside—which we ignored or shrugged off, continuing to play hopscotch or Chinese jump rope.

For the first time, I was on the outside looking into my peer group, and it was unsettling. Up to that point, I had considered myself a master at being able to navigate what I viewed as two worlds—my school life, where I enjoyed the praise that came along with being considered bright and excelling in my studies, and my regular life at home and with my neighborhood friends, where quick-wittedness and street smarts won the day. Now, it seemed as if I had been found out. My brother, who was always considered cool because of his sense of humor and athleticism, and gave me a little more credibility, was nowhere to be found.

To complicate matters, I too thought LaShawnda and Karen were nerds and saccharine-like. They didn't say *fuck* or *shit,* talk about boys, or sneak cigarettes. They were also flat-chested and skinny and had no butts—well, just like me. They were nothing like the girls I was accustomed to hanging out with, who wore bras and red lip gloss. Karen and LaShawnda were good girls and proud of it. They did not care that they did not have boy-friends or if they were teased. I cared. I cared a lot.

"You all failed," Mrs. McCabe chided as she handed back the black-and-white maps of Africa with low scores written in giant red numbers at the center of them. For the past week, we had been studying Africa. Our assignment was to memorize the entire continent, all fifty-four countries, including placement, for a test at the end of the module. I got only ten of the fifty-four countries correct. The "10" was like a flashing neon sign. I folded the paper neatly into a square and tucked it into my backpack. It was safe there.

"Unbelievable," she continued. "Not one of you got more than twenty countries correct. Tonight," she instructed us, "take your test home, have your parents sign it, and bring it back tomorrow." The stern look on her face told me that this was non-negotiable. There would be no losing the paper or forgetting to have it signed. "On Monday, you will be tested again and your final grade will be doubled."

On the way home, the paper was like a weighted stone on my back. How would I explain it to my mother? Should I forge her signature? Should I just not give it to her and deal with Mrs. McCabe tomorrow? What could Mrs. McCabe really do to me besides make me stay after class to write standards, a repeat of the same sentence over and over, until my fingers went numb or my wrist gave out?

"Mom, can you sign this?" I waited just before it was time to go to bed before I gave the map to her.

"What's this?" She looked puzzled.

"We had a test and were supposed to memorize all of the countries in Africa," I explained.

"She wanted you to memorize all of these countries. Hell, I don't think I could have done that. That woman's crazy." She threw her head back and laughed into the air. Good, she was on my side. She inspected the crinkled paper further. Her face turned sour. "You missed all of these?"

"Yes," I replied, embarrassed. "Everyone failed, the entire class. We have to take the test again on Monday," I added for context. I held my breath. I could tell she was searching for an appropriate response.

"Find me a pen," she commanded. "You better study." Her head bowed as she signed next to the grade, denoting she had indeed seen it.

"I will." I was relieved that she did not make a big fuss or try to punish me because it was what she thought she *should* do in the situation. I retreated to my bedroom, tucking the paper into my backpack for the next day.

I spent most of the weekend studying for the test. My mother never inquired about how it was going or attempted to help me study. To her, I knew what I had to do and I just had to do it.

No matter how much I had come to dislike Mrs. McCabe, I did not want to disappoint her and committed myself to doing well on the test. When she returned the test the following week, "54" was scrawled across the top of the paper. I was beaming and proud, but her flat facial expression told me I shouldn't be, that this was expected.

Mrs. McCabe represented my first real encounter with performance expectation, the idea that if you set the bar high enough and expect individuals to reach it, for the most part, they will. Up until that incident, I had cruised along, minimally challenged and with little expectation to do more or to excel. In fact, part of the reason I was able to do well or meet the standard was because the bar was set so low. It was fine if I did my work, but if I did not, there was minimal pushback or consequence. This was the case for most of the Black and Brown students in my classes. Every once in a while, we got a teacher who cared, but for the most part, we were passed along from grade to grade whether or not we mastered grade-level expectations.

To recapture my street credibility, I decided to sell candy during recess. As soon as the bell rang, I was swarmed with buyers. I had purchased the candy the previous day from the ice cream truck and sold it to the sugar-starved kids at a premium. It was brilliant. Karen, the Filipina, rented out her calligraphy pen for twenty-five cents for ten minutes; I figured candy would be an even better sell. Seeing the demand, my brother joined in on what was now becoming the family business. We convinced my mother to take us to Smart and Final, the wholesale warehouse, to purchase candy to sell. She agreed and admired our hustle. To her, we were learning what it takes to make it in the world.

"Give me that," a shrill voice yelled over my shoulder. All of the kids who once had been waving crisp one-dollar bills had scattered, and Mrs. McCabe was pulling forcefully on my purse strap. She snatched my brother's bag of candy too.

"Hey, give it back. You can't take our stuff," I protested with my small hand balled into a tight fist against my corduroy pants. We had been caught. Between the two of us, there was about ten dollars' worth of candy left to sell. When I returned to class, I watched helplessly as Mrs. McCabe snipped the tops of the candy wrappers and dumped each piece into the trashcan. Who did she think she was?

When I got home from school, I pleaded with my mom to talk to Mrs. McCabe and to get back the money she owed us for throwing our candy in the trash. She agreed. I was looking forward to my mother giving Mrs. McCabe a piece of her mind the same way she did those women in our neighborhood who stepped out of line. There might even be a fight, and I was sure she would win.

The next day, when I returned home from school, there was a crisp ten-dollar bill on my dresser drawer.

"What happened?" I asked eagerly. "Did she give you the money? Did she apologize for taking our candy away?" I wanted blow-by-blow detail. Did they fight?

"Don't worry about it," she said as she took a long drag of her cigarette. "You got your money."

"But what happened?" Despite my insistent prodding, she refused to answer any of my questions. In hindsight, I am sure the school phoned my mother to let her know what had happened. The discussion, however, I am certain, focused on our behavior, a sure violation of the school code of conduct, as opposed to our right to sell candy and be compensated for lost revenue.

The school year was nearly over, and I could not wait for summer and to be out of Mrs. McCabe's class. Although I was slated to return to her classroom as a sixth-grader, I quietly lobbied for Ms. Keller, an easygoing White woman who listened to the Beastie Boys and was dating a Jamaican man. When the class assignments arrived in the mail, I was relieved that I would not have to suffer through Mrs. McCabe's attitude another year. My brother would also be close. He was in the classroom next to mine with Ms. McBroom.

I spent the summer with my new best friend, Leticia, a raven-haired Mexican girl with glasses, who lived around the corner from my house. I visited her mostly because I was not allowed to bring people to our house without permission. Even when I was allowed, I was so embarrassed by the marijuana smoke wafting throughout the hallways that I almost always made up an excuse to go to her house.

Leticia's house was different from mine. The walls were covered with pictures of Jesus Christ on the cross with a thorn-laden crown, and hand-knitted blankets were draped over tables and the arms of the couch. There were no men, no commotion, and no smoke.

Like me, she shared a room with her sister. Her sister was older and had a boyfriend she spent most of her time talking to on the phone or in his car, parked in front of the house. When we entered the room, she called us *putas* and left in search of a quiet place to finish her conversation.

"I think he would like me."

"No, me. Why would he like you? He's not even Black." She had a point, I thought.

"He's so cute," I said dreamily. "He might like me. You don't know."

We were lying on her sister's bed, looking up at a poster of George Michael with a scruffy beard, tight blue jeans, a pair of dark sunglasses, and a leather jacket. His hair was perfect. I am not sure what it meant to like me, but George Michael was my new biggest crush, second only to Michael Jackson and neck and neck with Prince.

"I'm hungry," I announced as my stomach noisily interrupted our debate over who would make a better girlfriend for George Michael.

"Let's go find something to eat." We rolled off of the bed and walked the short distance to the kitchen in search of sustenance. The only thing we could find was raw chicken swimming around in a tub of water in the kitchen sink.

"*Abuela, tengo hambre,*" Leticia yelled into the living room to her grandmother, who was sitting in an oversized chair watching television. In all of my visits to Leticia's house, *Abuela* never once moved from that chair, no matter what time of day it was.

"Let's make the chicken," she said. "And some rice."

I knew how to cook by watching my mother, and believed I could fry chicken. Leticia reached into the cabinets underneath the sink, pulled out a large pot, and began to fill it with water.

"What are you doing?" I asked indignantly.

"I'm cooking the chicken. You have to boil it."

"That's not how you cook chicken, you fry it. You need flour and Crisco. Do you have any Crisco?" She stared blankly at me.

"What's Crisco? We have this." She held up some kind of liquid oil. The words on the bottle were in Spanish. My eyes traced the bottle in search of familiar words. I could not discern whether it was what we needed to make good chicken.

"I guess it'll have to do." As we seasoned the chicken with salt, pepper, and spices I had never heard of before, Leticia's sister walked past the entrance to the kitchen shaking her head. We ignored her, convinced she'd want a piece of chicken after it was done. The oil crackled as we dipped the droopy chicken into the flour and flung it into the pot. I was charged with flipping the chicken. In reality, I just poked it with a fork, since Letitia was afraid of the hot oil that popped uncontrollably and clung to anything it came in contact with, including flesh.

"How does it taste to you?" I already knew the answer—horrible.

"I told you we should have boiled it."

"It's not that bad. Put some ketchup on it." We stuffed down the chicken and rice and returned to admire the George Michael poster a little while longer before I went home.

The rest of the summer was a blur. On most days, I hung out with Leticia or Lolita, a full-chested Black girl who resided with her mother in a camper outside the house of one of the neighbors. The camper was tight and every inch of it was crammed with stuff—pots, pans, and empty food containers and bottles. The backseat doubled as the bed and there were shirts, pants, and shoes strewn about. We played with her Ouija board and played hangman and other games that did not require much movement. Although I wanted to know why she lived in a trailer instead of a home, I never asked. I knew the answer would be too much for me to absorb and for her to explain. It was beyond her control. How could she possibly explain her lack without taking some ownership or blame for the situation, as children often do in these circumstances?

I was afraid for her. The camper did not feel safe to me, especially at night. What if someone just came in while she was sleeping? The lock on the door seemed makeshift at best. And because she was developed, I saw how men looked at her or inquired about her age from her mother. "Damn, she sure is fine. How old is she?" they would ask with big Cheshire cat grins. "Thirteen," her mom would respond laughingly, not at all alarmed by their interest in her young daughter. Her mother left her alone in the camper for hours while she drank and caroused in the house. I am not sure Lolita was even enrolled in school.

My brother had all but abandoned me for friends who could run faster or hit a ball harder than me, including Alex, the girl across the street who played baseball in the local league and was the star pitcher on the team. I could not compete. I was looking forward to starting the new school year and making new friends.

Ms. Keller had classroom rules that she laid out on the first day of school: No bagging—slang for making jokes at someone else's expense—no fighting, raise your hand before you speak or get out of your seat, and do your best. I thought these rules were easy enough to follow. She didn't seem like much of an enforcer, and I knew if I broke the rules, there would be little consequence. Others felt the same way as they talked over her, walked around the classroom, or refused to do their work. Exasperated, she would plead with us to focus and to stay on task. To make matters worse, there was a Yoohoo epidemic sweeping the campus, and several boys, including Eric, the class bully, drank huge bottles of the sugary drink at lunchtime, making the rest of the day hell for Ms. Keller. The drink was eventually banned.

In our class, there were two reading groups: the eagles and the crows. Ms. Keller spent a significant amount of time with the crows and their math-group equivalent, helping them to sound out words and to solve math equations that should have been mastered long ago. She tried desperately to bring the crows up to speed, but language barriers and the fact that critical fundamental building blocks had been glossed over in previous years ensured that it would not be an easy feat. By the time they had mastered one lesson, we were on to the next. It was a never-ending cycle.

To help us learn, Ms. Keller used rap music and invited us into her life, telling us about her boyfriend, how much she loved reggae music, and where she shopped for groceries. She lived in our neighborhood, she said. Each week, she took one of us out for a meal after school to get to know us better. Because we were a class full of brown kids, she wanted us to see her as more than a White woman and our teacher.

It was a lost cause as far as I was concerned. She was an outsider and would never be allowed into our world fully. What she would come to know about us would be what we wanted her to know about us—nothing more. She would have to inter-pret on her own, decipher the meaning of our interactions, our slang, and our silence on her own. And her understanding would be only partial, mitigated by her experience of growing up in a separate world.

"Do you live with your mom?"

"Yes, and my brother and sister," I replied. I did not mention Stevie because my mother still received public assistance and I was told not to mention him at school or around people I didn't know.

For my meal with Ms. Keller, I requested to go to an outdoor hamburger stand that served chili cheese fries, my all-time favorite. After we ordered, we chose an orange table with a matching circle bench to finish our conversation. She continued to ask questions.

"How long have you lived in La Puente?"

"About two years."

"Where did you live before here?"

"L.A."

"Why did you move?"

"I don't know. We just moved." The food could not come fast enough. I could tell this was her moment to create a bond that could be leveraged in class. I was becoming a difficult student, and my behavior was inconsistent. I was bored. I bothered the crows when I finished my work, and I was loud. I discovered that I could use my voice—I could raise it to jolt the room in my direction. Ms. Keller needed me on her side.

"Do you know what your name means?" She looked anxious and eager to tell me. I stared blankly, unsure of just where she was going with this.

I had never thought about my name before. It was just my name—an awkward name, often misspelled, mocked, or mispronounced by most of the people whom I came in contact with.

"It's the name of a Native American princess. When her father died, she was the only descendant, but because she was a woman, she was not allowed to lead her tribe."

"Really," is all I could muster as I stabbed the chili-drenched french fries with my plastic fork. Why was this woman going out of her way to know me? Why did she care about my name and what it meant? I was suspicious. It did not matter how many questions she asked or how much she told me about myself, I would not let her in. There was so much I could have told her, but I resisted because I knew she could never understand my life or the people in it. There was nothing she could do to help me or to bridge the deep divide that separated our lives. I did not want to be someone's charity case or for her to feel sorry for me. I was strong. For the remainder of our lunch, I cascaded from one nonsensical topic to another in an attempt to keep her probing questions at bay.

Following that lunch, for years I told that story to anyone I encountered who wondered about the origins of my name. On occasion, I added my own embellishments, like the name of the tribe, Cherokee or Iroquois, depending on my mood. In my version, the princess in the story was a humble warrior who would rather denounce her birthright than bring disgrace to her tribe. It was my way of controlling the narrative.

My brother joined the school band. He was learning to play the trombone. The previous week, he had come home with a permission slip that said he needed to rent an instrument in order to participate. He pestered my mother until she packed us up into the Trans-Am and headed to the local music store to pick out a horn. Every afternoon, he holed up in his room practicing. He sounded horrible. It was like an angry elephant ensnared in a poacher's trap had taken up residence in our home.

"What's that noise?" one of the men who visited asked my mother.

"Lanny, he's learning to play the trombone," she said with a slightly boastful lilt in her voice.

"Why?" He began to laugh. "Why doesn't he play football or something like that? That's better for boys."

My mother was silent, unsure how she should respond.

"Lanny, cut that noise out. It's giving me a headache," she yelled down the corridor. "It's too loud," she said to the man.

My brother stopped playing and turned on his television. The sound was different now. It was that of canned laughter and commercials, not of music.

The following week, my mother was called to our school for a second time that school year. This time, it was to speak with Ms. McBroom, my brother's teacher. When she arrived at the classroom, he was sitting at a long wooden table with a thick scowl on his face, arms crossed. I was with our mother and tried to lock eyes with him to let him know it would be okay. He avoided my gaze. I took a seat at one of the empty desks.

"Thank you for coming to meet with me. Today, we had a big problem." My mother's back was stiff and her purse dangled on her forearm. "Usually, Lanny is not a problem, but today he got really upset when I asked him to have a seat."

"I don't understand. You brought me all of the way up here because he wouldn't sit down?" My mother sounded exasperated. For this woman's sake, I hoped that there was more to the story.

"When he wouldn't sit down, I told him to sit at a table away from the class to reflect on his behavior. As I walked over to talk to him, he mumbled that he wished he could shoot me and that I was dead."

My mother's eyes grew large as she cut to my brother. He fidgeted in his chair, looking defenseless and without explanation for what Ms. McBroom had said.

"I thought you should know," Ms. McBroom explained. "Is there anything going on at home that I should be aware of? He usually doesn't give me any problems."

"No. I'm not sure what's wrong with him. This is really not like him," my mother tried to explain in her best June Cleaver voice. She sounded like a cross between the woman in the Palmolive dish soap commercial and one of the White women on the soap operas. It was her practiced White voice.

"We're going to put a note in his school file and he will be suspended for one day."

"I understand," is all my mother said as she motioned to my brother and me to stand up. She didn't know how to defend him. Her task in that moment was to smooth things over so that he wouldn't be expelled and Child Protective Services wouldn't open an investigation. She had succeeded on both counts. As we walked the corridor to the parking lot, I could feel the heat radiating from her body. She pulled out a pack of cigarettes and beat it on her palm until one dislodged and fell into her hand.

"What the fuck happened?" The lit cigarette was dangling from her lips. "Now you got me coming up here to the school and these White people looking at me like I'm crazy."

We were silent as she accelerated around the corners and ripped down the street into our driveway. I wanted to speak for him. Lanny would never shoot or hurt anyone, let alone Ms. McBroom. He had never been in fight, did not curse, and still allowed me to treat him like a rag doll. I wanted to tell her that it was her fault that she did not know that he was struggling in class. He wasn't doing his homework and was falling behind. She should have known, I thought. She was his mother.

"Give me that trombone," she growled as we walked through the side door of the house. "If you can't listen to your teacher, you don't deserve to be in the band." My brother stood in the entryway of the kitchen as he tried to process what he was being asked to do. His feet were glued to the floor.

Don't do it. I tried to send a telepathic wave to him to let him know that I was behind him if he decided to fight back, to say no.

"Now," she screamed. "Do you want me to beat your ass? I'm taking it back. You're not going to waste my money."

He scurried to his room and returned with a large black box that held the trombone. He handed it over and she placed it in the center of the dining room table. "Get out of here." My brother turned around and retreated to his room.

Why did she do that? Why would she take away the only thing that he cared about and that he had committed himself to? I was seething. I wanted to snatch it back and tell him to play as much and as loud as he wanted.

"Are you mad?" I asked as I walked past his room.

"Nope."

"You don't care that she took your trombone?" I wanted him to feel what I was feeling, a mixture of anger, confusion, and disgust. I wanted for the two of us to exact a plan of revenge or at least to get the trombone back.

"Nope, I was getting tired of playing it anyway." He turned his attention to the television, his arms folded behind his head. I searched his face to find an opening, but there was none. He had accepted that he would never play the trombone again.

death is here

When I lived in Inglewood, I went with Clearlie to the doctor for her checkups. The hospital was a forty-five-minute drive from our house. The doctors and nurses treated Clearlie with care.

Clearlie was brave. She did not seem to mind being poked with needles, having her breathing monitored by a machine, or being asked to cough so that they could check the color of her mucus. When the needle reached through her skin in search of blood, her face was expressionless, and she was still. As soon as it was out, she shifted her body and returned to the conversation at hand.

She was going to die. I found this out after she was awarded a trip to Disney World by the Make a Wish Foundation.

"I want to go to Disney World too," I told my mom soon after Clearlie announced she was going. "How come we can't go with her?" It seemed like such a magical and fun place, per the commercials.

"We can't go," she said matter-of-factly. "It costs too much money and you have to take an airplane. Clearlie's going to Disney World because she's going to die. The Make a Wish Foundation is for kids who are really sick and don't have long to live. They don't expect her to live past thirteen."

This information hit me hard. I knew that there was no cure for cystic fibrosis, but I was unprepared for the possibility of my life without Clearlie. I wanted to know when she going to die. Would it be next week, next month, or next year? I needed time to prepare. How would it happen? Would we be playing together and suddenly she would collapse on to the ground, her eyes closed forever? Would I be far away, unable to say goodbye?

I sat in the first pew in the church, adjacent to the tiny casket that held her body. In the casket, she looked washed and scrubbed of all of her color. Her arms were folded neatly over her abdomen, a pose that I knew she would never have held in real life. Her hands would be on her hips.

The money for her funeral was scraped together from donations taken up in our community. Everyone pitched in the little they had to make sure she received a proper burial. Despite her terminal prognosis, she did not have any life insurance.

I wore my Easter dress to the funeral, although the holiday had come and gone many months ago. My hair was pulled into four neatly parted ponytails. Although I felt I had outgrown multiple, strategically placed ponytails years ago, it was my special-occasion hairstyle. My brother was in his Easter suit as well, along with his shiny leather Stacy Adams shoes. My mother wore black, and so did everyone else.

The whole family was there, including Clearlie's dyke great-cousin Mona and her lover, Rhonda. I knew Mona was a dyke only because, in the funeral procession of family and close friends, my mother called her one through the window as Mona rolled past slowly in her Toyota. Being a dyke was a bad thing, I assumed. I could tell from the way it spewed out of my mother's mouth that it was a thing I should not be.

There were people I had never met before at the funeral, including Clearlie's father. I had seen him once in passing, but never at her house for a visit. Was he sad? He really didn't know her like I did. Did he regret not spending more time with her?

I cried for my friend and for the loss of our friendship. She was gone. And I was not there when it happened. I was in another city, making new friends and on new adventures without her. I felt guilty that I didn't ask to be driven to L.A. to see her or to call to check on her. I am not sure my mother would have driven me the thirty or so miles in an hour of traffic to visit, but it would have been worth asking.

My mother sobbed uncontrollably. It was like she, not Shirley, had lost a daughter. The preacher was in mid-sermon. He patted the sweat from his forehead with a cream-colored handkerchief and paced the small area in front of the pulpit. I was not quite sure why he was talking about sin and the need for repentance instead of Clearlie, but I tried in earnest to follow his lecture.

"You have got to get your life right with the Lord before it's too late," he advised. "You never know when your time will run out. God will forgive, but only if you come before him and surrender. The flames of hell burn always, but salvation is forever." He turned to the casket. Clearlie's lifeless body was used as a case in point for the need for all of us to get busy repenting, praying, and possibly joining his church.

My mother seemed deeply affected by his words. She squeezed my hand and promised between sobs that we would return to church. I nodded, but knew it was the moment rather than any real commitment to living a virtuous life that had prompted this promise. We had not been to church in years. The last time she had made such a declaration was at my *PaPa*'s funeral a few years prior. He'd had a heart attack and passed in his sleep, found by one of his lady friends. He was only fifty years old.

His funeral was different, almost a spectacle. All of his buddies were there, including a few of my mother's former lovers. There were also plenty of women in attendance—several of them staked a claim to him. A woman in a red dress and heels grabbed my mother's hand before the service and whispered softly in her ear, "Yo' daddy was a good man." My mother's face turned from sorrow to repulsion as she pulled away from her grip. There was also the woman who had a five-year-old daughter with him. Technically, his new daughter was my aunt.

The preacher talked about my *PaPa*'s life as if he knew him. The man he described was honest, a hard worker, and a good father. He was someone you'd like to know or at least to meet. Linda Rose was wailing. Her back hit the cherry wood pew as she rocked back and forth. Without notice, she leapt onto the casket, causing the wreath of flowers to fall to the floor. The sight of her brown body, hands stretched, reaching for him in death, as she never had in life, was unreal. "Daddy, Daddy, Daddy," she cried. Three men had to pull her down and away. She continued to weep as they escorted her down the aisle and out into the vestibule. She continued to lash out, her body giving way to grief.

I was horrified and amused at the same time. Her sudden movement had jolted the church and maybe Christ himself. In that moment, we realized who we were there to memorialize—an imperfect man.

There again with God as her chief witness, my mother vowed that we would go to church every Sunday.

wedding day

We rushed around the house in search of something old and something new. The preacher was
waiting in the living room, ready to perform the
ceremony. He sat on the couch in a brown suit
and tie, sipping ice water. My mother did not
know she was getting married today. It was a
surprise, another gift from Stevie.

"Elaine, this is so romantic," Linda Rose
squealed as she pulled out a green dress she had
worn when she was crowned homecoming queen
at Compton Community College. It was a little
big for my mother, but it would have to do. It was
the best they had. My mother swept her long,
wispy hair into a loose bun and slid on a pair of
disco heels. She looked beautiful.

"I'm nervous," she said. "Do y'all think I should
marry him?"

Yes, we replied in near unison. We were swept
up in the excitement of the moment. It did not
matter that it seemed as though she could not say
no. That the preacher's being there implied that it
was already a done deal. She just needed to walk
down the hallway, the improvised aisle, into the
living room, and say yes. I put on my Easter dress
and brushed my hair back into a slick, high
ponytail that grazed my earlobe. I did the same for

my sister, Kamilah. We sat on the flower-covered couch and waited for my mother's grand entrance.

It was a brief ceremony, and there was no cake or celebration afterward. Stevie and my mother spent the evening out and returned the following morning. This was her first marriage, and we now had a stepfather. I wasn't quite sure if I was ready to give up the idea, still lodged in the back of my head, that my real father would come back for us.

That same year, my mother also enrolled at a fledgling for-profit school, to pursue a paralegal degree. Although she was quite comfortable with her life and did not want for anything, she had a desire to finish something, to be independent just in case things didn't work out between her and Stevie.

In their recruiting brochures, the school claimed that it did not matter if applicants had never finished high school. That, she was told, was a technicality and would be overlooked given her newly gained credentials. The school seemed legitimate and guaranteed her a job after she graduated. Each day she fought eastbound traffic to attend morning classes and studied during the evening, out of sight of anyone who might question her realness or authenticity as a drug dealer's wife. The books were thick and seemed to contain all she needed to know to become a qualified legal professional.

For her graduation, she wore a blue gown and

cap. The proud families, including ours, flooded the rented auditorium as each name was called and the graduate walked across the stage. For most of the families there, I could imagine the graduation was a milestone delayed or complicated by life. I am certain my mother wasn't the only high school dropout to walk across the stage that evening. I was proud of her and her new career. She was a professional and would go to work in pantyhose and a skirt, just like the woman who lived next-door to us.

"I was fired," she said quietly, her neck craned out of the car door as she pulled into our driveway. She had been employed for only a few weeks and had worked for a young, White lawyer in Los Angeles.

"Why?" I asked, puzzled by her announcement.

"He tried to hit on me and I told him I wasn't into that. So I quit." The words swirled like a small tornado in my head. It did not make sense to me. Did she really quit because she refused to have sex with her boss? Did bosses really do that? I believed her and thought he was a pervert.

Later, I found out the lawyer's wife had called my mother a maid when she saw her vacuuming the office. She did not approve of his hiring such an attractive aide and demanded that she be fired. He complied. Telling me initially that he'd hit on her was her way of hiding the humiliation and powerlessness she felt for being fired so abruptly. Even in her shame, she was adept at creating a world that was uncomplicated by the messiness of racism, classism, and, in this instance, sexism.

After about six months of searching for work, my mother returned to the college where she had received the paralegal certificate and demanded clarification on its value. She had taken out thousands of dollars' worth of student loans and needed them to pony up on their job guarantee. As reinforcement, she took along with her another student who had also had a hard time finding a job. After being brushed off by several different college officials, the two threatened to file a complaint against the college with the Better Business Bureau or whomever else they could think of in that moment. Fearing their cover would be blown, the college forgave their debt in exchange for their signing a non-disclosure agreement. And just like that, my mother was unemployed without a degree and back to square one.

There were eyes watching me. I could feel them whenever I undressed, when I slept, when I walked through the house, and even outside my bedroom window. The only place they were not was at school.

"You're not my daughter. That's why I can do this to you." He had called me into his room when my mother went to L.A. When she returned, I would be at the foot of her bed, frozen, out of my body, watching television. "What are you doing in here?" she once asked. Before I could answer, he did. "She's just watching television with me. No big deal." She never asked again.

It was 1989 and I was in junior high. I was excited about the new school year and all of the promise it held. There were different classes with several teachers. I immersed myself in extracurricular activities and enrolled in classes I thought I should be in whether or not I had been assigned to them. I was an average math student but decided to enroll in advanced algebra. That was where all of the smart kids were, and that was where I wanted to be. And because I continued to get good grades, the counselors never questioned me and assumed I knew better than they did where I should be. I am also not sure they received many requests like mine.

Since my experience with Mrs. McCabe, I had given up on my attempts to impress teachers or win them over. It never paid off in any significant way. I was also growing tired of having to prove myself. The teachers, not unlike the social service workers who processed our paperwork for cash assistance, had their ideas and assumptions about me and the other kids who looked like me. And they treated us accordingly. The messages we were getting from all over were clear: There was only so far that we could go.

I decided to become a cheerleader. I thought I was pretty enough. My hair was long and straight enough. And my mouth was loud enough. I missed varsity tryouts because my mother refused to allow me to go. She would not sign the permission slip or give me money for the uniform. Her decision making was arbitrary and highly dependent upon her mood. There was no such thing as a simple request. We had to ask more than once before we received an affirmative answer. Months later, when they created a junior varsity squad, she relented and I tried out along with fifty other girls and made the team.

In the mornings before school started, all of the girls stood in the front of the school as boys at least ten years older than us drove by in their low-rider cars, playing loud music. The lucky girls got called to a car and were whisked away before the first bell rang. "Cover for me," they would yell back as the car door slammed shut. I had perfect attendance.

"Breyann's pregnant. Did you hear?"

"No. By who?"

"Some dude. Her daddy's friend," my friend Michelle explained nonchalantly. Her boyfriend sat between her legs as she braided his hair. "That's why you have to be careful," she warned.

"Be careful about what?" I wondered. I nodded in agreement, not wanting her to know that I had no idea what she was talking about.

The summer before seventh grade, my period started while I was out on a bike ride. I felt an intense cramp shoot across my stomach, but assumed that it was because I had ridden over a pothole. I found out otherwise when I went to the bathroom.

My mother, to mark the occasion, purchased a small bouquet of carnations and a box of Teen Spirit maxi-pads and placed them on my dresser drawer. She then popped the *Miracle of Life* video into the VCR and left the room. This was *the talk*—a video, a box of pads, and carnations. "Keep your legs closed and don't get pregnant," was all she ever offered in terms of advice.

Breyann was in the eighth grade. She was a year older than me and on the varsity squad. She was beautiful, with cinnamon-brown skin and long curly hair. She had long legs that seemed to be made for short cheerleading skirts and a chest that filled out the varsity jackets of the guys who lined up to see her wear them. She wore heavy mascara and lip gloss that made her mouth sparkle. Now, she was pregnant; she was a bad girl, and the baby was proof of her promiscuity.

According to the rumors circulating around the school, the guy had disappeared once he found out she was pregnant. He was still around the neighborhood, but unavailable to her. She was no longer a cheerleader. Her stomach had betrayed her. It wasn't too long before Breyann disappeared as well. She stopped coming to school and I received random updates every once in a while about her from Michelle.

She was going to be a mother and have a baby shower where she would receive diapers, baby powder, blankets, and onesies. It was supposed to be a celebration, but it wasn't really. How could she take care of a baby? She was only thirteen.

From middle school to high school, I probably encountered more than two dozen or more *Breyanns*—young girls impregnated by men several years their senior. To be sure, there were a few girls who got pregnant by guys our age, but it was rare. There were never any conversations about accountability, consent, or the derailed futures of these girls. Nor about the predatory behavior of the men who lay in wait as girls as young as twelve walked home from school or visited friends' houses down the street or around the corner.

When a new baby arrived in our neighborhood, we all took turns paying visits to the newborn and its mother. Bedrooms that were once filled with teddy bears and posters of the latest teen heart-throb had become nurseries seemingly overnight, with diapers and Similac formula stacked neatly in crammed corners. The financial responsibility for the babies' care often fell upon the shoulders of the mothers of the young girls, who were themselves struggling to make ends meet. In a sense, they too became new mothers.

I spent my afternoons and evenings in front of the television as the now-familiar hum of the house roared on. From somewhere we had gotten a copy of Spike Lee's *School Daze*, a drama-musical, set in Atlanta, Georgia, about students at a historically Black college. I watched it nearly every day. The Black people on the screen fascinated me; they were different from us. They had problems and concerns that seemed other-worldly, almost trivial. Hair texture. Skin color. South Africa. They weren't preoccupied with survival, money, hunger, violence, or not getting pregnant by some random boy or man. *School Daze* was my introduction to the Black middle class and the kids who lived there. Somehow, their lives didn't seem real to me.

When I wasn't on the couch, I sold newspapers door-to-door for the *Sun*, the local paper. My boss was a jelly-filled White man with long, thin, black hair just past his shoulders. His scrawny mous-tache barely provided cover to the top of his lip.

He picked us up in the evenings at around 4:00 p.m. at McDonald's. From there, he dropped us off in random neighborhoods to sell sub-scriptions. The van trolled the neighborhood until we knocked on every door on the block. I was a decent salesperson and sold at least ten subscriptions a day, fifteen on a good day. The prize for the most subscriptions sold each month was a small trophy and bragging rights. To get people to purchase subscriptions, we told them we were raising money for a trip to the state capitol, in Sacramento, and that the more subscriptions we sold, the greater our chances for going on the trip. It was a lie. There was no trip to the state capitol. We were paid weekly, under the table, for the number of subscriptions we sold.

The other salespeople, if you could call us that, were White. Only they didn't look like the White people I saw on television. They wore dirty sneakers and their jeans were worn down to the thread with holes in them. They had crooked teeth and dirty hands. As we whipped through neighborhoods, Guns N' Roses and Metallica blared through the speakers. I pretended to mouth the words although I had no clue as to what they were saying. It all sounded like a bunch of screaming to me.

One evening as the door slid open, and right as I hopped in after my route, a boy with dark short hair and flaming acne along his jawline called me a bloodsucking nigger. I was stunned into silence and crawled into the corner of the dark van. It was the first time anyone had looked me directly in the eyes and called me a nigger and I had no context for knowing the circumstances

184

under which I would be referred to that way. The word cut like a knife, but I had no retort.

That night as I exited the van, I felt heavy and discombobulated. I had been nice to everyone and pretended to like their music, bobbed my head and everything. I was also a hard worker, outselling all of them in my first few weeks. I was playing by the rules.

The following week, I called in sick. I needed a break to sort out my feelings and to digest all that had happened. I didn't understand these people. Why were they so mean? Why did it seem like I was never a part of their club? Was it because I was Black? A girl? Both?

When I returned to work, I was told matter-of-factly by the fat White man that the pay I had already earned would be docked for the week I missed, leaving me with about fifteen dollars for a full week's worth of work. He told me that my not showing up had cost him money and that he would not absorb the loss. That's bullshit, I thought. First I had been called a nigger, now this. I quit on the spot and asked to be driven home. I had my limits and they had been reached. Besides, I had already saved up enough money to buy the daybed I had seen at a local furniture store. It was beautiful and made me feel special, like the girls on television whose parents doted on them and bought them whatever they wanted. I was going to make myself such a girl.

home street

"I don't care what you do, I want that house," Stevie said as he handed over a leathery brown bag full of cash to the real estate agent.

"I understand. I'll work it out. Don't worry about it."

He had no job, no verifiable income, no bank account or tax return. Everything would have to be fabricated, invented out of thin air. This was not a problem for the real estate agent. The money was not to buy the house. It was the fee to get around the systems that held the American Dream at bay for people like Stevie.

We were moving again. I was at the tail end of seventh grade, and it was time to go. Stevie, who had narrowly escaped arrest following a high-speed chase on his motorcycle, was anxious to get away from a place he believed had become compromised and therefore unsafe. This time he wanted to buy, no more renting, he said.

The American Dream was boarded up and the grass was dead. The front door was not a door at all, but a long piece of particleboard with a padlock on it. The interior and the backyard were no better. There were holes in the walls and doors hung off their hinges. Weeds and wild brush stretched up to the windowsills. The house was at the end of a cul-de-sac across from a park.

"What do y'all think? This is going to be our new house. Everyone will have their very own room," my mother said as she walked around the house making a mental checklist of all the work that needed to happen to make it habitable.

I didn't know what to think. We were now about two hours outside L.A., farther away from everyone and everything I cared about in Inglewood. The sun was dry and unforgiving here, as if it had positioned itself for a rest in this town and now refused to leave. I did not see any kids playing, not at the park or on the street. The quiet was unsettling.

I could see in my mother's eyes that she had plans for the house. It was going to be her very own mansion. She would paint it, plant flowers, rip the weeds out by the roots, and install new cabinets, floors, and a doorbell for the neighbors to ring. Since her mother had passed, she had never quite felt at home in any one place. This would be an opportunity for her to create a beautiful place of rest. She did not know, however, that it was a house built on quicksand.

San Bernardino, our new home, is the poorest city of its size in California and, after Detroit, the second-poorest in the U.S. It is a majority-minority city, with more than half of its population Black or Latino. Our neighborhood was mostly

Black, with no Whites and few Latinos. The only race mixing that occurred, from my recollection, happened in school, and barely there.

The move was uneventful, not unlike the ones before it. The only difference is that I had my daybed and a new, flowery, Victorian-like comforter that swept the floor and draped neatly over the sides of my bed's metal frame. I chose the bedroom in the back of the house, away from the commotion that I was all but certain would ensue once we settled in.

We were not allowed to play outside or go to the park. And it was not until school officially let out that I noticed that tons of kids our age lived in the neighborhood. In fact, there was a foster home two doors down with at least ten kids living there. Every afternoon, they played baseball, dodgeball, and tag in the cul-de-sac until the streetlights flickered on right before dusk. We watched them enviously as we toiled in the hot sun, helping my mother plant flowers and fill the walkway leading up to our front door with shiny white stones. They saw us too.

My mother did not trust the neighborhood or the people living in it. She decided unilaterally that it was best if we kept to ourselves. Fewer problems and opportunities for people to get into your business, she said. In her mind, she was better than the people who waved at her as they drove past our house and pulled into their garages.

She was from the city and had money and cars. And her children were well behaved.

The neighborhood looked fine to me, not much different from the ones we had lived in before. All neighborhoods, I assumed, became dangerous only if you ventured onto blocks where you had no business going. You figured out what was safe by talking and listening to the people who lived there. If you could, you avoided the unsafe parts of town, unless of course that was where you lived.

San Bernardino was like that. You knew where to go and not to go. The other side of the park, for example, was bad. Not bad as in *don't go there ever* bad, but bad like *be cautious* bad—*watch your back* bad. Gangs controlled the neighborhood blocks. The Delman Heights Bloods claimed the area between California Medical Center and Cajon Boulevard. The California Garden Crips claimed the area bordered by Baseline, 16th Street, and Lytle Creek Wash. And the Little Zion Bloods claimed their namesake apartment complex and the area between Highland Medical Center and 16th Street, a street shared with the California Garden Crips. If you lived on any of these blocks, the boys who patrolled the streets and hung out in their cars were not gang members but probably your brother, your cousin, or the guy you grew up with. There was love and affection for these boys. Today San Bernardino has more than three dozen active gangs or sets.

Luckily for us, and unbeknownst to my mother before we moved in, our cul-de-sac and the few adjacent blocks were outside staked gang territory. What this meant is that we had a small degree of freedom and did not have to worry about gunshots or death meeting us on our doorstep.

We lived a few doors down from the Carters: a wife, a husband, and their three daughters. Mrs. Carter, a cherub-faced, heavyset woman, made her own clothes and was the neighborhood snitch. From what I had gleaned from my mother, Sam, the youngest daughter, belonged to her current husband, Mr. Carter. The other two girls, both teenagers, were from a previous relationship, and their father was out of sight. She and my mother bonded over their perceived shared experience and bad luck with men. The two oldest girls were wild and self-styled rappers. Akeely had left home as soon as she turned eighteen, and Birdie, fifteen and too young to leave, struggled to follow her mother's rules about curfew and boys.

All three of the girls were stunningly beautiful. I kept my distance because my mother talked horribly about the daughters when Mrs. Carter was not around.

"You mark my word, one of them is going to end up pregnant," she would say to me.

To let her tell it, there was nothing worse than a *hot in the pants* girl or a pregnant teenager. Both things, I assumed, she had once been. If I took a nap in the afternoon, she asked if I was pregnant. If I ate too much for dinner, she asked if I was pregnant. She never asked if I was having sex, which would have been the most logical first question; she always focused on the nightmarish end result.

"If you bring a baby in this house, you've got to get out. You can't stay here," she would warn me. I am not sure if she meant it, but I did not want to test it. I did not put anything past her. I also wasn't sure that I wanted to ever become a mother. She made it seem like such a struggle, a burden. In my head, I was fashioning a life for me that did not include any of what I had seen—a life far from here. I just had to get there.

My mother told Mrs. Carter about Stevie's plumbing business and all of the plans she had for the house. She had become masterful at small talk and the details of our manufactured life. She also invited Mrs. Carter over for dinner, something she never offered to any of our previous neighbors. She needed someone to boss around. We lived too far for any of the men from our old house or their girlfriends to visit.

"We'll be back. Don't open the door for anyone. Don't open the blinds," she instructed as she grabbed her purse and jacket and headed toward the door. "If you need anything, go to the Carters'.

She's watching the house too." We nodded. She took my little sister with her. They would be gone for at least six hours.

As soon as I was certain they were gone and not coming back, I announced to Lanny, "I'm going outside."

"She told us to stay inside."

"So, who cares? Let's just go out for a little while. We'll be back inside before they get home." I had become tough-ish and defiant, both at school and at home. I had my own mind and decided that if a rule didn't make sense, when no one was around or I could get away with it, I would not follow it. And staying inside on a hot summer day was the very definition of making no sense. Not wanting to be left behind, my brother followed me out the door. I was sure if we were caught, he would blame me. I was okay with that. I was often the fall guy. It came with the territory of being the eldest.

We walked to the center of the cul-de-sac, right in front of our house, where there was a baseball game going on. "We want to play. My name is Pumpkin and this is my brother Lanny." The game stopped as everyone gathered around to introduce themselves: Wardell, Annie, Papa, Ishmael, Kenyon, D'aja, Tiffany, and a boy named Spike. Wardell and Papa, we discovered, lived on the other side of the park.

We joined the game. I ran as fast I could around

the soda can bases and my brother hit the ball as hard as he could. We needed to make a good first impression so that we would be asked to play again another day. I knew Mrs. Carter would tell that we were outside, but what did I care? We had new friends.

seeing with
only these eyes

The poor are made to believe that they are getting what everyone else is getting—that our schools are the same, our hospitals the same, and our neighborhoods are equipped to produce doctors and lawyers. But they are not.

Poor people and their neighborhoods receive only a fraction of the resources, and institutional and structural support, that middle- and upper-middle-class people and communities receive. In fact, growing up poor and in impoverished neighborhoods lowers children's chances of going to college, limits their future income, and influences the kinds of jobs they will hold as adults. Rather than becoming lawyers and doctors, they are more likely to work in the service industry or hold lower-skilled, manual labor jobs.

All of the schools that I attended from elementary through high school were average at best and failing at worst.

However, growing up, I naïvely believed I was receiving the same quality education as other students across the country and that I had an equal shot at success. I did not know, however, that elsewhere, students attended prep and private schools meant to funnel them to the most elite colleges and institutions. I also did not know until my first year of college that Head Start and food stamps were for poor people.

When I realized the truth, I was angry and felt like I had been cheated. The idea that I was excelling was suddenly placed within the context of the conditions in which I, and those surrounding me, had grown up. In the real world, I was behind, and the gap between me and my middle-class and upper-middle-class peers— between what I knew and what they knew— seemed insurmountable.

There was nothing around me, or that I could see, that signaled directly that the road ahead would be hard and filled with land mines meant to derail my friends or me. I did not know that there were real kids, not just those on TV, who had more and were being prepped for success. In all fairness, they did not know about me either.

away

"She can live with you."

"Do you want to live with us?" my aunt Glo asked as she swiveled around to face me. She was milky red, almost white, with freckles and fine, chestnut hair. My aunt Glo was married to my father's brother Monk. Her family cut ties with her because she married my uncle, a man they saw as beneath her because he worked with his hands. We were the only family she had.

I was unsure how to answer. I looked into my mother's face to see if it held an answer. It did not. She wanted me to leave. I was becoming a nuisance and harder to control. It was my mouth, she said.

That spring, I had written a short story about a girl who wanted to be a lawyer and who was being touched by a man. It took me days to write and I was careful not to use real names. When I was finished, I took it to my mother and read it aloud.

"What do you think?" I said, hoping that she would know that I was the girl in the story and that I needed help.

"It's a good story," my mother said, her eyes connecting with those of my aunt Linda Rose, who had been visiting us for the weekend. I wanted her to hear it too. "How did you come up with it?"

I shrugged my shoulders. I wanted her to fill in the gaps and to stumble over herself in a rush to embrace me. I wanted her to tell me that she knew all along and that everything would be okay. I wanted her to avenge me like Linda Rose had done for her daughter years earlier. She did not. Instead, she reached for her pack of Newports on the kitchen counter.

I stood there under the brighter-than-usual dining room light until the carpet began to feel like tiny razors stabbing at my feet. Say something! My throat hurt and I felt choked.

I was jolted from my trance when my mother turned away from me and began a conversation with Linda Rose about nothing in particular. It was as if I hadn't confessed or told on him. After a few more moments of stillness, I turned and retreated down the long hallway back to my bedroom, landing hard on my daybed. I tucked the crinkled paper inside the diary I had been keeping for the last year or so. It was a birthday gift from my mother. She said she had given it to me because I liked to write.

It was now a few weeks before the end of summer and the start of ninth grade. I was fighting at home, literally. Lanny, once my only confidant, became my chief adversary. The understanding we'd once shared about our life and how upside-down it was had faded, replaced with his fierce defense of it. He had accepted it. It was his way of surviving. For a while, he allowed me to sleep with him in order to avoid Stevie. At night, I would curl up in a tight ball at the foot of his bed, knowing that I was protected. After a while, he stopped allowing me to do that.

Now, he too thought I was a troublemaker. And so we fought. We rumbled through the house and chased one another from room to room. He had grown stronger and I was lucky that I was not seriously injured. I felt betrayed and abandoned.

In my last year at Martin Luther King Jr. Middle School, I had been suspended twice: once for fighting a girl named Angela over a boy named Vern and another time for not removing my sunglasses fast enough when requested to do so by the principal. Sunglasses were considered contraband, along with blue or red bandanas and a host of other items that were listed in our student code of conduct. I did not hear Ms. Oliver above the clank and noise of the lunchroom when she asked me to take them off. And when I did manage to read her lips and her sudden gestures toward her own eyes, as if she herself were removing sunglasses, she had already snatched me from my seat and guided me to her office.

Ms. Oliver did not want to know why I had not complied with her request. For her, there was only one answer: I was being defiant and she needed to regain control.

It was an open secret that she did not like us, the neighborhood kids. She treated us as though we were a burden upon her very existence.

During lunch, she walked between the long, brown tables clutching her walkie-talkie. The static-y device was a direct link between her and the school security guards, who could be summoned promptly if there was an issue. Our table, filled with loud talk and boisterous laughter, seemed to garner more than its fair share of her attention.

Our saving grace was her jovial vice principal, Mr. Vincent, a Black man who talked to us and saw us for what we were—children. He was the one who had recommended me for the gifted and talented program a couple of months into the new school year. Since Mrs. McCabe's class in the fifth grade, I had been tracked out of the gifted and talented program. However, every time I moved to a new school and my transcripts were reviewed or an observant teacher noticed that I was ahead of the curve, I would be reassigned.

The gifted and talented learning cluster was an insider's club and treated like an island unto itself within the school. It was also where most of the highly trained teachers and White kids in the school were. The difference between how the students in the gifted and talented cluster and the others students were treated by teachers, admini- strators, and even the janitors was obvious. We were the good kids. If anyone was going to "make it out," or go to college, it was going to be us.

When I joined the class or the learning cluster, both the teachers and students were suspicious. How did I get there? How long would I stay? Was I *Black* Black? Did I know how to behave? For the first few weeks, I felt like I was being evaluated or that the teachers were looking for a reason to send me back.

There were never more than one, maybe two, kids of color in any of the classes. And if there were more than two, by the end of the semester the Black or Latino kids, not the Asian kids, were tracked out, meaning they were sent back to a remedial or otherwise less challenging learning cluster. No one ever asked why; it was just assumed that we couldn't hack it.

The truth is that there was a hostile undercurrent for students of color in those classes. The teachers ignored us and waited for us to fail. The White students included us in conversations only for group projects, when they were forced to do so. When and if we excelled, it was viewed as an anomaly or fluke. For some students, I imagine the invisibility, isolation, and constant feeling of never being good enough drove them out. I brushed off these feelings and told myself that I belonged there as much as any of them. I knew they could not kick me out. I could stay as long as I did the work and wasn't disruptive.

I was under no illusion that those kids or the

teachers in those classrooms were my friends or a part of my community. In between classes, at recess and during lunch, I rushed back to my friends to hang out. They understood me. I did not have to pretend to be quiet and obedient, contain my laughter, or act White. I was one of them.

I had a boyfriend, DeWayne. He had a flat top and was in all of my classes before I was moved to the new learning cluster. Although I still wore a training bra, he thought I was *fine* and told me so instead of doing his work. He was not my first, but my second boyfriend. Previously, I had dated Wardell, who lived on the other side of the park in our neighborhood with his grandmother and brother Papa. He was smart and skinny just like me. For those two reasons alone, all of our friends thought we should be together and that we made a good couple. Wardell was quiet and liked to hold my hand. The relationship was short-lived. We broke up shortly after I received a whipping from my mother for walking to the park with him without her permission.

"You're suspended," she said through her thin, pursed lips.

"Why, I didn't even do anything?" I pleaded. I did not mind the day off from school, but I did not want to get a whipping. These days, both my mother and Stevie belted me frequently for seemingly minor infractions—not doing the dishes properly, not being nice to my sister or allowing her to play with my things, wearing lip gloss, talking back, fighting with my brother, not cleaning the toilet well enough—nothing I did or said was ever right.

I also did not want to be home alone with Stevie, who was often there during the day, resting until he returned to the streets of L.A. to work at night. It did not matter if I were sick or had the worst cramps imaginable, staying home was not an option.

What a *bitch,* I thought as Ms. Oliver handed me the paper outlining the suspension and my alleged crime. It was a yellow carbon copy; the white original was reserved for my mother.

When my mother arrived to pick me up, she was in her freshly pressed Laid Law uniform. After being unemployed for nearly a decade, she had gotten a new job as a bus driver for the local school district. On a visit to a Kmart one afternoon, she noticed a woman in a blue uniform sitting at a table. Curious, she stopped by, and the woman explained that they needed drivers, that no experience was required, and that my mother would be trained. Seeing an opportunity, my mother completed the application on the spot and was shuttling kids door-to-door within a few months.

The ride home was quiet. There was nothing I could say to convince my mother that my behavior did not merit a full-day suspension—the White woman had spoken. I was guilty. There were no two sides to the story. She dropped me off at home and returned to work to finish her route.

Back then, I wished that my mother had done more or been more present in my school life. She just wasn't. I believe this was the case for most of the parents in my neighborhood. They were called to the school only when there was trouble. They were never invited to engage the teachers and staff as peers or colleagues or asked for their input about the curriculum—something I now know is commonplace in middle-class schools and communities.

My mother, along with the other parents, was treated as if she were deficient, a bad mother. In the eyes of the teachers and administrators, she was apathetic and disengaged, a part of the problem. Her experience with and perception of her child was secondary to the opinions held by those in charge. I imagine she must have felt powerless within a system that she had very little experience navigating successfully. As a result, she kept her distance, interacting with the system only when it was absolutely necessary.

I wanted to be saved and to have someone come to my defense. In this moment, it was my aunt Glo. She was doing her best to rescue me without appearing to do so.

"Answer her," my mother prodded. I could tell she was becoming anxious and a little agitated. "You can come home to visit on the weekends."

We both knew that was a lie. The distance and traffic alone made that a near-impossible feat on a weekly basis.

"Yes, Pumpkin. We'll bring you back down here to visit whenever you want or if you get homesick," my aunt Glo chimed in.

Although she knew everything, my aunt Glo's tone was even. I had told her about Stevie, the beatings, and how my mother did not believe me. I asked her to help me and that is what she was attempting to do.

If I answered yes, I would give my mother what she wanted and increase the depth of the ocean between us. If I declined the offer, I would be stuck at home and would most certainly never have another opportunity to escape unless I decided to run away. And I did not have the guts to run.

"I'll go." My tone was definitive and matter-of-fact.

"Okay," my mother said. "You'll have to do what they say."

"I know."

There were few goodbyes. My mother signed over guardianship and I was gone.

The green stucco apartment building was nondescript. If you had been searching for its address, you would have passed it several times before realizing you were already there. It was on a busy main street with a mix of bars, apartment complexes, and random businesses. On one side of us was a gay bar with dark tinted windows and on the other a big, old house filled only with women. My uncle Monk cautioned me to stay away from both. He said the women practiced witchcraft and the men going in and out of the bar could not be trusted.

The two-bedroom, first-floor apartment was small and sparsely furnished. I shared a room with my cousin, Monk Jr., an only child. At only seven years old, he wanted a big sister, and I fit the bill. He followed me around the cramped quarters and hung on my every word.

I felt safe in my new house. There were no fights, beatings, or harsh words being hurled my way. I could be a teenager and obsess over teen-aged girl things like clothes, hair, boys, my body, and music. I found a hairdresser, named Boo, who cut my hair in an asymmetrical bob with a long ducktail that reached the center of my back. I told him about my boy troubles, my friends, and how nervous I was about my first day of school. He listened patiently and offered sage advice as he crimped my hair with hot marcel curlers and applied holding spray that made the curls stiff and unmovable for the next couple weeks, until my next visit.

My uncle worked nights, and after my cousin, little Monk, went to bed, I watched television and listened to my aunt Glo's stories about when she was a high school track star and everyone called her Rabbit because of her stature and speed.

"Here," she said as she twisted off the cap of a Seagram's wine cooler and handed it to me. She had a beer for herself. It was her second one. I sipped the berry-flavored, fizzy drink as we watched television in the dark. It tasted good and felt cold as it slid down my throat. We did this every night.

"I wrote my father today," I announced non-chalantly in between sips.

"You did?" she asked, pausing and placing her beer on the side table next to the bed.

"Yes, I'm hoping he'll write back."

"What did you say?"

"Nothing, really." I attempted to downplay the gravity of what I had just let slip out.

I hadn't seen or spoken to my father in years. When I decided to move with Aunt Glo and Uncle Monk to Long Beach, I thought I would see him more often and that we might become father and daughter again.

My hopes were dashed when I inquired about his whereabouts and was told by my uncle that he was locked up. He was in a prison in Norco, in Riverside County, a city closer in proximity to San Bernardino than to my new home. I did not ask why he was in jail. I just assumed it was drug-related.

Prison and the criminal legal system were ever-present in my life when I was a child. At some point, my father, my cousins, and most of my uncles had all interfaced with the system. Whenever I heard that someone had been stopped by the police, gotten roughed up, or been arrested, I accepted it as the way things were.

My uncle Monk visited my father regularly and told him that I now lived with him and my aunt Glo. Uncle Monk had given me his address so that I could write him. My father wrote me back for a while, and then the letters stopped coming. I didn't inquire about why they had stopped or ask my uncle to deliver a message on my behalf to him. I knew better than to foist my expectations upon others.

Years later, my father told me that he had continued to write but that the letters were intercepted by Uncle Monk at the request of my mother, who had sent word that she did not want me to write or visit him in jail. My father said he was infuriated when Monk told him that he would not bring me to visit or would no longer allow me to write him. My mother had the final say on the matter.

My new school, Woodrow Wilson Classical High, was two long bus rides away from our house. It was located in the Signal Hill neighborhood of

Long Beach. On the first day of school, the cheerleaders, band, and football team welcomed us with a raucous pep rally that filled the open courtyard. The seniors strutted through the halls and the nervous first-year students darted off in different directions to rotate classes as soon as the bell rang. There were four thousand students at Wilson, and I did not know anyone. Weirdly, I was comforted by this knowledge. I saw my anonymity as an opportunity to reinvent myself. Who would I be without the constraints and burden of my history and experiences? I was free.

I enrolled in all advanced-placement classes, including chemistry. I also signed up for dance and another elective in order to find my new crew. At lunch and after school, I hung out with the dancers, who attempted to show me new moves as Bel Biv DeVoe, Deee-Lite, and A Tribe Called Quest blasted from the speakers in the open square.

"Hey Nikki, come over here," Tina, my new friend, said, waving. "This is Booker and that is his older brother Derrick, you know him though, right?" I did know Derrick; he was a junior and super cute. His brother Booker was a smaller, slightly awkward version of him.

Nikki was my new name. It was a shortened version of my middle name, Nicole. It was also the name of the girl in that Prince song that I loved. I thought it had a nice ring to it. I did not want to be Pumpkin anymore, and Chataquoa was too cumbersome for a teenager. It also sounded too formal to me. The only time I ever heard it said aloud was when it was being read off a list.

"Hey," I said, smiling in Booker's direction. I had seen him around school and between classes. We stood in a closed circle making small talk and plans for the weekend.

"Ask your aunt if you can come over my house." Tina was a year older than me with big breasts and curvy hips. Her hair was crimped like a fan. She wore bright red lipstick, gold bangles, and long dangling earrings. I met her younger sister first, in my dance class, but the two of us did not click. Tina with her sophistication and maturity was a better fit and was my new best friend. She also knew about things that I did not—like older boys and sex.

My last best friend, Shay-Shay, short for Shaylyn, in San Bernardino, was a lot like Tina. Because of my puniness and the fact that I seemed like a nerd who was trying too hard to be bad, they were both protective of me. They would not let anyone bother me and if necessary would fight for me.

Shay-Shay lived across the park and had been sent from L.A. to live with her father because of the violence in her neighborhood. Her mother was also overwhelmed by her boy craziness and worried that she might end up pregnant.

We bonded immediately and became inseparable.

When I spent the night at her house, we dyed our hair with tropical punch Kool-Aid, listened to music, and hung out with her older sister and her boyfriend. At night, Shay-Shay and I shared a bed while her sister and her sister's boyfriend spooned in the other. Her father never checked on us or questioned why we always slept with the bedroom door locked.

When Shay-Shay visited my house, she was in awe. "This is your house?" she asked. "Look at your bed. I wish I had a bed like this and room to myself. You're so lucky." I didn't say a word. I only nodded. I didn't want her to know the truth about me or us. I felt like a fraud.

After a few months in San Bernardino, Shay-Shay moved back to L.A. to live with her mom. We promised to write one another, and we did for a while. In her letters, she talked about the boys she had met. She had a new boyfriend who lived in the same apartment building as she did. He was older and they had sex, she told me. He also bought her a Bart Simpson short set from the Swap Meet. She said that she loved him and hoped to be with him forever. Though it wasn't the truth. When I wrote back I told her that I was happy for her and that he seemed like a nice guy. I felt like she was stupid and selling herself short—just like most of the other girls in our neighborhood. I eventually stopped writing.

• • •

"I'll ask her. She'll say yes. I'll just tell her your mom will be home," I said. Tina's mom was never home because she worked two jobs. She was a single mom and responsible for the care and feeding of five girls. One of them was Tina's cousin, whose mother had left her with them and had never come back. The family lived in a tiny two-bedroom apartment across town from me.

"I hate being so skinny," I complained. "I don't have no titties, no ass." I ran my hand over my backside. It went straight down to my leg, no interruption.

"Have sex," Tina said matter-of-factly, as if this was common knowledge. "It'll make everything pop out. You'll at least get some ass and hips."

"Really?" I said as I surveyed her body. She might be right, I thought. I wasn't ready for sex. I was scared of getting pregnant and thought sex made things more complicated than they had to be. I also wasn't sure how long it was supposed to last. According to the songs on the radio, it lasted all night, and I thought that was too much time to commit to any one activity. It might even hurt. I switched subjects.

"That movie was trash," I said. Earlier that day we had gone to the movies to see *Graffiti Bridge*, starring Prince. He was still one of my favorites.

"Yeah, it was weird. I thought it would be more like *Purple Rain*."

"Me too. I didn't get it."

"Are you going to go with Booker?" Tina asked pointedly. "He likes you. Derrick told me so."

I had been talking to Booker for the last few weeks, since we were introduced in the court-yard. He walked me to my bus stop after school nearly every day, and we sat together during lunch.

"I might," I said, trying not to let on how much I liked him. "What about that girl who likes him. Did he used to go with her?"

"No, they just had sex in that construction site by the school. He doesn't go with her."

By the following week Booker and I were officially a couple. A lot of girls liked him, but he had chosen me—the new girl.

Booker was the first boy I french kissed. On the way to the bus stop one afternoon, he stopped short, turned my body toward his, and grabbed my waist. I pulled back, not knowing what he was about to do.

"Kiss me."

I looked away, grazing the tip of his angular nose with my own. My body was hot and my skin felt wet and sticky. Suddenly, I had on too many clothes. The only kisses I had given in the past were close-mouthed. This dude wanted me to use my tongue.

"Close your eyes."

I complied and moved my hand up toward the

small of his back. His lips were soft and he used his tongue to part mine. Before that day, I imagined my teeth would get in the way or that I would be at a loss for how to move my tongue around to meet the other person's. He was a slow and deliberate kisser. I followed his lead. When he pulled his lips away from mine, my eyes were still closed. I wanted another one. It felt so good.

"I'll see you tomorrow."

"Okay," I said as I floated onto the bus. The worn smell of the seats and the roar of the engine pulling off into traffic snapped me back to reality.

Sometimes I went to class and sometimes I did not. It depended on my mood. I felt it was okay to cut school as long as I continued to get good grades and did not fall behind in my work. None of my teachers noticed when I was gone or inquired about my whereabouts. At Wilson, the unofficial rule was that if you got out of the building without one of the security guards catching you, you were safe. If you were caught, you got in-school detention and a truancy warning, which included a call or letter home to your parents.

After the first bell rang, Tina and I slipped out of the side of the front gate. Our plan was to be back before the start of lunch. The cold morning air was at our backs as we walked briskly up the street toward the flashing green light.

"What do you want to do?"

"Let's get something to eat. Let's go to Joe's."

We walked the main street until we reached the diner-like hole-in-the-wall that doubled as our headquarters on the days we ditched school. As we turned to walk in the door, a guy in a black, two-door car stopped Tina. "I'll be right back," she yelled as she motioned for me to continue into the restaurant. I got a large order of french fries and a soda for the two of us to share. What was taking her so long? I wondered.

"Let's go with him," she said when she came into Joe's. "To his house. He's waiting for us outside. He said he will bring us back to school when we're ready."

Was she out of her mind? We didn't know him. He could kill us, chop us up into little pieces, and spread them in the Pacific Ocean. We were supposed to be in school, learning.

"It'll be fun. Don't be like that. If you don't go, I'll have to go by myself." She knew just what to say. I didn't want to be perceived as a square, a nerd, someone who didn't know how to have fun. And she was my friend; I couldn't let her go alone with some strange man.

"All right, I'll go," I said reluctantly. "But I have to be back by lunch time. I have chemistry and we have a big test coming up." I grabbed the fries and soda from the counter and followed her to the car.

The guy had just gotten off from work. He

214

worked the night shift and was tired, he said as he sped down the street. He had stopped at Joe's to get a burger before he went home to get some rest. Tina's hand was on his thigh. She was faster than I had originally thought.

We entered the on-ramp of the freeway and continued to drive further away from school. In the backseat, I tried hard to memorize everything—the green and white signs above the guardrails, the back of his head, and the details of the inside of the car—just in case I got away and Tina didn't.

About twenty minutes later, we pulled off the highway and drove up to the back of a small house. He lived with his mother, who was not home. She worked the morning shift, he said. The blinds were drawn and the house was dark, making everything appear brown, even the white walls. The long sofa and armchair were covered in plastic. The house smelled like mothballs and Ben-Gay.

The guy led us to the back of the house, into his bedroom. Once there, he pulled his work shirt up and over his head, exposing his muscular chest. Tina shot me a look and moved her eyebrows up and down. She approved of his body. I rolled my eyes. This girl was a piece of work, I thought.

Although he invited us to sit down on his bed as he reached over to pop a cassette tape into the boom box that sat on his overcrowded dresser, I propped myself up against the doorframe and folded my arms.

Tina looked at ease. She sat on the edge of the bed, surveying the room and the guy. As the music played, she began to move her body to the beat, gyrating back and forth. I made a mental note to myself to not ditch with her again. She was out of control.

He bent down and whispered something in her ear. She shifted her weight off the bed and walked over to me. She guided me by the shoulder into the hallway.

"Can you go in to the living room?" she asked. Her voice was low and discreet.

"Why?"

"So we can be alone."

"But you don't know him and you told me before we left Joe's not to leave you alone."

"I changed my mind," she said. "You said he was cute, right?"

"Yeah, but . . ."

"Well, then."

"We should go," I said in a hushed but firm voice.

"Stop trippin'. I'll be back." She was annoyed with me and probably wished I hadn't come with her. After she closed the door, I went into the living room and tried to watch television. The only thing on was game shows. After about ten minutes, I knocked on the bedroom door. Tina poked her head out. "What do you want," she said, not fully believing I was at the door.

"When are you going to be out? I'm bored and thirsty." She slammed the door in my face.

Instead of going back to the living room, I hung a left into the kitchen and let myself out the back door. I walked to the corner to see what street we were on and made a mental note of the license plate number on the back of the car—just in case.

After a few moments, I returned to the couch. I flipped on the television to drown out the sound of the music coming from the bedroom. She was unbelievable, I thought. Eventually, I fell asleep on the plastic couch and was awakened by Tina shaking my elbow. "Let's go," she said. "What time is it?" I asked. It felt like hours had passed. "Don't worry, you'll make it back in time for class."

The guy dropped us off back at Joe's. I was annoyed at Tina for leaving me by myself and said very little to her as we walked the long block back to Wilson.

"Hey, you two. Come here," a voice commanded. It was one of the school's security guards—the mean one. We had been caught.

"Where are you two coming from?" he asked. We didn't have an answer. We had never been caught. We stood there speechless. "Let's go to the office."

I did not care, because it was our first time

being caught. I knew the worst that could happen is that we would get detention for the rest of the day. It seemed like a pittance to pay, given that I had missed more than a week's worth of school and we were only a couple of months into the semester.

I had never been to detention before. It was a place reserved for the kids in the remedial classes who acted out or gave the teachers a hard time. That was not me. After lunch, detention was served in the lunchroom with the lights off. There were rows and rows of kids who sat with their heads down on the table or staring up at the ceiling. We were not allowed to talk or get up from our seats. To do so would extend our time.

I recognized some of the kids, but not many. It was common knowledge that some kids spent their entire school day in detention. And no one cared. There were few White kids and hardly any girls in detention. Because I was a new face and looked as if I did not belong, the detention teacher allowed me to sit at the front of the room and do my homework.

My home life was easy enough to navigate. For the most, it was quiet and uneventful. My aunt and uncle asked few questions as long as I was home from school on time.

"Look at this," he said as he opened and

slammed shut the oversized kitchen drawers. "This is ridiculous."

It was mid-afternoon and my uncle Monk's day off. My aunt Glo was asleep and unaware that she had been found out. The drawers were filled with what had to be more than five dozen empty beer cans, some smashed into small tin saucers.

"I only saw her drink one or two a night." I tried my best to defend her, but he wouldn't have any of it. I didn't understand. They never fought. It was true he complained about her to anyone who would listen—she couldn't cook, clean, or do anything right as far as he was concerned. When he berated her, she never talked back or attempted to defend herself.

"She's a drunk. She didn't even have enough sense to throw the cans in the trash so I wouldn't find them." He had a point. Maybe she wanted him to find them. When we watched television, she usually had one or two beers. Once I fell asleep, she continued to drink into the early hours of the morning. This was not my problem. My aunt Glo had saved me, and this would not change the way I saw her.

"It's just beer," I said, hoping to defuse the situation. I did not stay around to hear or see more. I never asked my aunt Glo about the cans in the drawer, and we continued our nightly ritual of drinking and talking.

The next day, instead of ditching with Tina, I

found a corner in the school courtyard to study for my upcoming chemistry test. The teacher allowed us to bring a postcard's worth of notes to class to use during the test. Because I hadn't studied, I didn't know what formulas to include and hadn't devised any shortcuts to help me remember the symbols or chemical bonds. I was fucked. To compensate, I folded a sheet of paper in quarters and wrote on every side, hoping I would be able to use all sides during the exam.

When the bell rang, I gathered my books and rushed to class.

"You have forty minutes for the test. You can use your notecard, but nothing else," the teacher instructed as he passed out the exam. I pulled out my big sheet turned notecard and placed it on my desk. I was shaking and my eyes darted around the room. It was as if the questions were in a foreign language; nothing looked familiar to me. And there was nothing on the front side of my sheet that provided any help. As I flipped the sheet over, it fell out of my hand and onto the floor.

"What is this?" the teacher asked, examining the sheet, eventually unfolding it so that all eight by eleven inches were exposed. "Are you cheating?" The whole room pivoted to my direction. He took my exam and threw it in the trash. "Go to the office," he ordered.

I pushed my chair away from the desk, gathered

my things, and walked out the door. My ears burned and I was embarrassed. I couldn't hack it. I did not belong. Instead of going to the office, I went to Joe's. I needed some time alone to think.

I slumped down in my usual booth and put my head on the table. I had never been a cheater, but now I was. And the worst part was that I had been caught. There was no way I could go back to that class. My eyes began to sting as tears fell from my arm onto the table. I was glad my head was down and my hair covered my face. To people walking past the booth, it looked as though I were napping. I was failing and probably going to receive my first F. In the past, I had never studied and still got good grades. I didn't understand what was happening. I was letting myself down.

I did not know how to study. Sure, I knew how to crack open a book, but I did not have any strategies or techniques to learn or master the information. For me, studying meant reading over the same pages a few times while watching television or listening to music. I didn't take notes or highlight important sections, concepts, or terms. I also never studied for more than thirty minutes at any given time. And if a concept was difficult or I didn't understand it, I skipped over it and went on to the next lesson. There was no one around to tell me to study or to ask me about my progress in my classes. I could do whatever I wanted.

There was a slam book going around school. The spiral notebook, usually started on its way by an upper classman, posed provocative questions about random topics, from sex to who had the best body in school. Whoever received the book was obligated to candidly answer the questions being posed. The answers to the questions were usually biting or clever retorts meant to get back at someone who might have wronged the respondent.

When the book got to me, around second period, to the question *Who's a slut?* I answered Meccah, the girl who'd had sex with Booker. I didn't write her name but alluded to her through a reference to the construction site. When the book reached Meccah, she read my entry and was furious. "I'm going to kick that bitch's ass," she told Tina who stood by as Meccah filled in her entries. By lunch, word had gotten back to me that Meccah wanted to fight me after school, in front of the big black gate. "That's fine," I said. "I'll kick her ass."

The only problem was that I didn't know how to fight. When I fought Angela in middle school, I just swung my fist in the air with my eyes closed and pulled her hair. The fight was broken up once her cousins jumped in and tried to get a few hits in on me. I was relieved, because if I had gone on for much longer, I would have had to run or back down.

Today, I would have to fight again. This time, I

would not have my friends or my brother to help or to make sure it was a fair fight. Since that incident with the guy the week prior, I had kept my distance from Tina. We were still friends, but we didn't hang out as much. I knew she would not jump in or stop the fight if I needed help. Still, I had to fight Meccah or everyone would think I was weak and I would lose all street credibility.

Our match was the first big fight of the school year, and everyone was planning to watch, including Booker. A few people I barely knew showed up at my last class to escort me through the courtyard and out to the front of the school. They wanted to make sure I didn't slip out the back entrance or the side gate. As we walked, my stomach turned flips and I felt like I was going to throw up.

"You call me a slut?" Meccah asked as she stepped in front of my face, her shoe pressing on my big toe. It hurt. She was much bigger and stronger than me. Her earlobes were torn from a previous fight, during which someone had ripped out her earrings.

"Yeah, bitch. I did." Who was I in this moment?

We were surrounded, as if in a boxing ring with no exit. She took the first swing, and it connected with my head. I closed my eyes and began to propel my arms like a windmill. I had hoped I was connecting, but I wasn't. She was bobbing and weaving like a prizefighter. When she tired of my Three Stooges shenanigans, she grabbed my hair, wrapping it around her fist, swung me around, and threw me onto the ground. I knew what was coming next—she was going to get on top of me, punch me in the face, and slam my head into the ground.

Before this could happen, a boy who had been crushing on me and was a fellow nerd pulled me out from under her. He held my hand and bulldozed through the tight crowd, who wanted me to stay to finish the fight.

"Are you all right?"

"Yeah, I am." My heart was pounding and my hair and clothes were a mess.

"Why did you fight her?"

"I don't know. I had to."

He shook his head. "Well, you got a few good licks in," he said, imitating my windmill. I laughed. He was funny. Why hadn't I paid him any attention?

As I boarded the bus, I was thankful it was Friday. No one ever got suspended on a Friday, so I was safe. I also had the weekend to think about what to do to recover from the fight and chemistry. I had not been to class since cheat-gate.

"I want to go back home."

"Why?" My aunt Glo looked confused as she took a pause from chugging her beer. She placed the cold can on the nightstand.

"I don't know." I had no reason, at least none that I felt like sharing. I was embarrassed and humiliated by the fight and the chemistry test. I felt out of control and exposed. It was harder than I thought to start over.

"You don't have to leave. We don't mind taking care of you." After the first couple of weeks of my living there, my mother had stopped sending money to help with food and cover my living expenses. And she supposed I felt like a burden on them.

"I know," I said. "I miss my friends and my old neighborhood." I made up something that sounded believable.

"What about Stevie?"

"I'll be okay." She took a long swig from the can. I turned my attention to the television. My mind was made up.

The following Monday, I checked myself out of school and cleared out my locker. I told the office clerk that I was moving back in with my mother. She didn't flinch, only handed me the forms that needed to be signed by my guardian so that my records could be sent to my new high school.

By the time Stevie arrived to shuttle me back to San Bernardino, my bags were packed and I had already said my goodbyes.

not poor, poor

My room remained unchanged. My bed was made, and the pillow sham with the pink and yellow flowers was still fluffed. I unpacked my clothes and waited for my brother to get home from school. My mother was still at work.

"You're becoming a woman now. And there is going to be conflict between you and your mother. Two women can't live in the same house together without one thinking she should be in charge," Stevie said, his body propped up against the frame of my bedroom door, as he watched me fold my shirts, shorts, and pants into neat squares.

"She's my mother. I don't want to fight with her."

"I know you don't, but she's getting insecure now. You're challenging her," he explained. "You have breasts and ass, you're not a little girl anymore." What did my ass have to do with anything, I thought.

His tight white T-shirt hugged his round belly, which bent the waist of his jeans downward. Although he wore a belt, he did not need it. His neat haircut and long sideburns, which reached past his ear, made his face appear smaller than it actually was. I hated the way he smelled and how he always coughed up large chunks of phlegm and had to be excused to spit it out in the bathroom toilet.

I had written my mother a letter while I was away and apologized for the trouble I had caused within the family. I wanted a second chance. Now that I was back, I was desperate to fit in. I needed guidance, and Stevie was available to shepherd me. I knew, however, that it came at a cost.

"I'll help you out, keep her off your back," he offered. He was going to be the buffer between us. He was going to be a real, live, in-the-flesh mother-daughter translator.

At the time, I believed I did not have a choice other than to accept his help. My mother, although fiercely independent, was still very traditional when it came to her husband, and did whatever he said.

"Hey," my brother said as he poked his head in the remaining space in the doorframe and squeezed past Stevie into the room. I nodded my acknowledgment. He was an inch taller and more handsome than I remembered. His chest poked through his shirt, and his arms had minor ruptures. He had been lifting weights in our garage and hitting the red punching bag that dangled in the middle of the unfinished rafters. He was becoming a man.

I wasn't sure if I should give him a hug or smile, so I did nothing. He did not reach for me either. Stevie turned away and walked toward the kitchen.

"What happened? Why did you come back?" Lanny wanted to know.

"I didn't want to stay there anymore. It was boring." I could tell that he didn't believe me. However, he did not care enough to probe. He stood idle in the center of the room and watched me as I continued to stuff my drawers with clothes.

"Okay, well, I'll see you later. I'm going down to Ish's house."

Ishmael lived down the street from us, in the middle of the cul-de-sac. It was the house where all of the boys hung out. They played video games, talked about girls, lifted weights, and did whatever else I imagined teenaged boys did. Ish's mother, the resident den mother, Sonia, was a tall thin woman who wore skinny heels and a long, synthetic ponytail. A nurse, she saw that Ishmael always did his homework and performed well in school.

When I visited the house, usually to drag my brother home for dinner, it always smelled of a combination of sweat, man feet, and corn chips. I also noticed older men slinking around the house. Similar to our house in La Puente, there were always people coming and going. Rather than go inside, I yelled from the sidewalk into the nearest bedroom window, my high-pitched screams eventually driving my brother from the house. My mother did not like Sonia. She did not trust the house and tried in vain to keep my brother away from it.

"Come help me get these groceries out the car," my mother called through the house as she struggled to lift two full bags already in her hands onto the kitchen counter. I raced down the corridor, past the dining room table, to help her.

"Hi mama," I said, pregnant with anticipation. I made my way to the garage and to the open trunk to help with the bags. "Hey, Pumpkin," she replied flatly.

Wasn't she happy to see me? I wanted more from her. I wanted her to tell me that she missed me and that she was happy I was back. When I was in Long Beach with my aunt Glo, we spoke about once every couple of weeks. Our conversations were short and to the point, unsentimental. There were no "I love you's" or plans made to visit. This was the first time I had seen her in months. After the bags were unloaded, I milled around the kitchen hoping she would ask me questions about my stay with my uncle Monk and aunt Glo. She did not.

On the way back to my room, I passed my sister, Kamilah, now five years old. She dragged two of her favorite Barbie dolls and their pink Corvette into the dining room to play within sight of my mother while she prepared dinner.

The two of them were close, and I resented it. They talked, hugged, and snuggled with one another. My sister's room was filled with an abundance of shoes and clothes; a custom-made toy box that overflowed with dolls; and a television and VCR. And if she wanted anything that belonged to me, she cried until she received it. I lost a Cabbage Patch Kid doll, half of a set of Bonnie Belle lip gloss, and numerous other things to her whim. From her birth, I kept a mental tally of all the things and the ways my mother treated her better than me.

I was Kamilah's surrogate parent, a role I also resented. As the oldest, in my mother's absence or when she did not feel like being bothered, I cooked, bathed my sister, and rocked her to sleep. Once I overheard a group of my mother's friends comment on how bad they felt for me because I was stuck taking care of a baby who wasn't mine. Initially, when I heard it, I chalked it up to their jealousy of my mother, rather than their keen observation of the heavy responsibility I carried at such a young age.

I wanted to feel differently about my sister. In my attempt to tamp down my resentment, I bought her Christmas gifts with money I had saved from babysitting, tried to teach her to read, and calmed her fears when she confessed to me that she was afraid that she would not advance past kinder-garten. These efforts were not enough and were thwarted by my mother, who often played us against one another. She did this with my brother as well. It was clear, the tide of the house was too strong; I was on one side and they were on the other. As a result, my sister kept her distance and only visited me when no one was watching.

I could hear the crackling of the hot grease from my bedroom. The salty aroma of fried chicken filled the air. My stomach began to turn on itself in anticipation of the meal to come. When I arrived at the dinner table, my favorite meal was served up on the plate—fried chicken, Rice-a-Roni, and corn from the can. She had made it for me.

I was confused by these moments of care and attention from my mother. I knew that she made the meal because it was my favorite, but would never admit it. I felt like a yo-yo and in a constant state of yearning for her love.

My mother drove the short yellow school bus, the one for children with special needs. Instead of meeting the kids at a designated bus stop, she picked them up and dropped them off at their respective houses. As a result, she became friendly with many of the kids and their families. Each day when she got off work, she regaled us with stories of the kids from her route. When we acted out, she reminded us that we were lucky and better off than the kids she drove around daily.

"Get the door," my mother yelled from the back of the house. Her bedroom was across from mine.

The doorbell was ringing in rapid succession. "Stop ringing the bell," I demanded as I swung open the door. I didn't recognize any of the faces on the steps. My brother, curious to see what all the commotion was about, met me in the vestibule. He didn't know these kids either.

"Is Ms. Foster here?" the tallest one asked. She was dusty-looking and her clothing ragged. The rubber band at the nape of her neck had the enormous task of creating the illusion of a pony-tail out of her short, coarse hair.

"Yeah, she is," my brother replied. "Mom, there's some people out here looking for you."

We were expecting my mother to shoo the four young paupers away when she arrived at the door. Instead, she invited them in. They filed into the dining room and sat around the table. They were dirty and unkempt. My brother and I stood next to one another watching them as they fidgeted. The room smelled different now, musty.

"How did y'all get over here?" my mother asked.

"We walked."

"Y'all did. That far. In this heat." She could hardly believe it. She had dropped them in front of their house not more than an hour ago.

"This is Brigette and her brothers and sisters. She rides my bus," my mother explained as she introduced them to us. Midway through the school year, she had scribbled our address on a scrap sheet of paper and extended an invitation for Brigette to come over to visit whenever she wanted. Now, she was here in our dining room with her siblings in tow.

"Are y'all hungry?" my mother asked as she moved toward the kitchen. "Are y'all thirsty?"

"Yes, ma'am, we are," the oldest one said, speaking for the group. My mother pulled out some bologna, Miracle Whip, cheese, and bread and made a round of sandwiches. She also gave them strawberries, Oreo cookies, chips, and little plastic bottles filled with juice all of our food. We watched as they ate, refusing to join them.

To fill in the silence, my mother began to talk. "They live across Baseline, down that dirt road. Do you know where I'm talking about?" We shook our heads. We would not help her out.

"You do, you do," she insisted. "It's across from that field and that big ditch. There's a couple of houses up behind there." We were polite, but chilled in our responses. If we showed too much enthusiasm, their visits might become a regular occurrence. And we did not want that.

"Pumpkin, maybe you can hang out with Brigette." Was she insane? I had a reputation to uphold. The lanky girl's body folded into itself as she read my facial expression. Feeling bad, I made an effort to clean it up by offering to watch music videos with her—in the house, where no one would see us together. She had holes in her shoes. I also wasn't sure we would have much in common. I was certain by the looks of her that she did not have a boyfriend.

After they left, my mother told us more about them. They were poor, she said, very poor. And she felt sorry for them. They lived in a small shack across the main intersection, about a thirty-minute walk from our house. The house had dirt floors and barely any running water. They were on welfare and the mother was *slow,* my mother explained, barely able to take care of herself. And the children took care of themselves.

When she wanted to be, my mother was quite generous and compassionate. The biggest caveat, however, is that she had to be in the mood. Additionally, the people she was helping had to be worse off than she was or remind her of something she never received when she was a little girl. In the case of the pauper children, Brigette reminded her that there were others who had less than even she did when she lost her mom and was forced to move to California. And now, she was living large, albeit on drug money, and could help the less fortunate.

After that day, Brigette and her siblings continued to visit us regularly. Each time they did, the foursome ate and drank until their bellies were overfull. My brother and I maintained our distance and treated them like charity cases. They could never be our friends. They dressed differently and had less than we did. They, not we, were poor.

sonnie's got a baby

I hung out with D'aja, who lived at the top of our block with her grandmother, aunt, and cousin Spike. Before I moved to Long Beach, I hung out with Annie, Ish's girlfriend, but when I had returned from my short respite in Long Beach, she had moved away. While I was bummed that Annie had left, I understood the transient nature of my neighborhood. People were always moving in or moving out, some with very little notice and some with urgency.

Spike and D'aja attended St. Aquinas Catholic School and were mostly out of sight during the week. My mother thought D'aja was good for me and allowed me to hang out with her on weekends. D'aja was beautiful, with catlike facial features and long, thin black hair. Her body was muscular and she walked high on her toes.

Her house was dank and ill lit. When I came through the black metal privacy gate, I was quickly ushered to her bedroom. There, we sat on her teddy-bear-filled bed and talked about boys. Honestly, the only reason I was even there was for her cousin Spike, the cutest and seemingly most mature boy on our block. I pretended to listen as she whined about the lack of available Black boys at St. Aquinas and her desire to transfer to the local public school. Where was Spike? My day was always made when he popped his head in to say hello and flashed his big-toothed grin my way. Soon after, I would make up an excuse to leave.

Spike was the only boy I had ever even considered losing my virginity to. He seemed experienced and as if he knew what to do in the bedroom. I was quickly disabused of this notion when my mother confronted me with my diary in hand. She had found it and read the entry about Spike and what I imagined the two of us would do together if we were ever alone.

"Who is Spike?" she demanded to know. The diary was on my large, triple-stack stereo next to her. In that moment, I wished it had legs so that it could run to me. She grabbed the little pink book and started to leaf through the inked pages. "Who is he?" She was growing impatient.

"Quincy, D'aja's cousin." I decided to give his real name instead of the one we called him because he was an excellent football player and kicked the ball across the field with little effort. No person should ever be introduced formally as the pointy thing at the bottom of a cleat, I reasoned.

"That boy down the street?" She reared back in disbelief, her face seemingly disgusted by the very thought of him. "You're not going down there anymore. Do you hear me?"

"Yes." I was embarrassed and wanted to snatch back my private thoughts. She had no right.

"Do you want to get pregnant?" she continued.

What kind of question was that, I thought. Of course I didn't want to get pregnant. I was thinking about sex, not having a baby. In my mind, those were two separate things. Most of my friends were having sex and had been since middle school. As far as I was concerned, my not having had sex was a liability. I felt out of place in many of our conversations. They talked about how good sex felt and how it made them feel like a woman, more mature.

In retrospect, I know they were exaggerating about how good it felt. They had to be. They were performing for the group of us. To admit that it hurt, was coerced, or "didn't feel that good" would have been a reflection of their lack of experience or their inability to please the guy.

"No," I replied.

"If you are doing something, let me know. We can go to the clinic and get you some birth control." She sounded exasperated and defeated.

Birth control? This conversation was moving way too fast. I did not know any girls my age that used birth control. If they did, they never talked to me about it. I wanted the conversation to be over. But it didn't end. She continued for about ten more minutes about how boys just wanted one thing and that I would be stupid if I gave it up to him. I continued to nod with my hands clasped in my lap. I tried to look as virginal as possible.

When she tired of speaking into the air, she turned to leave, dropping the book back onto the speaker. What about the entries about Stevie, hadn't she read those too? If she did, she did not mention them. On the way out, she reminded me not to go down to that boy's house again.

My friend Sonnie from across the park was back from Philadelphia. She was a year younger than me. We met at Martin Luther King Jr. Middle School. She was the cousin of one of my brother's friends. While she was away, I had spoken to her a couple of times over the phone. The last time we spoke, she said she had a surprise for me. When she arrived by Greyhound bus later that month, we met in the park, a halfway point between our respective homes. I was happy to see her. Her hands were full, clasped around the plastic handles of a stroller. She maneuvered around it to give me a hug. The cooing coming from below distracted me.

"Did you expect my baby to look like this?" Her mouth was turned up at the corners and her eyes were bright. I could tell she was proud and wanted me to match her feelings in kind. I was at a loss for words. I was not expecting her surprise to be a crying, pooping, around-the-clock care-needing baby. A tattoo or new boyfriend, yes. I also thought she might tell me that she was moving back to San Bernardino. Unfazed by my lack of enthusiasm, she continued.

"My baby is cute," she said as she reached into the stroller and pulled him out. She bounced up and down and walked in small circles. The baby was colorless, with soft curly hair, the opposite of Sonnie's charcoal-colored skin and coiled locks. Was this really her baby? In school, she was a prankster and a bit immature. Was this one of her jokes? Who did this baby belong to?

"The daddy is Mexican," she announced. "My baby gon' have good hair."

"Look at his outfit," she said as she lifted up his doll-like feet to expose the Nike swoosh symbol on the bottom sole. "Hold him. Doesn't he smell good? Babies smell so good."

I pressed him tightly against my body and walked slowly to the closest bench. She was right; he did smell good. I knew how to hold a baby, but felt like he might slip out of my hands. My grip was tight.

I could not believe I was holding Sonnie's baby. About a year ago, all she cared about were boys, her hair, and clothes. And her grandmother was her primary caregiver. She also never had any money to buy ice cream or candy from the ice cream truck after school. Did that all change now that she had a baby? Did she have money now?

Was she suddenly mature and able to provide for another human being?

All of these questions and more swirled around inside my head. However, I knew better than to ask any of them. I did not want to make her feel inadequate or that she couldn't do it. It was none of my business. She appeared happy and to have it all under control.

The baby started to cry and arch its back toward the sky. I held him a little tighter so that he would not tumble onto the rubber playground mat. Without skipping a beat or ending our conversation, Sonnie reached down into the diaper bag that hung from the arm of the stroller and pulled out a bottle filled with milk. She took the baby from my arms and began to feed him. It was one smooth transaction. I had to admit, she looked like she knew what she was doing.

"You got this mothering thing down," I said.

"It's hard," she replied. "I can't go to school and take care of him at the same time. I tried. I'm going to go back to get my GED when he's a little older."

I nodded. It seemed like a workable plan to me.

"Are you going back to Philadelphia?" I asked. Philly seemed so far away, foreign. It might as well have been France or China. "What's it like there?"

"Yeah, I'm going back. My mother is helping me to take care of the baby," she said.

"Philadelphia is the same as here, but funner. I can do whatever I want and the guys are fine."

The baby slept, entangled in his blanket, one foot hanging over the side of the stroller as I walked Sonnie to the edge of the park before turning back to go home. Our lives were so different now.

My mother's preoccupation with my becoming pregnant was something I never understood as a teenager. In reflection, I am almost certain that it had to do with her becoming a mother at an early age. For her, the fear of my becoming pregnant was as real as her fear of my brother being killed or sent to prison. Perhaps it was much worse, because she had lived through the struggle of being a teenaged mom and knew on a very visceral level how it slowed dreams down to a molasses pace and made dangerous choices seem like the only ones available. It was a different kind of prison.

cell block high

On television and in movies, urban schools are often portrayed as dangerous, inadequate, and teeming with teachers and staff who have checked out. In some portrayals, these schools are literal war zones. More times than not, the parents are rendered as absent, drug addicted, abusive, or neglectful. In the White mind, which I assume these depictions are meant to appeal to, these narratives are comforting and congruent with dominant perceptions and beliefs about poor and low-income communities.

What is harder to imagine, though, is that these schools are much less characterized by danger and violence than they are by benign neglect, understood as a willful denial of access to equal resources, equipment, supplies, qualified teachers, and vital social networks. On the surface, these schools look and function like many others in America, including schools in middle-class neighborhoods. The bells all ring at the same time. However, they are far from equal.

A large part of the difference is the expectation of what students in predominantly Black and Latino schools will become when they leave the school system. If, as a nation, we believe consciously or subconsciously that these students will drop out, go to prison, get pregnant, or end up in low-wage jobs, the system or institution will bend to those expectations and treat the students accordingly. The environment, including the teachers and helpers, will also reflect those expectations.

I checked back into school with no problem and, once settled with my schedule, decided to look for my old friends from middle school. As it turned out, most of them had gone to our rival high school, Cajon. I saw some familiar faces, but none were a part of my old crew. I decided to lie low until I figured out what was what.

To get to school each day, I caught the bus on Magnolia Street, two blocks over from my house, on a shade-filled street of modest, single-family homes. Once off the bus, I walked the long block to N Street, where San Bernardino High was nestled. The school was not as nice or as grand as Wilson Classical, but it was much easier to navigate. Many of the classes were held in bungalow-like classrooms on the back of the lot.

San Bernardino High had five learning clusters: honors, college prep, remedial, English as a second language (ESL), and special education. The students in these clusters rarely interacted or crossed paths other than at lunch or between classes. The ESL students were partitioned off in a corner of the main building. The special education students were housed in a building that was superficially disconnected from the campus. Neither group had much contact with other students, and neither was fully integrated into the culture of the school. They were not cheerleaders, football players, or student class officers —they were invisible.

The remedial learning cluster is where the school placed all of the gang-bangers, class clowns, and other students who were chronically absent or truant, hard to manage, unmotivated, socially promoted, but not developmentally delayed. For some reason or another, the students in those classes were always up and walking around. They came and went as they pleased. Rarely was the teacher at the head of the classroom delivering a lesson. Some of the students shifted their desks to play cards, board games, or dominoes, all kept in a closet and handed out by the teacher at the start of class. They played until the bell signaled that it was time to switch classes. At the time, I thought they had it made, but now I know better. They were doomed. They would never be able to compete, and many of them would drop out altogether. And no one would care.

The classroom was like a legal holding cell, only without the bars. By law, they had to be there, but that was it. No one was going to make or force them to learn. As far as I could tell, the main job of the teacher/babysitter was to prevent a fight from breaking out, stop the kids who were present from leaving campus, and keep the noise to a level that would not disturb the other students.

I needed a break from chemistry and enrolled in college-prep biology instead. It was an easy enough class, I thought. I also heard we would get to dissect a frog, which sounded interesting to me. The biology teacher, Ms. Randall, had over-processed, bleached hair and wore too-tight polyester pants that made a whipping sound as she paced back and forth in the front of the room. She was a good teacher and seemed to genuinely care about whether or not we grasped the concepts or learned.

"Take out a piece of paper," she said as she flipped out the lights and turned on the overhead projector. "Write this," she instructed us. "It's a letter to your parents about the lack of school supplies and equipment to run a proper lab."

We complied and turned over our notebooks to a blank sheet of lined paper to begin our respective letters.

Dear Parents:

I am writing to let you know that we do not have any paper to make copies or supplies for our biology lab. There have been deep budget cuts and it is not fair to the students or the teachers. The San Bernardino County Unified School District has a responsibility to provide supplies and equipment to teachers in order for us to do our jobs.

Sincerely,
Ms. Randall

She waited patiently until we finished penning our protest letter. "You'll receive five extra-credit points if you bring it back tomorrow signed by a parent." As if in the calm following an exorcism, she exhaled and turned to the day's lesson. She had done her part.

The following day, only a few students returned the letters. To make matters worse, before we began our work for that afternoon, Ms. Randall was forced to apologize to the class for asking us to write and deliver the letters to our parents. She said in the most sincere tone she could muster that it was inappropriate. While apologizing, she kept eye contact with the staff member who had been sent from the front office to make sure the message was delivered. Apparently, a parent had called the principal and complained about the letter and our involvement in what was an administrative matter.

Before that day, I had no reason to believe there was anything out of the ordinary with overly worn textbooks, broken telescopes, missing lab equipment, or the need to transfer assignments from the chalkboard or an overhead projector. I assumed that this was the way it was at all schools. But it wasn't. I was beginning to realize that some schools were better than ours.

The first new person I met at school was Rachel, a round-eyed girl with a gap in the center of her smile. Between classes, I followed the music to the gym and noticed her dancing to a choreographed routine. She was such a smooth dancer; her feet barely touched the floor between moves. Entranced, I grabbed a seat in the front row of the bleachers alongside the others already perched to continue watching the show.

After they finished dancing, Rachel and the two other girls joined us on the long, wooden row of benches. I had promised myself that I would not cut class any more, but this was a special case. I needed to make new friends. Through the next class period, the group of us stayed in the gym, listening to music, dancing, and talking. Through our conversation, I learned that Rachel was the co-captain of the San Bernardino Pacesetters, a local drill team housed at the Boys and Girls Club.

At lunch the following day, she invited me to sit with her group of friends—Sakinah, Krissy, Larry, Bernardo, and Craig. Sakinah was Rachel's best friend. She had long acrylic nails, gold chains that clung to her chubby neck, and rings on a few of her fingers. Her hair was shiny and *laid*. When Rachel introduced us, Sakinah was sitting on her boyfriend's lap and barely acknowledged me. Her boyfriend, one of a set of twins, was a gang-banger and drug dealer from Delman Heights. He had a Jheri Curl and wore beige Dickie's work pants, a crisp white T-shirt, a Black Raider's jacket, and white Nike Cortez sneakers. He was also grossly overweight.

Krissy, Rachel's first cousin, was the captain of the Pacesetters and the resident beauty of the group. She had everything—long wavy hair, light brown eyes, thick legs, and an older boyfriend named Maurice, who was the captain of the drum squad for the drill team. The rest—Larry, Bernardo, and Craig—were good guys who stayed mostly to themselves and out of trouble. By default, they became my new crew.

Rachel was a virgin like me. She liked boys but also feared getting pregnant and thought being a virgin was a good thing. She was untouched, she said. That was one way to look at it, I thought. Up until that point, I had not given much thought to what it meant to be a virgin or how pure it made me. If anything, it had seemed like an unnecessary weight.

She was also different from my best friends in the past. She cared about school and doing well.

She also wanted to go to college and leave San Bernardino, just like me. To my lawyer, she planned on becoming a psychologist. For hours, we would sit together in her home or mine, plotting out our lives, from the number of children we would have to our husbands' attributes. We also practiced signing our professional signatures and sketched out our dream homes. Our signatures were purposefully sloppy, so as to not be easily forged, in case we had to sign important docu-ments someday.

Rachel lived around the corner from my house with her grandmother, mother, brother, sister, two cousins, and aunt Leigh. Her mother was a nurse's aid in a local hospital. After work each day, her mother retreated to their shared bedroom, closing the door to the outside world. Rachel and the others were frozen out until bedtime. Her aunt Linda lived up the street and a couple of blocks over. On occasion, Rachel stayed with her when her grandmother's house became overrun with relatives.

Rachel's aunt Leigh was young and beautiful with hair that fell below her waist. Although she did not work, each morning she got dressed and applied a full face of makeup. She spent her days posted at the front room window, watching the activities on the block and brushing her hair. Her man, David, was locked up for dealing drugs. Until his scheduled release in a few years, she and her daughter, Brandy, were living in the family house along with everyone else.

For the most part, Rachel and our group of friends stayed out of the fray in our neighborhood. We did not pass judgment or pretend to be better than the gang-bangers, young moms, or drug dealers. We understood the choices they were making and why.

a place called home

The Boys and Girls Club on San Bernardino's West Side was located in a warehouse-like building on the corner of Ninth and Mt. Vernon Streets. It was across the street from the Hostess Bakery outlet store. The outlet sold slightly expired bread and cupcakes. When we could, Rachel and I pooled our money to buy a fruit-filled pie or a taco from the stand on the corner.

The Club was unlike any place I had ever been. It was home to the San Bernardino Pacesetters. Rachel, the co-captain, invited me to watch the squad practice. She thought I should join the team. I was hesitant because I knew I would need permission from my mother. She would also have to shell out the money for the modest Club fee and purchase my uniform. I just never knew with her.

The main room of the Club was bright, with a large television and a stereo. One wall was covered with mirrors, and the others had posters and pictures of the drill team in action. Couches and loose chairs filled in the space on the floor. It was a place for kids in the neighborhood to hang out, to keep out of trouble and out of harm's way. Mr. Herndon and Rachel's paternal grandmother ran the day-to-day operations of the Club.

The other staff was welcoming and knew all of us by name.

The Boys and Girls Club became my place of refuge. After school, Rachel and I walked the two or so miles to get there, passing the housing projects and all of the things that were happening around us along the way.

Shortly after we arrived, Rachel turned on the music and began to dance in the mirror. She nudged me to join her. I did. As we were free-styling, her cousin Krissy came through the door. She dropped her bag onto the floor and joined us. I eased back against the wall as the two of them fell in step with one another and started to perform a routine I was sure they had practiced before. After about twenty minutes, the room filled up, and we all moved to the oversized gym.

"Everyone get in line and take your positions," a voice from behind the group of us yelled. It was Ms. Parker, the team's director. Her daughter Kelly, who helped with the team and mentored some of the girls, followed her. I stood on the base-line of the basketball court, along with the other parents and neighborhood kids who had come to watch the team practice. The show was starting.

Bombombadum. The drums roared, creating an echo throughout the gym, and the cowbell rang out. This was a full-fledged band, similar to the one in school, only without the horns. These guys learned to play the drums by watching and imitating. There were no expensive lessons, only a desire to learn and participate.

The girls, with their bangle earrings, overly styled hair, and thick legs, marched with the precision and focus of Radio City Music Hall Rockettes to the center of the floor. Krissy, the captain, commanded the forty or so girls using only a whistle and her hands. She was like a maestro conducting an orchestra. I was mesmerized. By the time practice was over, I was convinced. I had to join.

The San Bernardino Pacesetters had been started in the 1960s by Marie Genest, a teacher at Martin Luther King Jr. Middle School, to provide local West Side youth with positive activities that they could be proud of and give them a sense of self-efficacy. When the school dropped the program, she moved it into the community until it found a permanent home in the early 1990s at the Boys and Girls Club of San Bernardino.

I was a member of the drill team for a full two weeks before I asked my mother if I could join officially. She agreed without much fanfare or pleading on my part. I am still not quite sure why she said yes so easily. She purchased my uniform, consisting of white majorette boots and a short black dress with a silver-sequined sash. In the boots, my legs were like two beanpoles, and the dress was like a short tent. It never filled out quite as nicely as the other girls'.

During practice, I soon realized that I wasn't as rhythmically gifted as I had originally thought. I was placed in the back of the troupe and promised an opportunity to move up if I proved myself. Only the best got a slot in the front row.

"Pumpkin, do you know when to move?" Ms. Parker shouted in my direction. "You move when it's your time to move." Oh, shit. She was calling me out in front of everyone. I swallowed hard and tried to maintain my focus.

There were so many steps and routines to remember. I believed I was dancing as hard as I could, at least my pounding heart told me so, but I guess not. There was so much pressure. I did not want to let the team down. They had become my new family.

"Davita, this is not a booty-shaking group, this is a drill team. We do precision," Ms. Parker thundered.

She continued to watch as we glided across the floor in and out of formations. Her ultimate goal was to make sure not one hand, arm, or step was out of sync.

"Las Vegas is coming up. If you're not ready, you're not going," Ms. Parker threatened the room as she hit her palm with a rolled sheet of paper. The sheet held the names of those she planned to take on the road trip to Vegas. I did not want to be crossed off the list. To ensure I remained a part of the performance squad, Rachel rehearsed with me between official practices.

To raise money for our trip to Las Vegas, we held fund-raisers. We washed cars, sold candy, and baked goods. The Club was always in danger of shutting down due to some looming financial crisis. One time, the local radio station held a fund-raiser over the Christmas holiday that consisted of Santa Claus threatening to jump from the roof if we did not meet our fund-raising goal. It was morbid, but it worked, as enough money trickled in to save the Club.

"The trophy cases don't lie," read an article about our squad in the local newspaper. Our squad was the best, and we won every competition, locally and nationally. When we marched in holiday parades, hundreds of people surrounded us and followed us down the streets. When we were on the schedule to perform, the gymnasiums were filled to capacity.

Las Vegas was the site of the biggest drill team competition in the country. And we were the team to beat. I had moved up to the center of the squad and was prepared to help lead our team to victory. We traveled the four hours from San Bernardino to Las Vegas by charter bus and stayed at Motel 6. Las Vegas was the farthest I had ever traveled outside California. This was a big deal for me.

The room was electric and the crowd roared as

we edged our way onto the slick floor. Our faces were stern as we focused on Krissy's white gloves and the whistle that hung from her lips. The drummers two-stepped onto the floor, twisting their drums in the air and setting the tone for the show to come.

The twenty or so of us who had made the cut marched slowly onto the floor and slowly turned to face the row of judges. We stood at attention as Krissy marched forward to greet them and to deliver a solo performance. Her moves were deliberate, each one landing like a hammer on the judge's table. It was hard-core and amazing. When she turned away to meet us, she had the crowd eating out of the palm of her hand—so much so that the security guards were summoned to push back the people who had rushed the floor for a better look at what was next. We exploded. Our hands were on fire, and the flames were fanned each time we moved into a new formation. The crowd went wild. We took first place in the competition.

For many reasons, my experience as a part of the Pacesetters was meaningful. Most of us on the team made our way to the gymnasium every day not because we had to, but because we wanted to be there. We did not have parents shuttling us to and from practice, pinning their hopes and dreams on our success. Without prompting or cajoling, we showed up, many of us walking miles to get there. The squad gave us a sense of purpose and belonging.

The routines were challenging to learn and took an extraordinary amount of discipline to master. We invested a lot of time, holding one another accountable and helping the weakest one among us. We did this, I believe, because we were a part of this thing that was larger than ourselves. All of our hard work had paid off. We were the best, and that knowledge could not be taken away from us, by anyone.

Because of the way we dressed and wore our hair and makeup, strangers could easily have dismissed us or pegged us for delinquents, throwaways. For the most part, our schools, our homes, and society had written many of us off.

Following that trip to Las Vegas, I decided that I could create a home outside my home.

a light

I needed an anchor, something to keep me from drifting away. And school was it for me. By eleventh grade, I had joined every club I could. I was a varsity cheerleader, co-president of the Black Student Union, a member of the Future Black Leaders of America, and a member of our Mock Trial team, an organization for aspiring lawyers. Academically, I was enrolled in the Phoenix Honors program and took Spanish and French simultaneously. I also had a zero-period trigonometry class that began one full hour before school started.

My mother had no clue about my school life or any of the classes I was taking. She only saw the grades on my quarterly report cards. The grades were what she used to measure my progress. Her chief concern was whether or not I flunked out, and her only goal was for me to graduate. This was all right with me, because I did not think she would understand what I was learning or my ambition beyond high school. And I did not want to make her feel bad for not being able to help me.

Now in the tenth grade, my brother attended San Bernardino High as well. However, most people did not know we were related. Since my return from Long Beach, there had been so much animosity between us at home that we avoided one another at school. He was in remedial classes and had become the reigning class clown. Everyone thought he was hilarious and circled around him as he made comedic observations about life in our neighborhood or kids scuttling by to their classes. I did not find him amusing at all.

He played football and was quite good. That was until he was booted from the team for smart mouthing the coach, who was also one of his teachers. Not only did the teacher refuse to let him play football: He also banned my brother from his class for the remainder of the year. Not even Ms. Craig, the principal, could talk the coach into letting him back into the class. During that class period, my brother went to the gym or sat in the counselor's office.

The deep rift between my brother and me was baffling and at times outright unbearable. We had been so close as small children. Now, we were enemies. I could not walk past his bedroom without the fear of being pounced upon or chased. And when necessary, I fought him, clawing at his face and body as if he were a stranger on the street.

For me, the fighting was about the loss of our connection and the feelings of abandonment and resentment I felt toward him for not protecting me as I had done for him when we were younger.

He too was surviving, the best way he knew how. He could not help me, lest he risk the favor he curried with my mother, which was slight at best. His strategy was to fly below the radar and make as few waves as possible. Whatever my mother said was gospel. When she asked his opinion about something I had done wrong, he almost always agreed that I was out of line or at fault. I resented his cowardice.

"Black people's history began at slavery," Mr. Kuhn said from the front of the room.

A hand shot up in the back of the room. It was biracial militant Brad. He wore his curly hair in a picked out Afro and had piercing hazel green eyes. He took issue with this statement.

"How do you figure that?" He asked pointedly. "Black people, Africans, had a long history way before they got to this country." Mr. Kuhn, our history teacher was unshaken. He continued.

"Black people were brought here as slaves and didn't really create history, per se, until the civil rights movement in the 1960s."

"Black people helped to build this country," Brad retorted. His voice was raised as he preached to the room. I did not know whom to believe. I had never thought about it before. The only history I had learned about Black people up to that point was related to Rosa Parks, Martin Luther King, Jr., and the famous March on Washington.

I was scared for Brad. He, Anna Lisa Zavala, Arlene Lee Soy, and I were the only people of color in the advanced placement history class. Both Brad and Anna Lisa were new to the Honors program. I had Spanish with Anna Lisa and knew she was smart. She belonged.

After class, Brad tried to pull me to the side to explain his point of view and how he thought Mr. Kuhn was prejudiced against us. "Don't you see it?" he implored me. I did see it, but didn't want to admit it. Brad was making waves, and I didn't want any part of it. I knew what could happen to him, us, if we spoke up or out too loudly.

For the rest of the class, and until Brad was tracked out after only three weeks, Mr. Kuhn ignored Brad's flailing hand. Anna Lisa left too. She never spoke in class and always looked out of place. There was nothing I could do to help her. Before the first quarter was over, there were only two of us left.

Brad would not be in our history class to help us to untangle the Rodney King riots that occurred in the spring of 1992. King, a Black man, was mercilessly beaten by four White police officers while a dozen more watched, following a high-speed chase on the interstate. Although the incident was videotaped by a bystander and showed King being struck more than fifty times with batons, the officers were acquitted. During the trial, the video played on a loop on most of the local news stations. And the beating was the talk of the community.

When the riots broke in L.A. following the verdict, the racial panic reached our distant school, more than one hundred miles away. Ms. Craig locked down our campus and declared a state of emergency. The fire alarm rang out, and we were told to stay in our respective classrooms.

"Now, everyone remain calm," Mr. Kuhn advised. "No one's going to get hurt if we just stay put and wait to hear from Ms. Craig. We'll leave when she tells us it's safe." "Safe from whom?" I wondered.

As I scanned the room, the White kids looked anxious and in need of definite reassurance that nothing would happen to them. After a few moments of silence, it finally dawned on me: safe from *us*. They were protecting the mostly White kids in the room from *them,* the Black and Latino kids who might also be upset by the verdict. In that moment, my skin felt like it did not belong on my body. I felt like an intruder, an outsider-within.

L.A. was burning. The neighborhoods I once walked and visited as a child were engulfed in flames, and no one was doing a thing about it. On television and in the newspapers, the residents were portrayed as savages and as shortsighted for burning down their own neighborhoods. The truth is they were not allowed to go anywhere else. They were contained; an invisible fence surrounded them.

For fear that they would be harmed, the police and paramedics were given orders to stay out of those areas. Mayor Tom Bradley called in the National Guard on the fourth day of rioting only because the Downtown Civic Center area was threatened. By then, billions of dollars in damage had been done and entire blocks had been reduced to debris.

The King verdict was preceded by the fatal shooting of LaTasha Harlins, a fifteen-year-old Black girl who was shot in the back of her head while buying a bottle of juice from a local corner store. The storeowner, Soon Ja Du, believing Harlins was attempting to steal the drink, had confronted her, and a scuffle ensued. As Harlins turned to leave, she was shot. She died clutching two one-dollar bills, the money she intended to use to pay for the juice. Du was indicted on a charge of first-degree murder but received only probation and a five-hundred-dollar fine. Following the verdict, the judge in the case noted that although Du had reacted inappropriately, her reaction was understandable. I suppose she meant that if she, the judge, had found herself in a similar situation, she might have reacted the same way.

The Rodney King riots and the LaTasha Harlins verdict represented the first time I attempted to place myself within a larger social context, as both a Black person and a girl. LaTasha was only a year older than me. She was brown, just like me. And she wore her hair like I sometimes wore mine.

As a result, I felt vulnerable. At the time, I couldn't find anywhere in society or around me that said that my life or what I became mattered. And the places and neighborhoods I called home were not worth protecting or saving. I was slowly coming to realize that the systems, structures, and institutions in our lives caused us more harm than good and were not designed to protect people like me.

Advanced placement history had a reputation for being the hardest class in the learning cluster. If you received a grade lower than a B in the course, you could not graduate with Honors. The course's difficulty, however, had little do with keeping track of important historical moments but a lot to do with Mr. Kuhn's grading.

He proctored the multiple-choice exams from an overhead projector as we bubbled our answers on Scantron sheets. After we turned the short forms over to him, we never saw them again. Instead, about a week later, he read our grades aloud to the entire class. He gave us the grades he thought we should have. His favored students, or the ones whose academic reputations preceded them, always received As.

I was suspicious of my grades on the exams. When I asked to see my tests to better understand where I had gone wrong, Mr. Kuhn said that he had disposed of them after recording the scores in his grade book. I thought he was full of shit, but there was nothing I could do about it.

Although I had studied for the tests and kept meticulous notes, I never received any higher than a C on any of the tests. At the beginning of the school year, Mr. Kuhn introduced us to the notetaking method created by an education professor at Cornell University in the 1950s. It made sense to me, and I used it religiously.

I believed there was a glass ceiling in many of the advanced placement classes for the Black and Latino students, including myself. Many of the teachers, all of whom were White, believed they were doing us a favor by allowing us to remain in the classes. We had to constantly prove ourselves but be careful not to visibly outperform the other students, particularly the White boys. Doing so meant an overcorrection by the teacher to soothe their egos and restore the order of things. I believe this was not deliberate but was, rather, an unconscious bias.

For example, in my government class, Yuri, the other Black girl in the class, and I were teammates on the mock presidential election simulation. The exercise was worth 50 percent of our overall class grade. Everyone competed against one another. They never saw the two of us as a real threat. However, by the end of the simulation, there were only three teams left—two teams of White guys and us. Everyone was shocked. They had under-estimated us. We also had the most campaign cash left and were poised to win. After a short huddle between the two other teams, the teacher allowed them, the four White boys, to join together in order to win. It did not matter that this was a clear violation of the rules or that in reality a four-person presidential ticket would never be elected. The most important thing was that we were kept in our place.

Blythe Anderson was my guidance counselor. She counseled most of the advanced placement students and liked me. I checked in with her often to make sure I was on track for graduation. We also talked about colleges. She thought I should explore the University of California, Berkeley, or another of the University of California schools, because of in-state tuition. She said it would be cheaper than going out of state.

Before my conversations with Ms. Anderson, I had never given much thought to what college I might attend, what I might study, or how I would pay for it. I also had no idea about entrance exams, the application process, or how to choose one school over another. Save for geographic location, I assumed all of the colleges were the same. I did not know the difference between an Ivy League institution and a state college.

The rules for negotiating the higher education system were largely unknown and invisible to me. The conversations about what to do after high school in my community, in my family, or among my peers usually focused on immediate employment. Rarely was there serious talk about college, particularly a four-year institution. In this instance, information was currency. What I did not know could cost me dearly.

To bridge this gap, I listened carefully to the conversations that were happening between the White students in my classes about the impending deadlines for the PSAT or SAT, upcoming college fairs, or information that I felt might be useful when I decided to apply to college. I also relied heavily on Ms. Anderson and the other counselors for information.

"Are those new glasses?" Ms. Anderson asked, giving me a once-over as I flopped down in the metal chair in her crammed office. The line to meet with her was never long.

"Yes, I got them last week," I replied. I did not need them—my prescription was negligible, literally one step above reading glasses from the local drugstore—but thought they made me look smarter.

"You've been missing a lot of classes." Her back was to me, and her face was squinting at the computer screen. She waited for a response.

"Not that many," I offered up.

"Yes, you have thirteen absences for the quarter, not full days. You've been missing individual classes."

I did not have an explanation. Sometimes I needed a break between home and school. I would hang out at Burger King or in the office of Ms. Hayes, another of the school counselors. On some days, I would convince Rachel to join me. When she wasn't available I persuaded D'aja, who had transferred to San Bernardino High, to hang out with me. She never went to class and spent most her time in the bathroom practicing applying her makeup and combing her hair.

Seeing that she was getting nowhere, Ms. Anderson decided to move on.

"What do you need?" she asked. She was always eager to help me.

"I want to apply for this," I said, shoving the paper in her direction. "I need a letter of recommendation." She pulled the paper close to her face, then jerked it away. Despite her thick bifocals, she was blind as a bat. She was matronly with an over-rolled bob that did not move when she shook or nodded her head.

It was an application for the Rotary Club award. I had picked up the application from the front desk of the counseling office. The prize was a regional sleepaway camp with other student leaders and a write-up in the school newspaper. It was competitive. There was an extensive interview process, and only two students were selected from each high school. I had learned about the program because some of the kids in my class were discussing whether or not they should apply.

"Of course, I will," she said.

To prepare for my interview, I practiced the sample questions included in the thick application packet in my bedroom. My biggest competition was Arlene Lee Soy. Her older sister Allison had received the award the previous year, and Arlene's mother was putting pressure on her to win it too.

Arlene was biracial like Brad but lacked his racial consciousness. She did not hang out with any of the Black or Latino students. She talked like a Valley girl and took German as her foreign-language elective. Like me, she was also a cheer-leader.

The morning of my interview, I stood looking in the bathroom mirror, combing my hair, attempting to make it interview-presentable. I wore a peach, oversized men's dress shirt tucked into a tight black cotton miniskirt, off-black panty hose, and flats. It was the best I had. The shirt was my aunt Glo's. I had taken it when I left, without her knowing.

"You're such a fucking bitch," my mother said as she watched me brushing my hair. "Who do you think you are?"

I didn't have an answer. I did not know who I was or who I was attempting to be in my dressy clothes. My shirt looked mismatched with the skirt, and my panty hose were a size too big.

"Why the hell are you dressed like that?" Her eyes burned a hole in the side of my face. I was convinced she hated me. I continued to brush my hair. I wanted to make my ponytail as neat as possible.

About a month before, my mother took me to a hairdresser who, unbeknownst to her, was having an affair with Stevie. The hairdresser chopped my hair off, all of it. I believe she thought it would hurt my mother, but it did not. She did not care. In fact, my mother blamed me when I climbed into the car with tears streaming down my cheeks. "Oh, well," she said. "It'll grow back." I had no idea what the hairdresser had done until she swiveled me around to the large piece of glass that covered the wall in front of us. I now struggled with how to style it and make it Rotary Club–acceptable.

"I have my interview with the Rotary Club today," I managed to get out. My throat was tight, and I swallowed to keep from crying.

"Instead of worrying about the Rotary Club, you need to be worried about keeping this bathroom clean and helping out around the house." Recently, she had held my head in the toilet for not cleaning it well enough. I wanted her to leave, to stop talking. Eventually, she did.

I caught the bus to the Rotary Club. As I walked the block to the brick building, the hot sun forced my panty hose down to my ankles, where the extra fabric gathered into a puddle. By the time I reached the door, my forehead was wet, and the creases under both sleeves of my shirt were damp.

Arlene was already there. Her hair flowed down past her shoulders, and her dress was more than appropriate for the occasion. When she saw me, she leapt from her seat in the direction of the Sparklettes water cooler, dropping her note-cards onto the floor. I helped her pick them up. She was nervous, I could tell. She was called in first.

When she came out of the interview, I tried to make eye contact to see how it went. I wanted to know what questions they had asked and if she thought she did a good job. However, before I could ask her, my name was called—Chataquoa Mason. I hated it when White people said my name. They always got it wrong and made it seem as if it were my fault for their mis-pronunciation. It sounded foreign to them, I suppose. Their tongues and mouths were not made for names like mine. It was like I was being punished for not being named Lisa, Jane, or Jennifer.

I stood, used my clammy hands to pull my skirt closer to my knees, and headed into the room.

There was a panel of five White men with black tasseled hats around the long wooden table. When I entered, each stood to shake my hand. The inter-view lasted about thirty minutes, and I believed I had done well. The questions centered on what makes a good leader, why I should be chosen, how much I knew about the Rotary Club, and my extra-curricular activities at school. My answers were forthright and honest. They seemed impressed.

"When you shake hands with someone, be firm and look them in the eye. It shows your power. You don't want to be perceived as weak," the wrinkly White man said as I walked toward the door.

"Let me show you." He grabbed my right hand with his and shook it firmly. It did feel different. My handshake was soft, like a wet noodle. From that day forward, whenever I met someone, I shook his way.

The Rotary Club contacted the school principal, Ms. Craig, to let her know I had won the award and would be traveling with a group of other students from the region to the sleepaway leadership retreat in the woods. I won along with Ian, a White boy who was the smartest guy in our class and the eventual Valedictorian. We were both featured in a newspaper article.

Although I had very little interaction with her, I liked Ms. Craig. She was cool and everyone loved her, even the gang-bangers. Instead of suspending them, she hugged them. Jeremiah, Chris, The Twins, and the others were a welcome part of our community. When they were absent, she checked on them or inquired about their whereabouts. I believe this made a difference and endeared us to her.

Ms. Bowman ate her overstuffed baked potato and smacked on the tough piece of roast on her plate. Between chews, she talked to the group of us about Virginia State University, a predominantly Black college in Petersburg. Larry, Rachel, Bernardo, Craig, and I listened with rapt attention. I was still a little more than a year away from college, but the other four were shipping off at the end of the summer.

Every Wednesday, we met with Ms. Bowman in her classroom for the Future Black Leaders of America Club. Ms. Bowman was the special education teacher at San Bernardino High and a graduate of West Virginia State, a historically Black college in Charleston, West Virginia. On our campus, she had developed a reputation for getting Black kids into college. She saw it as her duty to help us, those of us she could.

"Rachel, did you get your enrollment paper-work back to Virginia State University?" she asked.

"Yes, ma'am, I did," Rachel said. "My mother won't fill out the financial aid forms. She said she don't want people in her business."

"You have to get her to fill them out. That's the only way you are going to get any aid or loans." She sounded exasperated, but not the least bit surprised.

"Larry, have you heard back from Tuskegee?" She had connections at many of the Black colleges in the South and used them to our benefit.

In one of our meetings, Ms. Bowman called me overzealous and told me to stop raising my hand to offer up solutions to problems I did not know how to solve, like getting an unwilling mother to complete financial aid forms. Now, I just listened as she doled out advice on how to navigate the application process. She was no-nonsense. I could not afford to be on her bad side.

food for all

"I'm hungry," Rachel said through the phone. There was no food at her grandmother's house, and everyone was starving, including the small children.

"When is your mother coming home from work?"

"I don't know," she replied. "It doesn't matter, she doesn't have any money. She doesn't get paid until next week."

Since we had become friends, Rachel was my lifeline. She listened to my stories and assured me I was a good person, not a troublemaker. She saw what I saw. When she spent the night at my house, she saw the small circle of light from the flashlight that searched the bedroom for the outline of my body. When Stevie saw I was not alone, he left.

We were plotting our escape together. She was going to Virginia State University in the fall and would write to tell about the life she was creating for herself and how it was on the outside, away from here.

"I'll bring you some food," I offered.

"How?" she demanded to know. She sounded nervous and relieved at the same time.

"I'll just put it in a bag and bring it over," I explained. "My mother's not home yet."

Our refrigerator was full, and I knew what would not be missed or what my mother would assume one of us, the children, had eaten. I eased open the refrigerator door and cabinets, careful not to make any noise. A slight creak would be noticed. My brother and sister were in the living room watching television. I could hear the muffled, canned laughter and prayed that a commercial did not come on and cause them to break for a snack or use the toilet.

I hurriedly filled a plastic Food 4 Less grocery bag with potatoes, an onion, a couple of packages of freeze-dried Nissin ramen noodles, some cookies, and one of the cheap steaks my mother purchased in excess for Stevie. The entire grab took no more than a couple of minutes. After the bag was packed, I held it at its lowest point, creating a large soccer-ball-sized mound so that it would not rustle when I moved around the room.

My body was shaking as I twisted the knob of the garage door and headed down the driveway. The front door made too much noise when it was opened. I walked briskly down the street, not stopping to speak to anyone. My mother would be home any minute. If she saw me, the first thing she would ask was what's in the bag. I was not safe until I rounded the corner. When I turned down Magnolia Street, my gait relaxed and I let the bag swing freely at my side.

"Here," I said as I was handing over the bag to

Rachel. She riffled through it, her hands combing over the contents.

"I didn't think you would do it," she said. Her face was thankful. She pulled one of the packages of ramen noodles out of the bag and placed the other items on the kitchen table. I watched as she cooked then ate the noodles. It was her dinner for the night. When she finished, she whipped up a meal for her siblings and cousins with what was left in the bag, putting the remaining package of noodles to the side for later.

"Are you excited about Virginia State?" I asked as we sat in the window of the front room. When her aunt Leigh took a break from her perch on the sill, we looked out onto the street and observed the comings and goings on the block.

"I'm nervous and excited all at the same time," she said. "I just want to do well—get good grades so that I can become a psychologist. Make my mother proud. I bet I'll meet my husband there too."

Our conversation reminded me just how much I was going to miss her and our talks. She had become such a huge part of my life. I did not know how I would make it through my last year without her, or any of my friends, for that matter. They were all seniors.

"My cousin from Las Vegas called me," I said, changing the subject.

"What did she want?"

"She said she would send for me to come there for the summer. I could work with her at Jack in the Box to earn money to buy school clothes.

My mother had all but stopped purchasing clothes for me and barely gave me lunch money any more. Rachel and I wore the same shoe size. We shared our shoes—I had two pairs and she had one.

I had not seen my oldest cousin Missy in nearly a decade. She was the daughter of my father's sister; when my father and I lost contact, I also fell out of touch with his side of the family. Missy had gotten my phone number from my aunt Glo, she said, and decided to give me a call.

"Do you think she's legit?"

"I don't know. She sounded like it. She said she wanted us to be close and to have a relationship."

"Are you going to go?"

"I might. It can't be any worse than being here. And plus, I could really use the money. The only thing I would miss is being here with you this summer before you leave for school."

"Don't worry about me. I'll be fine," she assured me.

We sat in silence, watching the cars roll past and thinking about the imminent shifts ahead of us. I was not prepared.

new mission

I stood high above the congregation in a long white robe, bonnet, and underwear with my arms crossed against my chest. The water-filled tank awaited me. Pastor Tinkel stood behind me and nudged me to the top of the stairs. Rachel was behind him. She was next.

The water was cold as I waded in, careful not to splash. My robe floated above my waist as I settled into the basin. The pastor followed me inside. He spoke with righteousness as he placed his hand over the top of my head.

Lord God, our heavenly Father,
we thank you for your great goodness
in calling us to know you and to put our trust
   in you.
Increase this knowledge and strengthen our
   faith.
Give your Holy Spirit to this person,
that she may be born again and made an heir
   of everlasting salvation;
through Jesus Christ our Lord,
who lives and reigns with you and the Holy
   Spirit,
one God, now and forever. Amen.

Both of my cheeks filled with air as Pastor Tinkel gently submerged my head in the water. When he pulled it back up, the congregation erupted with applause, and the organ pipes began to sing. A woman in a black usher's uniform grabbed my hand and gave me a towel to pat my face dry. She led me to the back room, where I changed my clothes.

I had been washed in the blood of Jesus. It was the first step toward my redemption and the dedication of my life to the Lord. I was saved.

"Do you feel different?" she asked. Her voice was expectant. I could tell she wanted me to respond affirmatively. I searched my body for a sensation, a new connection, or a feeling of calm. There was nothing. Still, I nodded slowly as I slipped my head through the collar of my shirt.

"Good, that means God is with you. You have to make Him proud."

I had no idea how to make God proud. It seemed like such a tall order.

"Do you have a boyfriend?"

I hesitated, but decided to answer. I did not want it to appear as if I had something to hide. "Yes, I do."

I had started to date Larry, the co-captain of the Pacesetter drum squad. He was a mama's boy and worked at Kentucky Fried Chicken after school. He also had a car and pulled up to my house for a visit every time my mother left to play Bingo at the local Kiwanis Club. My brother never told because when she left, he invited his friends over and they shot dice on the slippery kitchen floor.

"Now that you've been baptized, you'll have to refrain from kissing, groping, and having sex," she said. "The Lord is a jealous and vengeful God. He is very patient, but great in power; the Lord punishes."

I was okay with the sex part, but I enjoyed kissing and sitting on the hood of Larry's car while he nibbled on my neck. This would have to stop. Everything good or bad that happened to me from that day forward would be the result of whether or not God was pleased with me.

Rachel's aunt Sheri invited us to New Mission Ministries, an apostolic church on El Toro Street in our neighborhood. She was evangelizing, doing the Lord's work by converting nonbelievers. When she initially approached us about going, I was reluctant and made excuses as to why I could not attend. Her syrupy tone and earnestness creeped me out a little bit. I had not stepped foot inside a church since Clearlie's funeral. Then, I was overcome with sadness and grief.

I also did not understand church culture or its politics. As a child, I had only gone consistently on major holidays—Easter, Christmas—or for funerals. To me, church seemed like an elaborate show with a sure pecking order. The men were on top and the women were behind them, running the church or quiet in the first few rows.

The pastor stomped around the pulpit, his words punctuated by the organ or the drums. As he spoke, the congregation shouted back their approval or sat in silence when he spoke about a sin that hit too close to home for them. The first few pews are where the most devoted of congregants sat and also where the Holy Ghost was likely to break out. When worshipers became spirit-filled, they danced and shouted as if on fire. God was inside them. And once they did, the music started up and eventually one, two, or three more people were up on their feet jumping and shouting, each one outdoing the last. Did God approve of all of this, I wondered.

Sheri lived in Riverside, about thirty minutes outside San Bernardino, with her husband and three children. She was a dutiful wife and mother. Her husband, Tony, was a deacon in the church, and her son TJ was a star football player being recruited heavily by top universities. She attributed all of her fortune in life to the grace and glory of God. And she promised that it could be that way for me too. I could have a good life. She was convincing. I also did not have anything to lose.

As a result of Sheri's promise, I began to attend

church regularly. Every Sunday, I walked to Rachel's house, Bible in hand, and waited there for Sheri to pick us up. When she did not go or we wanted to attend the youth program during the evenings, we walked the few miles there and back. My mother allowed me to go because she figured any church was better than not going at all. I went because I was hoping God would rescue me.

Over the next few months, I became a full-on Bible thumper. I carried the good book everywhere I went—to cheerleading practice, on the bus, and to class. I attended private Bible study in homes and memorized Scriptures. I figured the harder I prayed and followed the Ten Commandments, along with a few other rules spouted off from the pulpit, the more I would win favor in the eyes of God.

Sheri said that before I could join the choir or usher board, in addition to being baptized I had to speak in tongues. It was the rule of the church. It was to keep heathens and sinners out of service positions in the church. It was for the good of the church, she reasoned.

After church on Sundays, I stayed after service with other congregants. We were in a closed room with validators, who prayed with us until, magically, we started to speak in tongues.

The loud wailing sounded like an auctioneer trying to obtain the highest bid. I imitated and waited for the validator to recognize what I was saying was indeed god-speak, a special language understood only by God himself. It could not be interpreted. When I tired of praying, I opened one of my eyes to scan the room and to see what the others were doing. Some had gotten up and paced around the room, lifting their hands to the heavens. Others had dropped to their knees and shut their eyes and clasped their hands tightly. This was intense.

I returned night after night, hoping to be filled with the Holy Spirit. After about a couple of months of trying, the validator praised God for my deliverance and for speaking to me directly. I was officially saved. I belonged to the church.

The following Sunday, we all piled into Sheri's blue minivan and headed to a gathering at Pastor Tinkel's home. The palatial house sat atop a large windy hill. It smelled good inside, like Thanksgiving dinner—collard greens, ham, and baked macaroni and cheese. There were also plenty of cakes and pies. Outside, there was a pool and garden. Why was his house so big? Was he rich? Did God give him all of this? I wanted to know.

The church, with its gold cross sliced through its roof, was modest, nothing to brag about. It was on a main thoroughfare next to the local swap meet. Pastor Tinkel's house was far different from what I had imagined. I thought it would be simpler, Jesus-like. I was confused. I moved around the house, cautious not to knock anything over. There were antique vases and figurines everywhere.

Between the sermon and the Holy Ghost outbursts at church, the offering plate was passed, often more than once. The request for an offering was almost always preceded by a testimony from someone in the congregation, usually a woman. When she stood before the church, she attested to the goodness of the Lord or how she gave her last dollar, only to have it returned exponentially to her within a matter of days. "Praise God," Pastor Tinkel would shout into the microphone as he encouraged us to dig deep into our pockets. He also said that God knew our capacity to give and if we were withholding, God would hold it against us. Sometimes I threw a dime or a penny into the plate as it passed to let God know I was giving all that I could.

In retrospect, what I find interesting and perhaps most troubling is that most of the congregants at New Mission Ministries were working-class people barely scraping by. Many of them were single mothers. They believed that if they gave to the church, their pockets would be enriched. If it didn't materialize, they held on to the belief that if they were not rewarded on earth, their truest treasure awaited them in heaven. These women had very little money to give and sometimes denied themselves in order to replenish the church. Interestingly, Pastor Tinkel was living his lavish life now. He did not have to delay his blessing for another day.

Real disillusionment set in for me when Pastor Tinkel's daughter became pregnant by some dude in the choir. I thought we weren't supposed to be having sex.

Nina sat in the front pew, her face overcome with shame. Her young suitor, who had become a regular at church, was nowhere in sight. It was a huge scandal, one that could not be corrected with Scripture readings or repentance. Pastor Tinkel forced her to have an abortion, a procedure he vehemently condemned from the pulpit but now quietly advocated to save his own reputation.

This religion thing was more complicated than I had originally thought. I had joined because I figured I would get saved like Sheri and, miraculously, my life would turn around. God, however, was becoming harder and harder to please. I wasn't seeing any improvement at home. My prayers and chastity were not working. It was still hell. I decided to save myself.

"Don't do that," I mumbled.

"What did you say?" Stevie's eyes locked into mine.

"You heard me. Don't touch me." I meant it and straightened my back.

"Oh, you don't want me to touch you now."

I was silent. I had already spoken. There was no

need to repeat it. He heard me. Moments before, he had pinched my ass and rubbed himself up against my backside. It felt disgusting. There was going to be no more of this shit.

"Fine, have it your way," is all he said. I noticed a slight snicker on his face as he pivoted toward the front door. "Don't ask me for any more help. You're on your own."

Fuck you, I thought.

gone

The doors opened and shut as passengers got on and off. I had gotten on going the opposite direction from home, although that is where I should have been heading. I moved past mothers and children to a seat in the back, near the exhaust pipe. The roar and the heady, intoxicating smell of petrol always meant we were leaving, pulling off to another destination.

I pulled my feet up onto the hard plastic seats and rested my back on the window. My sneakers dangled over the edge into the aisle. I pulled out the crumpled newspaper from my backpack and began searching for apartments. I had already circled a few places, a one-bedroom, one-bathroom for $350 per month and a studio apartment for $250. I tried not to pay attention to the prices. I planned on getting a job to pay for it and to cover my other living expenses. Then, I pulled out the want ads and began to circle jobs. At sixteen, I found that my options were limited to fast food or retail. Both paid minimum wage, $4.25 per hour in the state of California, hardly enough for an apartment.

At the end of the route, I exited the bus and crossed the street to the Carousel Mall. I entered through Harris Department Store. The store was beautiful and the smell of high-priced perfume clogged the air. The saleswomen were dressed in suits with neatly coifed hair and perfect makeup. It was as if they were going to a fancy restaurant once they finished restocking the racks and ringing up customers. I was invisible to them.

As I drifted through the store, touching sleeves and glancing at price tags, I wondered what it would be like to have enough money to buy anything I wanted in there. I only shopped at discount stores or swap meets. My mother never took us to department stores because she said the salespeople made her feel dirty, unworthy.

"Would you like to try that on?" the skinny saleswoman asked. I had an arm full of hangers of clothes I wanted to try on that I had collected from the Young Miss section. I had beautiful dresses, slacks, shorts, jeans, and a few shirts.

"Yes, I would." I looked her in the eye as I handed over the merchandise. I was working to convince myself that I deserved to be there and had the right to try on clothes even if I didn't have any money to buy anything today. Someday, I would. I closed the door behind me.

The clothes hung on the hook on the back of the door, as my body was square in front of me in the long mirror. I pulled my shirt over my head and unbuttoned my pants. I had nothing. No boobs, no ass. My arms were so skinny that I could make a circle around them with my index finger and thumb. And my legs and thighs had circle-like welts on them from the extension cord used during my whipping a few days ago. I tried to ignore the marks as I slipped into the beautiful pink floral dress. I picked it from the rack because it reminded me of Arlene Lee Soy's dress, the one she wore to the Rotary Club interview. However, I did not look like her in it.

Before leaving the dressing room, I stuffed a pair of shorts into my backpack and hung all of the clothes back on their respective hangers. I did not want to leave a mess for the saleswoman to clean.

Summer comes early in the Valley. Before noon, the temperature had already reached one hundred degrees in our cul-de-sac. It was Sunday and my mother was out running errands. I was holed up in my bedroom on punishment. Instead of staring into space, I decided to make good use of my time by studying for the next day's final exam in English. It was the last week of school.

Dennis, Stevie's cousin, was visiting from L.A. My mother enjoyed his company and the attention. They talked for hours, and she was Queen Bee once more. Dennis was also her confidant and fed her information about Stevie's many infidelities. All of which he denied. Despite this, my mother remained faithful and made sure his dinner plate was kept warm in the oven no matter what time of night he arrived home. If he disappeared for days, she never complained or inquired about his whereabouts.

I knew he was a cheater because he often gave me blow-by-blow accounts of his encounters, complete with sound effects and simulated moaning. Women were falling over themselves to be with him, he said; even the neighbor's daughter Akeely.

He also told me that my mother had an abortion. "You would have had a little brother," he said. "But she didn't want to be a mother again."

I didn't know what to do with this information that poured into me almost daily. I was sad for my mother, for her loneliness and for what her life, and our lives together, had become. I could see she was playing the hand she was dealt, and she was losing badly.

I continued to listen, but did not allow his words to penetrate. There was nothing he could say to convince me that he was looking out for my best interests or to change the way I saw him. He was disgusting.

I was also on to him. He was playing both sides—me against my mother. He told my mother about our so-called confidential conversations, leaving out all that he had told me. He made it appear as though I trusted him and we had a special bond. This made my mother feel insecure. As a result, she often deferred to him about me.

Additionally, as if he were some kind of oracle, he prophesied that she and I would have to fight in order to settle our differences once and for all. It was inevitable, he said. My mother was growing sick and tired of my ways and of me. I was too good for the family and no longer wanted to obey the rules of the house.

The goading became more frequent and intensified after I demanded that he not touch me anymore. Instead, he beat me with an extension cord for the tiniest infraction. I was forced to strip down to my underwear and lie on my stomach on my daybed. He swatted me ten times, more if I moved or turned to catch the rope with my hand. After a while, I stopped crying when I was hit. I knew it would not make it stop and that no one would come to my rescue.

I was dying. I had to get out of there.

"Has anyone seen my shoes? The black ones," I asked as I searched underneath the beds and sofa, in the closets, and on the front porch. We often left our shoes on the porch to allow them to air out.

"I haven't," my sister responded as she slipped on a pair of shorts and sandals, preparing herself for a day of outdoor play. My brother hadn't seen them either. This was strange. When I asked Rachel about the shoes, she said that she had returned them to me. The last time she had seen them was more than a week ago on the front porch.

The doorbell rang. Since I was passing, I answered it.

"Can Kamilah come out to play?" the little girl asked. I recognized her. She lived in the group home three doors down from us. There were always new kids moving in and out of the house. Some ran away, never to be seen again. Others expressed their desire to stay, only to be shipped off to another home a week later. This girl had been there for a few months now.

"Kamilah, Salina is here." I yelled into her room. "What are y'all about to do?"

"We're going to go to my house to play Barbies," she responded. I continued to make small talk while my sister gathered her dolls to take with her.

"Are those my shoes?" I asked as I stared down at Salina's feet. She was quiet and her smile faded. She bowed her head.

"They are. Those are my shoes," I answered for her. Hearing the commotion, my sister pushed her way past me and out onto the front porch next to her friend.

Salina must have taken them from the doorstep on her previous visit. I was conflicted. I wanted them back, but knew that nobody steals a pair of used shoes if they don't really need them. They were also probably too big for her.

"Why did you take them?" I wanted to know.

She shrugged her shoulders. I bent my head down in order to nudge hers up, but it did not work. She would not make eye contact with me.

"You can have them," I said. Salina's body loosened. I could tell she was relieved.

"No, give them to me," my sister demanded. "I want them."

"You have plenty of shoes," I told her. My sister began to cry. She insisted that I snatch the shoes off of the girl's feet and hand them over to her. I refused. This was quickly becoming a matter of principle for me.

"Are you really going to let her keep the shoes after she stole them from the doorstep?" Dennis asked. He had made his way to the front door and was now trying to arbitrate. The vestibule was becoming crowded.

"She needs them," I rationalized. "She wore them over here. If she had another pair of shoes, she would have worn those instead of the ones she had taken from the steps."

There was no convincing the two of them. The only solution as far as they were concerned was to rip the shoes off Salina's feet, leaving her to walk home embarrassed and barefoot. We were at a standstill.

My sister bent down and tried to pry the shoes off her feet. Salina was unmovable, like a concrete post. In that moment, I could see her resilience and that she was a fighter.

"You can have them," I repeated in Salina's direction. They were my shoes and I could do whatever I wanted with them. I returned to my room to continue studying.

This was bullshit, I thought. I sprang from my bed and marched into my sister's room. One, two, three . . . ten, eleven—pairs of shoes. They were lined up neatly in her closet. Many had been worn only once or twice. I was furious. I should have been the one crying—I had just given up one of the only two pairs of shoes I owned, arguably, my good pair. She was such a brat.

My mother was back. I could hear her and Dennis from my bedroom discussing what had happened earlier in the afternoon. They were loud. She was unloading the groceries and preparing to make dinner. "She did what?" I heard her say. He repeated it for her:

"She gave the shoes to the little girl even though she had stolen them off the porch," Dennis said, his voice tinged with disbelief.

"And I wanted them," my sister chimed in. "And Pumpkin gave them to her."

Shit, I thought. Here we go. It was only a matter of time before I would be summoned to account for my actions. "Pumpkin, come here," my mother bellowed down the hallway. I drug my feet to the center of the dining room.

"Yes," I said, trying to pretend that I had not been listening.

"You gave that little girl your shoes even though she stole them from the porch?" My mother's summation of the story was correct. Coming from her, it sounded nonsensical and wrong. I could tell she was incensed. Maybe I should have taken them back, I thought. Things would be much easier right now. Instead, I was going to be punished and my restriction extended into the start of summer.

"Yes." I kept my answers short. No way was I going to get into an argument about this.

They started the story over from the beginning. Each time, it was grander and my actions inexcusable. In their version of events, Salina sounded like a seasoned criminal rather than a seven-year-old. It was all I could do to keep from rolling my eyes.

As Dennis and my sister told the story, my mother glared in my direction. "I should fuck you up," she said.

I didn't care. So fucking what, I thought. The shoes were gone. This brought me a little satisfaction.

"You should have just stayed in Long Beach with Monk. It's been nothing but trouble since you've been back." I had heard this before. I was unfazed. My only task in that moment was to not absorb the words, not allow them to wound me. I looked at the ceiling, down toward my feet, and then at the blinds that had been opened earlier in the day to allow the light in.

"Why didn't you give them to Kamilah?"

"She already has eleven pairs of shoes." This was a fact. My face was strained and pleading for understanding.

"You're just selfish," she offered up as an explanation for my actions.

"I'M NOT SELFISH!" I yelled. My voice snatched the air from the room. Why did I do that?

My mother raced from around the kitchen island and into the dining room. She struck me in the face with her clenched fist. The blow knocked me to the ground. She crouched down and continued to deliver punches to my head and face. Between hits, she attempted to pull me to my feet and ordered me to fight back. I did not.

I would never hit her. She was my mother. Instead, I curled up into a fetal position with my forearms pressed around my head to protect it. The rings on her fingers felt like jagged rocks. This will be over soon, I thought as she pounded my body. She would get tired of my not fighting back.

"Stand up," she growled. She had backed away. Her mouth had tiny bits of foam around the edges. Her eyes bulged and her chest heaved. I slowly unfolded my legs and released my arms from around my head. I used my hands to push the weight of my body upward. My body was vibrating.

"Stevie told you this was going to happen. I told you too. You should have just kept your mouth shut." She was screaming.

Dennis was in the background shaking his head. "I don't know why you didn't just give your *own* sister the shoes."

"Get out of here."

What just happened? Had I just survived the big fight? My hair was a mess and my scalp burned. That woman had tried to snatch me bald.

As I passed my brother's room, I tried to catch his eye, but his body was stiff and distant. He would not look at me. Certainly, he had heard everything. He knew what had happened. He could have helped me. Fuck him too.

I did not eat dinner and slept through the night into the morning. My head throbbed and my body ached. My pace was slow and my efforts deliberate. After I dressed, I went to the bathroom to brush my teeth and comb my hair. In the mirror, I did not recognize my face. It was swollen, and the lids of my eyes practically folded over onto themselves. My bottom lip felt tight. When I pulled it down in the mirror, I noticed blood trapped inside the skin.

I had to go to school. I had to tell Rachel what had happened and that I planned to leave. I left through the garage, grabbing my mother's oversized sunglasses from the card table and forcing them onto my face. They would have to do.

"What happened to you?" Rachel's voice was an amalgam of concern and disbelief.

"I'll tell you over there." I led her behind the special education building where no one would see my face or me. She gasped when I removed my glasses. Tears began to swell in the corners of her eyes.

"Don't cry," I told her. "You'll make me cry."

"You have a black eye," she informed me.

I nodded and put my glasses back on. My face wasn't that bad, I thought. She was making a bigger deal out of it than it actually was. I began to feel self-conscious. I wondered if anyone had noticed my puffy face in the cafeteria that morning.

"What happened?" she asked once more.

"She beat me up," I said matter-of-factly. I gave her the short version of what had occurred the day before.

"I'm leaving. I'm going to Vegas for the summer. I will come back in the fall when school starts."

"Do you even know those people in Vegas?"

"It's my grandmother, my aunt, and my cousins. I'll be fine." She wasn't convinced.

"I'll come back to visit you," I assured her. "And we can write." I didn't have time to convince her of my decision. It was already made.

The bell rang out.

"I have to go. I have an English final right now. I can't miss it." I did not give her a chance to respond to any of what I had said. I did not want to talk about my decision to move or what had happened the day before. "Don't worry about me," I yelled back. "I'll be all right."

I am not sure what I wrote on the exam. It did not matter. My head was swimming, and it was hard for me to concentrate. I just needed to make it to the end of the class. Although we were not allowed to wear sunglasses in class, Mr. Lyles did not ask me to remove mine. I took the test with them on. When I finished, I asked permission to leave and exited the bungalow and walked toward the back of the school.

My cousin Missy wired the money for my bus ticket through Western Union. In our phone conversation, she assured me that the job at Jack in the Box was still available. I spoke with my paternal grandmother, Josephine, to make sure it was okay for me to stay for the summer. She said she was looking forward to having me down.

"I want to go to Las Vegas for the summer," I declared as I stood in the frame of my mother's bedroom door. She had just gotten off from work and was resting on her bed. She still had on her uniform.

"It's just for the summer. I'm going to work

and save my money to buy school clothes. Maybe I'll send some home," I continued.

"I don't care, do whatever you want." I believed she meant it—do whatever you want. I had her permission.

I returned to my room to pack. I stuffed all of the clothes I could into a large, black plastic garbage bag. The rest, I left in the closet—my secondhand church dresses, my cheerleading and drill team uniforms. I put one outfit to the side to wear on the bus the following morning. I cleaned my room and made sure everything was in its place.

My mother dropped me off at the Greyhound bus station on her way to work. "Call me when you get there to let me know that you made it," she said as I exited the car.

"I will," I said as I slammed the door. I did not look back.

I had never ridden a bus long distance by myself. I struggled to the ticket counter with my heavy bag, which was developing small holes where my fingernails had dug in for a better grip. I had to be careful. The last thing I needed was for the bag to rip and all of my clothes to be strewn across the floor.

I rested the bag on the edge of my shoe as I reached in my pocket to pull out the money for the ticket. I then dragged the bag to the opposite side of the room to the vending machine to buy an orange soda. I still had a two-hour wait before my bus departed the station. I sat atop of my bag and waited for my bus number to be called over the speaker system.

When it came time to board, I rushed to the head of the line. I wanted to get the best seat possible, away from the toilet and the perverts who usually took up residence in the back of the bus. I gave my ticket to the driver and grabbed the seat directly behind him. I placed my garbage bag of clothes in the seat next to me.

I am never going back, I told myself as I stared out of the slightly tinted window at the broken lines down the center of the road. This was my last thought before I drifted off to sleep. My body collapsed into the seat, my head against my bag. I was exhausted.

in the desert

There was no job at Jack in the Box waiting for me. Missy was the family fabulist and often made promises she could not keep or told stories that were untrue. I'd had no way of knowing this about her since we had been out of touch. When I prodded her to speak to her manager on my behalf, she made excuses, telling me I needed to be patient. She was working on it.

Missy was two years older than me and had dropped out of high school in the eleventh grade. She now worked full-time at Jack in the Box. It was one in a chain of fast-food jobs she had worked since dropping out. Before her current job, she worked at Pizza Hut, she said.

My grandmother was a maid on the Las Vegas Strip at one of the megahotels. She was waiting for the new Debbie Reynolds Hotel to open. Having heard through friends at work that the hotel was offering better pay, a full forty hours of work per week, and benefits, she kept her eyes and ears open for more information in order to be among the first to apply for a position. My grandmother understood how these things worked and how to get a job. You had to be ready and willing to work hard, she said. Be the first one at the door.

Including me, there were thirteen people, three adults and ten children, living in a three-bedroom house. There were people everywhere, and the house was impossible to keep clean. On occasion, my cousins Katrina and Luvleen and I slept on an old, sunken-in couch on the front porch. The night breeze felt good against my skin. We did not need blankets or pillows, which was lucky because there weren't many.

Our nights on the porch came to a halt after my grandmother complained that it was not safe for three young girls to sleep outside. We could be raped or kidnapped and no one would know, she said. We thought she was overreacting, but we moved back to the cramped quarters with the rest of the family.

At the start of each month, my grandmother and aunt combined the little money they had left after paying the rent and utilities to grocery shop for the entire house. To get the most for the least amount of money, they shopped at the local discount grocery store in our neighborhood, where the meat always smelled and the vegetables were overly ripe. It was our only option. On more than one occasion, the household fell ill because the rotten meat we had consumed had been marked good for sale.

Our meals were cooked in bulk. Breakfast usually consisted of Albert's hominy grits with sugar or cereal with milk that was passed from one person to the next. For dinner, we ate beans and rice or, sometimes, just plain rice with butter. A few times a month, we had tacos or fried chicken. Rarely were there any leftovers.

"What are you going to do about a job?" my cousin Katrina asked pointedly as I sat on the living room couch watching television. It was one of those rare times when I had it to myself. I stretched out across the soda- and food-stained fabric. She flopped next to me. I moved my feet to accommodate her.

"I don't know." I shrugged my shoulders.

A few days after I arrived, my grandmother had taken us down to the Convention Center to look for work. There was an exhibition in town, and she'd heard they needed workers to clean up after the show. She and five of her grandchildren, in tattered clothing, showed up ready to work. Without explanation, they turned us away at the door. They said there was no work to be had. We walked the two miles back to our house, talking and joking along the way.

The truth was, I had not really thought about a job. I had come to Las Vegas to work, but I had also come looking for a place of refuge, rest. I was also still getting adjusted to my new home and all of the people who lived in it. Some I had met before, but many of the faces were new.

My cousins, particularly the youngest ones, looked like the four children who had visited my house in San Bernardino, ashen and unkempt. They wore the same clothes day after day and did not sleep in pajamas at night. Their hair was disheveled, and none of them wore shoes, even outside to play. As far as I could tell, no one brushed his or her teeth in the morning. We were related. Did I look like them to other people, I wondered. Was I poor without knowing it? I pushed these questions to the back of my mind.

Katrina's question was a good one, though. It had been nearly two weeks since I had arrived, and I was still unemployed. I also had no money.

"Tomorrow, I'll go down to the strip and find a job," I declared.

"Maybe I'll come with you," she said ardently.

I did not want her to come with me, but told her she could. I believed she would ruin my chances. We would be turned away just like at the Convention Center, I thought. Her jeans had holes in them, and her white T-shirt never looked quite clean. She also wore flip-flops wherever she went. And I was sure our job search would have been no different. By myself, I could convince someone to give me a chance and impress them with my interview skills and firm handshake.

I knew how to act in front of White people. I had learned from watching television and from observing the interactions between them in my classes. She did not. Katrina was rough around the edges. When she spoke, the words sounded jumbled, not in order. And when she was angered or told what to do, she erupted in verbal fits of *fucks, bitches,* and threats of violence. She used her strength and verbal assaults to silence others and as a defense against her vulnerability. There was no way she was coming with me.

The next morning, I tiptoed out of the side door of the house and to the bus stop while she slept. Later, if she asked why I had gone without her, I would say I tried to wake her, but that she did not hear me when I called her name. I believed the tiny lie was worth it.

To canvas the strip, I wore my good pair of jeans and short-sleeved shirt. The jeans were a mistake. It was already 103 degrees, and with no trees, the sun met me every step of the way. I was sweating profusely. My first stop along the way was the Fashion Show mall, a high-end shopping center in the middle of the long strip of hotels. I bypassed the fancy department store and made a beeline to the food court. I filled out application after application for those restaurants that said they were hiring. Once I had finished there, I continued along the strip, dipping in and out of noisy casinos in search of employment. My ears were beginning to buzz because of the loud ringing and sirens from the slot machines. My last stop without having to get on another bus was the Riviera Hotel and Casino. As luck would have it, I entered smack in the center of their food court. There was a Wienerschnitzel hot dog stand, Chinese restaurant, bakery, and Baskin Robbins ice cream shop, all in one line. Surely, someone would hire me.

"Excuse me sir, can I speak to a manager?" I asked in my most polite, White voice. I waited for the line to die down to get his attention.

"Why?" he asked suspiciously.

"I'm looking for a job and wanted to fill out an application." My eyes were pleading. I needed him to make the connection for me.

"Hold on a minute," he said, disappearing into the back of the restaurant. When he reemerged, he was with a woman in a long white jacket with a pen stashed behind her ear. She was the manager.

"How can I help you?"

"I wanted to fill out an application for one of the restaurants or as many that have openings." I tried to look eager and available.

"It's only one application. Each day, we assign everyone a different food station to work," she explained. "Wait for me at the side door and follow me to my office."

Her office was located in the busy casino and there was a little table outside it. "Have a seat," she said.

When she returned, she handed me an application and sat in the chair across from me.

"When are you available to start?" she asked.

I wasn't expecting to be interviewed. It was a welcome relief. The other places just took my application and said they would call me.

"Tomorrow . . . this week," I answered anxiously.

"How many hours can you work?" she asked. "We can't hire you if you can only work the weekends. Do you have your food and beverage card?"

I hesitated before answering. I didn't know what she was talking about. "No, I sighed."

"It's required by the state of Nevada. Before you can work in a casino, you have to get it. It costs twenty-five dollars. Fill out this application. I'll be back."

I used my best penmanship and wrote as fast as I could. I wanted to be finished by the time she returned. On the application, I marked that I was available to work from 10:00 a.m. until midnight, when the food court closed.

"Here, I'm done," I said, pushing the application into her hand. She looked it over.

"Here's the food and beverage application. It also requires that you get a TB test," she explained. "You have to bring the card back along with the test results before you can officially start. Come back on Friday." I had a job.

I spent the summer scooping, cooking, and serving food to the thousands of tourists who came through the door of the hotel. I worked forty hours per week and sometimes picked up a shift when someone called in sick.

The job itself was mundane. When we weren't busy, I watched videos on the television screens high above the tables in the center of the food court. To pass the time, I challenged myself to learn how to make all of the food from the different stations.

The Chinese restaurant was the hardest to master. The dishes and ingredients were foreign to me—moo goo gai pan, egg drop soup, and lo mein. To mix the food, I used a giant wok. The ingredients—bamboo shoots, oyster sauce, bean sprouts, and water chestnuts—came in huge cans with writing I did not understand. I followed the recipes written in a large notebook. After I was comfortable, I began to improvise. I was proud when customers returned for seconds or remarked about the taste.

Because I knew how to work all of the food stations and never took off from work, I was considered a good employee. And when a new food station or cappuccino station opened in the center of the casino, I was the first one asked to work there. When I worked inside the casino, I wore a see-through mesh top with a bra underneath. It was similar to what I had seen the cocktail waitresses wearing when they served drinks to their customers.

The female impersonators from the *La Cage*

show and burlesque dancers from *Crazy Girl* were regular customers and tipped well whenever they visited me. I scrambled to have their orders ready as soon as I saw them approaching the counter. They also gave me free tickets to their shows. For prom, I took my date to *La Cage*, and we sat in the front row. Dionne Warwick and Whitney Houston blew kisses to me from the stage. My date was befuddled.

"Hey mama," I said as I walked up the driveway toward the house. I was stronger since the last time I had been home. My voice was confident. The summer was nearly over, and my pockets were weighed down by my paycheck for two weeks' work. She was posted up in a lawn chair in the garage, smoking a cigarette. The overhang of the large door cast a dark shadow across her face.

"Hi Pumpkin," she said, clearing her throat.

I reached down into the seat and gave her a hug. She patted my back with her empty hand. The smoke from the cigarette crept into my nostrils. I pulled back to keep from coughing.

"Where's Lanny? Where's Kamilah?" I asked.

The house felt quiet, empty.

"Lanny's somewhere and Kamilah's at the people down the street's house." The family cat, Tippy, rubbed his back against the metal of the chair and came out between her feet. I've always hated that cat, I thought, as my mother reached down to rub his back. I believe the feeling was mutual.

"What happened to the Carters?" I asked. Their house was boarded up and the grass was high.

"They had to move. They got kicked out of their house," she said. "Remember when they took out that loan on the house and Ms. Carter was bragging about putting a pool in her backyard?" I did remember, vaguely.

"It was a scam. Those people took their house. Ballooned the payments and stole it right from under them. They had signed the paperwork so there was nothing that could be done. Now they live in an apartment in Riverside." She took a long drag of her cigarette and blew the smoke into the air.

"You coming home?" she asked.

"No, I'm going to stay in Las Vegas. Finish school out there."

"You must like it down there."

"I do. And I like my job." I was there to see Rachel off to Virginia State. It was her last weekend in town. I had only stopped by to tell my mother I wasn't coming back.

"Stevie's gone." My heart skipped a beat. The thing I had wanted for so long had finally happened, and I was not there to reap the benefits.

"Where did he go?"

She shrugged her shoulders. I waited.

"He has another family in L.A. Remember that woman who sent those diapers in the mail with that letter, her. He's with her," she said. Her voice was dispassionate, hollow.

"Some of his things are still here," she continued. "But he's not. He stopped paying the bills too. I had to sign up for food stamps."

"It'll be okay," was all I could offer up as consolation. I would help her take care of my sister and brother. She needed me. I began to send money home.

brighter

My grandmother and I moved into a two-bedroom apartment across town, away from the family house. I was the only grandchild without parents present. We lived like roommates. She worked nights and slept during the day while I was at school. During the evenings, I worked full-time at the food court and took the bus home after my shift. We rarely saw one another.

In every way, I was responsible for myself. There was no one to tell me what to do, when to wake up, to go to school or finish my homework. I had a routine and followed it religiously. I was determined not to become sidetracked or return to California. There were no second chances. My situation felt precarious, as if it could unravel at any moment if I were not careful.

My cousins, who had enrolled in school with me, stopped attending after the first few weeks of the semester. They were too far behind. Although they were old enough to graduate, each of them had less than a year's worth of credits. That year, they joined the ranks of the more than one million students in the U.S. who drop out of high school. There was no sense of alarm, and there weren't any attempts made by school officials to get them to re-enroll.

Valley High was similar to the other high schools I had attended. They all ran on the same tracking system. All of the middle-class White and Asian kids were in advanced placement classes. They had all of the privileges and clout within the school, and the rest of the students, mostly Black and Latino, were beholden to the rules and penalized for not following them to the letter.

Most of the Black and Latino kids were in remedial classes. Because of the way I dressed—baggy jeans, large bangle earrings, and sneakers—it was assumed that I belonged there too. My teachers were shocked when I entered the room and took a seat. When I first arrived at the school and handed my schedule to the advanced placement government teacher, for example, his first question, which he asked without skipping a beat, was whether I was in the wrong class. Embarrassed, I assured him that I belonged there. I recall feeling unworthy and as if I had done something wrong by being there. I could also feel the eyes of the other kids in the class tracking me to my seat. They too were suspicious of my presence.

Then, I did not make the connection between the way I looked and dressed and the assumptions made by my teachers and others about my intelligence and capabilities. I dressed and looked like everyone else in my neighborhood. I did not see anything wrong with my hairstyle, Air Jordan sneakers, or baggy polo shirt. However, the way I dressed was all my teachers and fellow students needed to see before turning me away or, in subtle but sure ways, letting me know I did not belong. To fit in, I began to change the way I dressed, wearing more form-fitting clothes and dresses. I stopped wearing large, dangling earrings. I made myself look like a baby doll, less threatening. I took my cues from the White girls in my class who shopped at the Gap, the Wet Seal, and Charlotte Russe.

My counselor, Mr. Dent, a squirrelly White man, was different from Ms. Anderson at San Bernardino High. When I visited him, he had very little to say and never spoke to me about college. He only verified that my courses from my old school would transfer and that I would graduate on time. Although I had fulfilled all of my basic requirements for graduation, I enrolled in physics and calculus and continued with Spanish and French. When physics proved too difficult, or when Mr. Olen, the physics teacher, went on a rant about video games, I went to the library to read or to write poetry. The librarian allowed me to come and go as I pleased throughout the day without question. Poetry was my new thing. In one of my classes, I asked my teacher if I could write a poem for my final project, and she agreed.

When I read it out loud to the class, everyone clapped. Although I didn't know much about the technical aspects of poetry, I felt like it allowed me to express myself without revealing too much.

I was comfortable in my classes and had learned how to navigate my two worlds seamlessly. I could be tough when I needed to be—scrappy and resourceful. I knew how to survive. I hung out with my cousins at home and with the other Black kids in the cafeteria during lunch. I shoplifted clothes from the local department store and roamed the Circus Circus Hotel and Casino with my cousins on the weekends in search of girls to fight. My heart pounded when we confronted a group of girls playing video games in the arcade and attempted to goad them into a conflict. I breathed a sigh of relief when, upon seeing the size of my cousins, the girls declined to fight us.

Simultaneously, and beyond the watchful eyes of my friends and family, I was meticulously learning the rules of how to succeed outside my neighborhood by observing the White kids in my classes. They had a different way of being in the world, entitled and less fearful. I too wanted to feel like I owned the world. My efforts paid off: I was nominated for homecoming queen, I wrote our senior class poem, and my Spanish teacher, the cheerleading coach, invited me to tryouts. I was one of them—one of the good kids.

"Can I please speak to Mrs. Bowman?" The school receptionist put me on hold. The classical music that played while I waited had become familiar. Why did they play this kind of music, I wondered, instead of rap music? I would not mind being on hold then. I could sing along.

"She's not available right now. Can you give her a call back a little later?"

She sounded annoyed. I am sure it was Ms. Lyle, who barely had time to look up from her magazine to acknowledge us when we visited the front office.

It was the middle of the school day. I was using the pay phone across the street from Valley High. I had been calling Ms. Bowman for the past few weeks with no success.

College was the topic of discussion in all of my classes. Everyone was applying, retaking the SAT and talking about where they hoped to go. They had their top choices and their safety schools. They spoke with such authority and certainty. With the exception of my vague conversation with Ms. Anderson about UC Berkeley, I had nothing to contribute to the conversations. Those conversations seemed so long ago and out of reach now.

I tried attending a local college fair to get a better sense of the application process. I had taken the morning off from work to attend and caught several buses to get there. When I arrived, I was overwhelmed. I did not know how to sort through all of the information on the tables or what criteria I should be using to decide which schools would be a good fit for me. The school representatives, while eager to help, grew annoyed with my lack of understanding of the process and my seemingly rudimentary questions. I did not know what a major was or what I planned to study. I was unfamiliar with the financial aid and application deadlines. I realized in that moment that I knew very little about going to college and all it would take to get there. I needed more guidance, some help.

"Hello, Ms. Bowman. It's Pumpkin—I mean Chataquoa." I had finally gotten through to her. "I need your help. I am trying to figure out where to apply to school." The other end of the line was silent. "Hello." I hoped that she remembered me and that she still didn't think I was overzealous.

"Where have you been?" She was shocked to hear my voice.

"I moved to Las Vegas to live with my grandmother." I tried to make it sound as normal as possible, like going to the dentist or taking a morning shower.

Ms. Bowman did not probe. I could tell she was barely paying attention. She dropped the telephone on the table to scold a student who had gotten out of his seat. It sounded like a mad house there. "Sit down," I heard her yell. The commotion did not stop.

"Where should I apply?" I cut to the chase when she got back on the line. I knew I only had a few minutes before she would have to go.

"Apply to Howard," she advised. "Send your application to the attention of Tawanna Banks in admissions. I have to go." The click of the dial tone prickled my ear. I had the information that I needed. I was satisfied.

"Mr. Dent, I'm going to apply to Howard University in Washington, DC."

He paused and cocked his head to the side. He looked puzzled. This was not the reaction I was expecting. I was hoping he would offer some advice on completing the application or talk about the other students he had known who had gone there.

"That's a really hard school to get into. They turn away more than half of the students that apply." The deep lines gathered at the center of his fore-head and furrowed eyebrows told me he thought that I was reaching for too much. He walked past me to the row of mailboxes. He pulled out a stack of large envelopes from his cubby. "Well, I guess it doesn't hurt to apply," he conceded.

I spent weeks working on my application. In

the package, I included a table of contents, my transcripts, the typed blue and white long-form application, a few of my favorite poems and a short story that I had written, a personal statement, and whatever else I thought would help my case. I also used the biggest words I knew, incorrectly and out of context, I am certain. When I was finished, I put it all together in a small binder and shipped it off to Washington, DC.

Besides Mr. Dent, my grandmother was the only person I told about my application and that I planned to go to college. It was a secret. I could not stomach the backlash, the judgment, or having to defend my decision to leave the neighborhood. My lunch table friends were having trouble passing the high school exit exams required to graduate, and I did not want to seem as though I was bragging. They already did not trust me because we were not in the same classes. If I didn't get in, I didn't want to be embarrassed or be looked at with the "I told you so" eyes.

little brother

"Pumpkin, I need to come to Vegas and stay with you for a while." I had not spoken to my brother since I left home the previous year. He sounded distressed, his voice hoarse.

"Some stuff happened and they're looking for me."

My heart began to pound. "Who, who is looking for you?" I demanded.

"Some dudes from Delman Heights. They think I had something to do with this guy getting shot and killed. The other day they came by the house looking for me. They called me outside. Spike was with them. He told me to stay inside, but I came out anyway. When I did, this guy put a gun to my head. Spike begged the guy not to shoot me. He put his hand on the gun and brought the guy's hand down. When he did, I ran back into the house. And the guy pulled off."

"Why do they think you had something to do with it?"

"I was hanging out at Doobie's house shooting dice when this dude came into the house with a gun and said he had just shot someone. The next day, I was at Ish's house and everyone was talking about it. I put two and two together and figured out it was the guy who had come into the house with the gun. I told Sonia, Ish's mom, that I had seen the shooter. She turned around and told people that I had something to do with the murder. It's not true."

That *bitch,* I thought. Her house was one of three drug houses on the block, along with ours and Spike and D'aja's. And because Sonia was entrenched in the neighborhood politics and connected to the local dealers, her words carried weight.

"I'll Western Union you some money so that you can buy a bus ticket," I said. "Come now."

Suddenly, my stomach was overwhelmed. I placed my hand over my mouth and raced to the bathroom. Before I could reach the toilet, the floor was covered in pink-colored chunks. Since I had left, I had heard stories of friends being killed or getting locked up; many of them were my age. A former boyfriend of mine, Clinton, had been shot in the head and left for dead in an alley. My cousin Michael was shot and killed on the way to school for wearing the wrong color. A drug dealer killed my uncle, a notorious addict. His death, unlike the others, made the eleven o'clock news. Death was all around us. The thought of my brother being shot dead in front of our house was too much for me to handle. He was still a boy and a good one. I had promised to protect him.

I sneaked past the security guard to the place

where the buses docked once they pulled into the station. There was a sign prohibiting non-passengers from going beyond the lobby. I ignored it. I wanted the first face that my brother saw when he exited the bus to be mine.

"Hey boy," I yelled as he lumbered off the bus. He looked as if he had just awakened from a nap. He pulled his hand over his face to freshen it up. I wanted to embrace him, but did not. Hugging was not our thing. I grabbed onto his shoulder tightly.

While we waited for his bags, he began to yammer on about the people on the bus—the lady who smelled like urine, the snoring man who annoyed all the passengers, and the baby who cried the entire trip. I listened intently and studied his face in search of the fear that I am sure was buried deep inside of him. It was undetectable. He was cracking jokes. He *was* funny, I thought.

As I watched him pull the two small duffle bags from the luggage hatch, a wave of relief swept over me. He was here with me. He was out of harm's way. And without my mother, we could be friends—sister and brother again.

accepted

It was almost time for work. On school days, instead of doing homework or hanging out with my friends when I arrived home, I had just enough time to put on my uniform and catch the bus to the casino for work. I took my job as seriously as I did school. I needed both. Work provided me with the money I needed to take care of myself and to send money back home to my family. School is what I hung my future on. It was going to be my ticket out.

"Pumpkin, Pumpkin," my grandmother exclaimed, waving a white envelope in the air. The edges were torn. It was clear that it had been ripped open and the paper stuffed back inside.

"You got in baby, you got in!" Her body jiggled with excitement. She shoved the envelope into my hand. "I couldn't help it. I had to open it," she said.

I unfolded the letter and began to read, my eyes dissecting each line for confirmation of what had just been said. I examined the dark blue imprint: Howard University. It was weighty, not a photo-copy. She was telling the truth. I had been accepted. I screamed and jogged in place.

My grandmother's eyes were gleaming and

filled with joy. I had never seen this look before on her face or anyone else's for that matter. It was pride. She was proud of me.

I stuffed the letter in my backpack and galloped down the stairs. I was in.

Once on the bus, I pulled the letter out and read it carefully. I let each word sink in twice. On my lunch break at the food court, I read it again as I ate my hamburger and french fries. I was careful not to get any grease or ketchup on it. It was my proof and I wanted to be able to whip it out if anyone doubted me.

"I got accepted to Howard," I said, almost boastfully.

It was Saturday. I was still in my work uniform and my face was oily from the shift. My black sun visor was covered in splatters and I smelled like fried food. On the weekends, I preferred to work the morning shift. After work, I took the bus to the family house so that I could hang out with my cousins.

"You did?" my cousin Katrina asked. "You're so smart, Pumpkin."

"When did you find out?" my other cousin asked,

"Last week, you want to see my letter?" I responded.

I held my backpack on my knee as I unzipped the small pouch on the outside and pulled the letter out. I started to read it.

"Let me see that." I turned to my left and twisted my head over my shoulder in search of the hand that had snatched the letter from my grip. It was Key-Key, my aunt Dina's husband. He was such a *dick*.

He cleared his throat and straightened his back. "Ahem, Dear Ms. Mason—" He read the letter mockingly and tossed it back at me when he was done. The letter I loved and treated like a golden ticket just a few days ago now sounded like a joke.

"You ain't goin' nowhere," he declared.

What did he mean? Sure, I was.

"How you gon' pay for it?" he demanded to know. His face was smug and his lips were pursed. If he'd had a moustache, he would have been twirling it.

Good question. Before then, I had never thought about how I would afford to pay for college. I just assumed I would get loans or grants like I had read about in all of the brochures. *Shit.*

Seeing an opening, he kept going. "You gon' be right here with us. Watch and see."

Fat bastard, I thought, as my eyes began to well up with tears. I batted my eyes and turned my head up toward the sky to keep them from rolling down my cheeks. I stuffed the letter back into my bag. Who the *fuck* did he think he was.

"I have to go." The small circle felt airless and constricted. Deep down, I was afraid Key-Key might be right, but conceded nothing. I would figure it out. I was leaving and there was nothing anyone could say or do to dissuade me.

"Can I please speak with Ms. Bowman?"

"She's not available."

"You told me to call back today at this time. I'll hold until she becomes available."

"We cannot tie up the phone lines. You waited yesterday and people complained about not being able to get through to us," the receptionist said testily.

"Okay," I said, deflated. "I'll call back later."

Ms. Bowman was my only hope. I needed to speak with her. She had gotten me into Howard, and I was sure she knew what I should do next.

My mother still had not gotten around to filling out my financial aid forms, and I was concerned she would not. I also knew that even if I got a job in Washington, DC, it would not be enough to cover the five-figure tuition. And I was tired of working and going to school. I needed a break.

I lost sleep worrying about how I would get to Howard. When I did sleep, my dreams were filled with anxiety and panic. In the dreams, I would plead for help from financial aid officers, college officials, or anyone who would listen. Each time, I was denied assistance.

As the weeks passed and time grew short, the intensity of the dreams increased. Once, I dreamt

I was locked out of a gate, and in another dream I was trying to climb over one.

"Ms. Bowman, you have to help me." It was after the first class of the day and I was standing in her door. I charged in the direction of her desk. She was startled.

"What are you doing here?"

I spilled it out in one long breath. "Ms. Bowman, you have to help me," I repeated. "I got in to Howard, but I don't know how I'm going to pay for it. I don't have any money."

My eyes were pleading, begging. She let out a deep sigh. She wasn't expecting me. I was supposed to be in a high school four hours away.

"Step outside. I'll call you back in a minute."

I did not want to leave. I wanted to stay and force her to answer me— How was I going to pay for college?

After a few moments, I turned and headed toward the hallway.

The building was as dank as I remembered. I paced the corridor and listened to the civics lesson being delivered in the classroom across the hall. I wished she would hurry. I was on a schedule.

After about twenty minutes, she motioned with her long acrylic fingernails for me to come back inside. I rolled my eyes and let out a long sigh. Finally, I thought to myself.

"I just spoke with Clarence Lee, the dean of Arts and Sciences at Howard University."

My breath was trapped inside my body.

"You have a full merit scholarship to Howard," she announced regally.

"For real!" is all I could manage to get out. I could not believe it.

She nodded. The expression on her face remained unchanged.

"They'll send you more information with your financial aid packet," she said.

I was bursting with happiness. Undeterred by her stateliness, I rushed her body, throwing my arms around her neck. My scrawny arms might have just made it around her full body. She patted my back.

By noon, I was on the bus back to Las Vegas. I had to work the night shift. I did not make any stops along the way, even to home. I had gotten what I had come for.

graduation

I walked around the car slowly, checking its tires and sliding my fingers along its side. The car was rusty pink, like a dusty rose. It was parked in the carport of our apartment building. My mother had driven it down from California.

"Do you like it?" Her voice was overwrought with nervousness.

"Yes, I do," I said as my eyes widened and I nodded like an out-of-control bobblehead. The truth is I thought it would be newer, more polished, like the cars a few of the kids drove at my school. For the last several months, I had been attempting to save up for a car, but most of my extra money was being siphoned off to pay for my senior class expenses—pictures, graduation invitations, the yearbook, my cap and gown, and prom.

She handed me the keys and stood by as I opened the door and slid into the driver's seat. "Unlock the door," my brother urged as he gripped the passenger side door handle.

"Are you going to tell her you don't have your license?" he asked pointedly as he burrowed into the leather seat across the center console.

"No, I'm not." I cut my eyes and whipped my neck in his direction. "And you better not tell her either. I'm going to take the test again next week." I had failed the test twice already. I put the key in the ignition and fired up the engine.

To compete with the sputter of the engine, my mother's voice grew louder. "The man I bought it from said that it was in great condition. He gave me a really good deal. I told him it was for my daughter who was graduating." She was talking to me through the semi-closed window. "I made sure it had an oil change before I took it on the road."

I listened as I adjusted the mirrors. I slid the seat back and forth on its track until my feet reached the pedals comfortably. I was as close to the windshield as one could be possibly be without actually going through it. I turned on the radio and found my favorite station.

I did not know how to respond. I had not seen my mother since the end of last summer. Then, she was sorting through her life and was ambivalent about my coming home. Now, here she was delivering a car to me in Las Vegas, a place she had previously visited only to gamble. It was a gift from her to me. It was surreal.

"I told the guy I had to get my baby a car. I saved up my little money until I had enough." She pinched her index finger and thumb together and pretended she was stuffing money into a purse.

"We'll be right back," I said. "We're going to take it for a test ride."

"Okay," she said. She clasped her hands

together and backed away from the car, which was a good idea, or she might have gotten run over.

"Just listen to me," my brother instructed as he guided me out of the tight stall. "Put it in reverse and take your foot off of the brake." I rolled back slowly.

I wasn't sure where my brother had learned to drive, but I hung on to his every word.

"Use your turn signal when you want to change lanes," he advised. I nodded. I eased out into traffic and turned into the lane closest to the sidewalk—just in case I needed to drive on it.

"Go faster. You're going too slow; cars are going around you," he chided.

"Shut up," I screamed. "You're making me nervous. Just chill out."

When I checked the side view mirror, he was right, cars were zooming past me. And the drivers looked annoyed. I accelerated a tiny bit. When we approached the stoplight I slammed on the brakes. We lurched toward the dashboard.

"I'm sorry," I said as I tightened my grip on the steering wheel and straightened my back.

"Turn left here."

I merged into the flow of traffic and continued to check all three mirrors simultaneously. With the brakes, gas, mirrors, and turn signals, this was hard work, too much to coordinate at one time.

"You drive like an old lady." I ignored him. We

made four long loops around the block. I was starting to get the hang of it.

"Go that way," he said pointing to the on-ramp.

"No, I'm not getting on the freeway." Surely, we would be killed, I thought. I imagined us in a multicar pileup caused by my inability to switch lanes properly, the very infraction that had caused me to fail the driving test twice.

"Just do it."

I took a deep breath, changed lanes, and followed the car in front of me up the incline.

"See, it's not that bad. Now, speed up." He was asking too much, I thought. The road began to curve.

"Turn, turn, turn," he yelled. I closed my eyes and took my hands off the wheel. Horns blared as cars swerved to the right and left of us. He grabbed the wheel with both hands and pulled the car back between the dotted white lines.

"Fuck, pull over," he said. "You almost killed us."

I was relieved. My heart was racing and my body was shaking. Once on the side of the road, he huffed around the front of the car into the driver's side while I climbed over the console into the passenger seat. He started the car and pulled into traffic.

When we returned to the apartment, my mother was retelling the car story to my grandmother.

"How was the drive?" she asked when she saw us.

"Good. It rides well." The fewer details the better, I thought. I made my way to the back bedroom. I needed more practice before my next driving test or I would certainly fail again.

"I'll see you in a few months," she said as she poked her head into the room. "For the graduation."

"Thank you for the car." I got up from the bed and walked over to the edge of the door where she stood. I wasn't sure what to do next. Should I give her a hug? A kiss? What was expected of me in this moment? She filled the silence.

". . . You know Kamilah wore your cheer-leading uniform for Halloween. It was too big for her though. She had your pom-poms and red ribbons in her hair. She said it made her feel like you."

I wanted her to stop talking, to stop being nice, and to stop saying nice shit. I could not absorb it. "Really?" is all that would come out. My questions were stuck in the back of my throat. Why did she buy me the car? Was she proud of me? Did she love me after all?

I avoided her eyes and her uneasy smile.

"Well, we're about to get back on the road. Call me if something goes wrong with the car."

"I will," I mumbled as I walked her to the door.

My brother and I were closer than ever. On Friday nights, we cruised the Las Vegas Strip in my new, but very used car, while listening to music. On occasion, the bumper would fall off in the middle of the street and one of us would have to get out of the car, scoop it up, and reattach it before the light turned green. That poor car; although I eventually passed the driving test, I was still a horrible driver.

The next few months were a complete blur. I wrapped up my senior year and worked to save money to fill the metal blue trunk that I would eventually take with me to Washington, DC. I meticulously purchased every suggested item on the dorm room list sent to all of the first-year students by the university. I also bought a flower-green comforter for my bed that reminded me of the one I had on my daybed back in California, Victorian and delicate.

I wore a sleeveless white polyester skirt suit, white panty hose, and shoes under my graduation robe. I had purchased the suit the week before from TJ Maxx. My hair looked the same as it always did, a clipped ponytail with bangs, nothing special.

The noise from the living room was growing louder and the creak of the door became more frequent. When I entered the room, it was suddenly filled with people. They had all showed up, all of them—my cousins, my aunts, my uncles, my grandmother, my sister, brother, father, and mother. I was the first in the family to graduate, and it was a big deal.

"Here you go, baby," my father said as he separated himself from the group and pushed a bouquet of Mylar balloons with a teddy bear dressed in a graduation gown and cap into my hands. It was the same arrangement that I would receive when I graduated with my doctoral degree in government and politics more than a decade later. His smile was broad, and his chest swelled with pride.

Overwhelmed, I made a beeline to the newest addition to our family. My cousin Luvleen had just given birth to a baby boy named Tony. We all took care of him and I knew he would be a sufficient buffer between me and everyone else. I exchanged the balloons for the baby. I held him close to my chest.

After a bit of congratulatory small talk, we piled into cars and caravanned to the Thomas and Mack arena for my graduation. There, I joined my class and waited to be escorted onto the floor.

As I sat in the plastic chair, a wave of loneliness washed over me. I could not shake it. I was supposed to be happy. I was in the top 10 percent of my class, I was on my way to college, and my family had put on their best clothes to celebrate me. This was supposed to be one of the best days of my life. Instead, I felt alone. The music, the speeches, and the applause sounded like a distant, muted echo to me.

I did not recognize the people sitting next to me. They were not my friends, and I would never see them again after today. I was glad. When they turned to me with tears brimming or reached to grasp my hand, I pretended not to notice. I did not want to hold their hands. I was ready to go.

i'll fly away

"Where to?"

"Howard University in Washington, DC. Do you know where that is and how to get there?"

He smirked and turned toward the large trunk and suitcase that were stacked next to the curb. "Is this all you have?"

Did he not hear me, I wondered. I raised my voice an octave. "Do you know how to get there?" I had never ridden in a cab before and I was not sure I trusted him.

"Yeah, I do," he finally answered. "It's about forty-five minutes away from here." I breathed a sigh of relief. I was almost there.

He loaded my things into the trunk, slammed it shut, and set the meter. I only had two hundred dollars and hoped the trip would not be too costly. It was all I had.

"Where you from?"

"California."

"Oh yeah, what part?" He seemed interested.

I hesitated. I did not know what to say. Where was I from? I suppose all over. I had lived so many different places and no place in particular for any length of time. I wanted to say Inglewood. It was the last place I felt at home and safe in my body.

"Southern California," I responded.

"Like where, L.A.?" he asked. "I've been there once. Beautiful place. Wouldn't want to live there though." Our eyes met in the rearview mirror.

This guy was beginning to annoy me. I just wanted to take in my new environment—the contour of the road, the names of the cities on the signs overhead, the license plates, and the people zooming by in their cars.

"All around," I replied flatly, hoping he would get the hint. I turned toward the window. I had never seen trees so green, so lush. They scraped the sky and the clouds, the few that there were, draped over them. I was in awe of this new city.

"Are you sure you're going in the right direction?" I asked as he made a right turn onto Georgia Avenue. It did not look like what I had imagined. The neighborhood was just like mine back home—nondescript convenience stores, men hanging out on the corners, and Chinese carryout restaurants sprinkled along the block. I was expecting it to be fancy, like the weighted logo on the letterhead of the acceptance letter.

"Yes, this is it," he assured me. "Not what you were expecting?"

"I don't know. I just thought—"

He interrupted me. "Around the campus is a little rough. The locals don't like the students that much either. Never have. They think, y'all are, you know . . ." He put his finger to his nose and smushed it upward. "A little snobby." He chuckled. "Don't worry about it though, you'll be fine."

What the hell was he talking about? Snobby? How could Black people be snobby or look down on other Blacks? It did not make sense to me. I waved my hand dismissively in the air.

"I'm going to Bethune Hall—2225 Fourth Street NW." I directed him from the paper that had been sent to me by the university. It also had Ms. Bowman's home telephone number scribbled on the bottom of it.

The cab driver made a right, and then a left, and then another right down a narrow street filled with cars. "What's going on?" I asked.

"People are unloading, parents with their children." He waited patiently as he made his way to the front of the line, close to the door.

When he got close enough, he parked the cab and popped open the trunk. I glanced at the meter and reached into my purse to pay him. "This is heavy," he said as he pulled on the handle of the trunk. He placed it on the curb next to my other suitcase. I handed him the money.

"Good luck," he said as he counted the money and gave me my change. He pulled off. Wait, what—no help up the stairs? He was already gone. There was no way I could get the trunk inside by myself. I stood there alongside my stuff plotting my next move.

As I did, I noticed something. There were parents—lots of them. And they were helping their daughters unload and climb the unstable-looking concrete stairs that led to our dormitory. They were laughing, hugging, and snapping pictures as they prepared for their final fare-wells.

In that moment, my heart and my confidence sank. I was alone. It never occurred to me to ask someone to take the cross-country flight with me or that parents did these kinds of things with their children. And no one, not my mother or my father, had offered to come with me. Perhaps, I rationalized, they did not know that they should have been here or that this was a milestone moment.

The trip was my first on an airplane, and I had certainly never traveled so far away from home. As my mother waved goodbye to me from the departure gate, I assured her I would be fine. I just assumed we were all coming alone. I was mistaken.

The scene was dizzying. I watched parents and daughters move past me with boxes, lamps, and various knickknacks. They barely noticed me. When they did, it was only to ask me to clear the way.

"Can I leave these here while I check in?" I asked the girl standing at the foot of the stairs directing traffic and answering questions. "Sure, just don't be too long. Other people are unloading too." To give myself space to think, I decided to leave my things on the curb and check into the dormitory.

"What's your name?"

"Chataquoa Mason."

"Hi Chataquoa, my name is Eminette. You can call me Emi. Welcome to Howard."

I did not like the way "Chataquoa" sounded. It was awkward. Chataquoa was fine in my neighborhood, because no one ever used it except for teachers on the first day of school, but not here. I hoped she did not repeat it and that others standing at the table next to me had not heard it. I needed a new name. Pumpkin would not suffice either.

"Where you from?" she asked as she flipped through the pages to find my name.

"California."

"There's a club for people from California. You should join it," she told me.

"A club?" I supposed she was just making small talk so I treated it as such.

I studied the top of her head as it pointed downward at the typewritten page. She was bald—intentionally, it appeared. I had never seen a woman with a close-shaven head who was not ill, especially a Black girl. She had chopped her beauty off and did not seem to care.

When she looked back up at me, her long

eyelashes hit the backs of her eyelids. Her skin was creamy brown and her teeth pristine. Maybe we could be friends, I thought.

"You're on the fourth floor. Here's your key and a copy of the house rules," she said. "No company or boys allowed in your room until after the first couple of weeks." Why did she say that? I wondered. Did I look like the type to have boys in my dorm room? I was a good girl, still a virgin, much to my chagrin.

"Thank you," I said, as I turned and walked back down the hallway and onto the street.

These Black people at Howard looked different from any I had ever seen or met. They moved with authority and were well dressed. I had worn my best outfit on the plane—a black-and-white romper, cream tights, and patent leather black Mary Janes—and now it felt not good enough, almost as if I were wearing rags.

And all of the girls were beautiful, polished. In my old high school, I was used to being one of only a handful of attractive, smart Black girls. Here, I was lost at sea. Everyone was beautiful, smart, and well spoken. *Shit.*

Cars were honking and maneuvering to find a space to unload. My things on the curb were becoming a nuisance.

"Excuse me sir," I said. "Can you please help me take my trunk up the stairs?" He was somebody else's father. I had watched him as he unloaded his daughter's luggage and took them upstairs. He looked happy to do it.

"Yes, I can help you," he said. "Is this all yours?" He lifted his baseball hat a little so that I could see his eyes.

I nodded and hoped that he would not change his mind. He was already sweating profusely, and his white T-shirt clung to his chest.

He grabbed the long trunk by the handles on each of the sides and carried it up the stack of stairs and up to the elevator. He returned for my suitcase.

"Thank you," I said. I was grateful for his help. I took the elevator to the fourth floor. Once there, I dragged my things out of the elevator and down the hall to my room.

There was a row of rooms on one side with a communal bathroom on the other. I peeked into the bathroom. It reminded me of the gym locker room at my old high school gym. The mirrors were hazy and the brown tiles were cold. Maybe we could put up some pictures or something, make it a little more homey, I thought.

My room was no different. It belonged in an orphanage. It was tight with only enough room for a bed, desk, and chair. I switched on the air conditioner. It cranked, made a noise, and then began to hum. I moved my hand over the vent to make sure it was pushing out cold air. It was hot.

Hearing voices, I went out into the hallway. I poked my head in the room next to mine. The people in the room paused their conversation and turned their attention to me.

"Hi, I'm Melanie, and this is my dad, Mr. Jackson, and my mom, Mrs. Jackson," the girl with the long hair and white K-Swiss sneakers said. Her accent was thick, southern. She reached her hand out. I shook it.

"My name is Nicole," I said. "I'm from Los Angeles, California." I had a new name and an origin place.

I wasn't a Chataquoa and had never been. I had also never met anyone White named Chataquoa. Nicole was my middle name, and it would be my name from here on out. It sounded professional, easy to say.

"Nice to meet you," she said. "I'm from Holly Springs, Mississippi." Where the hell was that? I wondered, but did not dare ask.

"Did you come by yourself?" she asked.

"Yes, I took a red-eye flight last night and had a layover in Phoenix. Everyone on the plane was so nice to me. My mother couldn't come. She had to work." I tried to rearrange the order of the facts and focus on my travels.

A girl came up from behind. The tight hallway was becoming congested.

"Excuse us, can we get by," she said. She paused briefly to introduce herself. "My name is Jade. I live in the last room at the end of the hall. And this is my mother." Jade was from New York. They were heading to the door of the common area with a bag full of trash.

I repeated my new name. "I'm Nicole. I'm from Los Angeles."

They tried to match me with parents. They could not.

After a few more minutes of small talk, I returned to my room and began to unpack. I made the bed first, then unloaded my suitcase. I put my pom-poms from high school on my desk. Before I left for the airport, I had rummaged through some of my old things still at my mother's house and decided to take them. Everyone loved cheer-leaders, and I could hide behind the visage of what cheerleaders are supposed to be—happy, pretty, pampered, and without worries—nearly the exact opposite of my life up to that point.

I was done. I had unpacked my entire room in less than an hour. I walked down to the end of the hallway to Jade's room. She was still unpacking and in deep conversation about which things her mom would have to take back to New York with her because they could not fit in the breadbox-sized dorm room.

I returned to my room and flopped down on the bed. I had no television or radio. To pass the time before lunch, I listened to the conversations through the paper-thin walls.

"Did you see that little girl from California. She's here all by herself." It sounded like Jade. She was talking to her mother.

"I know," she said. "That's so sad." Although I couldn't see her, I was almost certain she was shaking her head. She felt sorry for me. I drowned out the rest of their conversation. I couldn't take it.

I focused on the globular green flower on my bedspread and blinked hard to push back the tears. My door was still open and I didn't want anyone to pass by and notice me crying. I sat there working hard to convince myself that I was going to be okay.

To them, I was the little girl from California without parents to help her unpack. To me, I was the girl who made it.

what should be done?

What I have attempted to do in *Born Bright* is to take you, the reader, on an insider's journey into poverty in the United States. In my telling of this story, I tried to refrain from judging the behavior of, or choices made by, the people I wrote about, including myself. Growing up, I never considered myself poor, and I told the story from that perspective. It would have been easy for me to filter my childhood experiences through the lens of my professional training and education. But doing so would have made me no better than the policy-makers and legislators who use their experiences and backgrounds to write policies and create laws that do more harm than good to low-income and poor families.

I contend that the choices low-income and poor people make must be understood within the context of the environment in which the decisions are being made and the limited options available to them. Most often, they are constrained choices or the choice between the lesser of two problem-atic options. Poor and low-income people take calculated risks that on the surface might seem irrational to casual observers, but may be reason-able under a particular set of circumstances or their lived experiences of negotiating systems and institutions in society.

Take, for example, the story of Shanesha Taylor, a homeless mother who in spring 2014 left her two children, ages eighteen months and two years, in a car while she went on a job interview at a Scottsdale, Arizona, insurance agency.[1] The job paid significantly higher than minimum wage and would, if maintained, have put her on a sure path toward economic security. After about an hour left alone in the car, the children were found, unharmed, in the car by a police officer. Shanesha was arrested and charged with two felony accounts of child abuse. As a result, she lost custody of her three children and was sentenced to eighteen years' supervised probation with a set of strict stipulations, which included taking parenting classes. Is Shanesha a bad mother? Or was she faced with an impossible choice—leave her children and go on the interview or miss the interview and miss out on a job that would allow her to support her family? I am not sure what I would have done in her situation.

In the U.S. the poor have always been viewed as a problem or as the unseemly underbelly of an otherwise prosperous nation. At best, the poor are portrayed as victims of circumstances beyond their control. At worst, they are viewed as freeloading criminals trying to take advantage of the system at every turn. Since the 1900s, both of these portrayals have figured prominently in the types of programs and policies we have created at the federal and state levels to alleviate poverty and to create a more equitable society.

The story of Shanesha shows us that poverty is much more complicated than either of these myopic and partial descriptions of the poor suggest. These characterizations fail to accurately account for the ways in which poverty functions in America—it is, in and of itself, the true barrier to full economic security for low-income people and families. On every social indicator of well-being, poor people rank low or last. Poverty itself, including the conditions created as a result of it, is the number-one barrier to escaping poverty.

It is tempting to believe that at a particular point in our nation's history there was a full-out war on poverty, but it is simply not the case. It was more of a street corner fight with no clear winners or losers. The actual federal "War on Poverty" declared by President Lyndon Johnson lasted a scant five years, hardly long enough to sub-stantially decrease the number of individuals living in poverty or to significantly alter the conditions in communities that enable poverty to persist.

Both Republicans and liberals argue for differ-ent reasons that the War on Poverty failed to deliver on its promise to end poverty. This is true, it did. What is indisputable, however, is that in the decade following the declaration of the War on Poverty, poverty rates in the U.S. dropped to their lowest levels since the start of comprehensive record keeping in 1958, going from 17.3 percent in 1958 to 11 percent in 1973. Since then we have not witnessed a comparable decline in the number of individuals living in poverty. Today, forty-seven million people live in poverty—six million more than in 1964. Poverty rates are highest among Blacks, Latinos, and households headed by women. And although children make up only 24 percent of the U.S. population, they account for 36 percent of the impoverished.

What this tells me is that poverty is not arbitrary, which would mean that everyone had as good a shot at being impoverished as they had at being middle-class; rather, it is exacting. Those who are the most vulnerable, who are most likely to be marginalized in the labor market or in the economy, or who have been on the receiving end of historical racial and gender discrimination in most, if not all, of the systems and institutions in our society—these people are most likely to be poor. This is no coincidence.

For more than one hundred years, we have attempted to develop policies and programs to alleviate poverty by focusing almost exclusively on the individual or the family unit and the kinds of subsidies and social supports they need to maintain a basic standard of living. While these programs may have prevented individuals and families from falling deeper into poverty, they have not been successful at moving people out of poverty in significant numbers. This is the hard truth.

In addition to providing job training and social supports to low-income families, we must begin to pay attention to the conditions under which individuals are able to pursue opportunity and success in the U.S. In order to end poverty and to put children and families on a sure path to economic security, we must transform communities so that individuals, regardless of where they live, have the sufficient and necessary preconditions for success and opportunity.

Asking if we can do without welfare in the U.S. is akin to asking a farmer if he can do without water in a drought. He has no choice but to make it work. Families are doing the same; they are relying on a complex network of families, friends, and social services to make ends meet. Nationally, despite record-high unemployment in many impoverished communities, less than 1 percent of families receive cash assistance from the government.[2] And 18 percent of cash-assistance families have an employed adult, while 36 percent are child-only cases with no adult recipient. In 2013 the maximum monthly benefit for a family of three ranged from $923 in Alaska to a meager

$170 in Mississippi, significantly below the federal poverty line of $1,674 per month for a family of three.[3]

In a real sense, we are already doing without a robust social welfare system in America. Since the end of the War on Poverty, the social safety net has continued to erode, a trend accelerated under the Reagan administration. The erosion of the safety net over the last three decades has meant that in times of economic crisis and expanded need, families are unable to access necessary temporary relief. It is also more difficult for families who have left the welfare rolls or have cycled in and out of employment to access assistance or maintain benefits because of cumbersome reporting requirements and guidelines that ultimately push them out of the system.

The devolution of welfare programs to the states under the Personal Responsibility and Work Opportunity Act of 1996, which overhauled Aid to Families with Dependent Children (AFDC), also had an adverse effect on families in poverty. In the beginning, welfare rolls plummeted to record lows, and former Temporary Assistance to Needy Families (TANF) recipients entered the workforce, but these shifts were only temporary. Many women lacked the education or training to move up the career ladder or had caretaking demands that made it difficult for them to maintain full-time jobs. A weak economy aided by the 2007 recession and increased competition for jobs also forced many more into poverty and back onto the welfare rolls.

With smaller welfare rolls, however, some states began to divert TANF funds to fill budget gaps. In fact, some states have used the flexibility of the block grant to redirect TANF funds to supplant existing state spending, plug holes in state budgets, or free up funds for purposes unrelated to low-income families or children. They have also diverted funds to program monitoring, evaluation, and drug testing for recipients.[4]

At the onset of welfare reform, 70 percent of TANF funds were being used for basic assistance to poor families. By 2011, only about 29 percent of TANF funds were being used to provide assistance to needy families, and nine states spent less than 15 percent. Overall, state control has done very little to reduce poverty or to create a pathway to prosperity for low-income families.[5]

To improve outcomes for families, we need to rebuild the social safety net and develop a new set of systems at the federal and state levels that might completely replace existing programs and service models. This requires reimagining not only so-called antipoverty policies such as TANF, but education, housing, health care, and crime and community development policies and initiatives as well.

Specifically, we should implement a tiered system[6] of support for families, from those in need of short-term assistance due to unemployment, illness, or other life circumstances to those with the most significant barriers to economic security. These programs should not be limited to single parents. Assistance should be available to families who meet eligibility requirements, regardless of familial status.

Tier 1 would provide temporary cash or support assistance to low-income families to meet specific short-term needs, such as fixing a car, preventing eviction, or helping with unexpected caretaking responsibilities that might disrupt employment. Tier 2 would focus on support to low-income women who are unemployed with limited skills or with minor barriers to economic security, such as the need for child care or transportation. As a condition of cash support, recipients with school-aged children would enroll in education or training programs, including high school completion or literacy programs, or obtain employment. Young mothers should be encouraged to complete high school or its equivalency before going to work. Tier 3 would provide cash assistance and support for low-income women and families who have multiple barriers to economic security, such as mental health or addiction issues, chronic health issues or heavy caretaking responsibilities, or who are otherwise unemployable.

The level of cash assistance for families should be standardized across the states, with a minimum floor established at the federal level using a formula based on a self-sufficiency standard and updated poverty measures.[7]

It is estimated that by the age of three, children born into low-income families hear roughly thirty million fewer words than their more affluent peers. By the time they enter preschool or kindergarten, the gap is often too wide to close and can have long-term effects on school achievement and success. In order to close this gap, we should integrate early literacy programs within the health care delivery system. As with campaigns that encourage breastfeeding or counter Sudden Infant Death Syndrome (SIDS), obstetricians, primary care physicians, and pediatricians should begin conversations with parents and primary caregivers, from the first prenatal visit onward, about the importance of language development and literacy to healthy child development. Pediatricians should also provide a recommended list of age-appropriate books and word lists for parents and caregivers. For parents with limited literacy skills, programs could be formed in communities to help them provide ongoing support to their children.

Poor and middle- and upper-class children attend schools that are worlds apart from one another with regard to resources, teacher quality, and conditions. The reasons for the disparities and inequities in schools are myriad, and there is not enough room here to go into them in great detail. To increase educational parity and equity in low-income neighborhoods and communities, more money and resources should be invested in schools as well as extracurricular activities and appropriate bridge opportunities. By bridge opportunities, I mean experiences outside homes and communities that are meant to expose students to the larger outside world and that penetrate the wall of geographic isolation.

Most fundamentally, school systems should place high-quality teachers with the proper skills and training in classrooms to work with children with multiple barriers to success. There should also be trained therapists and counselors within the school setting to offer one-on-one sessions with students. It goes without saying that the overreliance on harsh punitive measures and the criminal legal system within the school setting in Title 1 schools should end.[8]

In the United States, there are approximately 2.4 million inmates in state, federal, and private prisons, a figure significantly higher than in any other country—a half million more than in China, which has a population five times greater than that of the U.S. The United States holds 22 percent of the world's prison population, but only about 5 percent of the world's people. Poor people and racial and ethnic minorities are more likely to be incarcerated than affluent or middle-class people.[9] In 1991 more than half of all state prisoners reported an annual income of less than $10,000 prior to their arrest, and in 2002 more than six in ten were racial or ethnic minorities.[10]

To build a more equitable society and to increase opportunities for low-income and poor people, we should reduce arrest, incarceration, and sentencing for nonviolent or quality-of-life crimes. In this same vein, federal social welfare programs and education loan and grant programs should be prohibited from using prior felony convictions for nonviolent or quality-of-life crimes in determining eligibility for services and programs.

Lastly, the prosperity of the 1990s and early millennium missed most low-income and poor people. Between 1993 and 2008, the top 1 percent of families captured 52 percent of total income gains, while the income of families in the bottom percentile significantly declined.[11] And although the Gross Domestic Product (how the United States measures its economic well-being) has grown steadily over the last forty years and topped 14.5 trillion[12] in 2010, the poverty rate has not substantially decreased.

The new global economy, characterized by a heavy emphasis on highly skilled labor, technology, efficiency, and the protection of the corporate citizen, has meant the certain decline of wages and standard of living for the average American worker, and for poor people in particular. Today, individuals with less than a high school diploma earn 28 percent less than in 1979 and are more likely to be employed in low-wage occupations with few benefits and little to no job security.

In the U.S., there are approximately thirty million people employed in jobs paying less than $9.00 per hour—that's $18,000 per year and marks the federal poverty line for a family of four.[13] The majority of the people employed in low-wage jobs are women and racial and ethnic minorities. Shockingly, it is possible for an individual to work more than forty hours per week and still have to rely on public assistance to make ends meet. Therefore, any antipoverty policy rooted in the economic reality of our time will have to seriously contend with the problem of declining wages and the proliferation of lower-wage jobs in the labor market.

The most recent recession and its effect continue to hobble those living in poverty and the one-paycheck-away, fragile middle class. The disappearance of work due to outsourcing and technological advancements, and the domino effect created by job loss in one sector that prompts layoffs in related sectors, creates fierce competition for available jobs. In a sluggish economy, with high unemployment and job scarcity, low-income individuals, racial and ethnic minorities, and mothers disproportionately bear the brunt because they may have barriers to work that include the need for child care, lack of trans-portation, and inadequate training or education, among many others.[14]

We need to increase wages for low-wage workers and ensure that their jobs are quality positions, meaning that they have flexibility, benefits, protections, and opportunities for upward mobility. Increasing wages for workers who provide vital services to the public could pump more than $18 billion into local economies annually. It would also decrease the dependency on social welfare programs and services by essentially transferring a big chunk of the financial responsibility from the taxpayers to corporations.

In order to build a more equitable society, begin to alleviate poverty, and chip away at the damage done by historical and cumulative disadvantage, we will need to create more connected commu-nities throughout the country.

Connected communities[15] are those that provide the necessary preconditions for individuals and families to achieve full economic opportunity from early childhood on. Connected communities are characterized by high levels of civic engagement and participation; strong, vibrant community institutions, including hospitals and schools; social and political capital that allow community members and actors to mobilize quickly when there is a threat to the community or when they need to access necessary resources, information, or bridging opportunities; and lower rates of violence, incarceration, and arrests.

Economically, connected communities tend to have lower levels of unemployment, higher median earnings, and higher levels of home and small business ownership. All of the afore-mentioned elements converge like puzzle pieces to create the necessary conditions under which individual members are able to pursue opportuities and maximize their potential without worry, harm, or stress.

Across the United States, communities and neighborhoods of concentrated poverty are more likely to be disconnected, meaning that the conditions of the community are not conducive to success or the maximization of opportunity. Members are consistently preoccupied with securing the necessary preconditions to pursue opportunity, including quality education, safety, access to adequate health care, stable housing, and access to resources and critical information needed to negotiate complex social and political institutions. Individuals who are able to succeed under these conditions are likely to be perceived as extraordi-nary or exceptional.

In cities such as New York, it is not uncommon for rich and poor neighborhoods to be separated by mere blocks or a short subway ride—a difference often monumental in determining everything from the quality of children's education to the number of grocery stores and healthy food options available to residents.

In Philadelphia, I studied two neighborhoods only blocks apart and found that in West Philadelphia, a predominantly African-American community covering all land west of the Schuylkill River, bounded by City Line Avenue to the north and the SEPTA Media Line to the south, more than 70 percent of residents lived below the federal poverty line and 30 percent of families were headed by single mothers. In addition to poverty, the neighborhood faced a host of other challenges, including high rates of incarceration (10.0 prison admissions per one thousand adults), low graduation rates (only 40 percent of residents had graduated from high school), a median income ($14,792[16]) lower than the national average, and a housing foreclosure risk score of 87 out of 100.

Conversely, when I looked just a few blocks over, at the Society Hill and Washington Square neighborhoods of Philadelphia, a predominantly White community bounded by Walnut Street to the north and Lombard Street to the south, I saw a different world. Less than 7.3 percent of residents lived below the federal poverty line, and single mothers headed only 6 percent of families. The neighborhood also had lower rates of incarceration than West Philadelphia (0.02 prison admissions per one thousand adults), high education rates (more than 65 percent of residents with bachelor's degrees or higher), a median income ($57,689[17]) higher than the national average, and a housing foreclosure risk score of 0.03 out of 100.

In writing this book and reflecting on the strategies and policies necessary for ending inequality and poverty in America, I recognize that there is no magic bullet or single proposal that will win the day. Inequality has become embedded in most, if not all, of the institutions and systems that govern our society. The pain and the burden of these inequalities, however, are felt most by those with the least power, resources, and mobility in our society. Our strategies must be multifaceted and guided by our shared humanity.

Once I was asked by a student following a guest lecture at a top university, "Where are you going with this and what do you plan to do next?" By "this," he meant my work and research on poverty and inequality. He had a hard time wrapping his head around why, given my current position, I was so concerned with the plight of those who had less or who were impoverished. My response to him was, "This is it. Working to reconcile public perceptions of the poor and their lived reality with policy is what I believe I am supposed to be doing."

His question, though innocuous in nature, provoked an internal effort to recall the moment when I first became interested in the question of inequality in America and the impact of disparate conditions on life outcomes and chances. It was in 1994, while I was attending Howard University and enrolled in an introductory political science course. I was a psychology major at the time, and the course was an elective that fit into my schedule.

On most days, Ms. Gruski, the professor, delivered her lecture from the head of the class. And although she tried to incite lively discussions, the class was mostly silent and without opinion. When we reached the module on poverty, Ms. Gruski began to talk about Head Start as a government-funded initiative for poor inner-city children and food stamps as a social welfare program. My ears perked up, and I began to focus on the discussion as she explained in very plain terms why people were poor and needed anti-poverty programs. This was also around the time that the nation was in a deep and contentious debate about welfare reform, led by President Bill Clinton.

I was rocked to the core by our conversation. As a child, I was on the receiving end of both of those programs. I had been poor and hadn't known it until that moment. I was a part of the large group of impoverished individuals we were reading about, a group for whom we hypothesized about what was best. The discussion was abstract. We talked about the poor as "them" and "they," and as others. Sitting in the small desk toward the back of the classroom, I felt a mixture of embarrassment, shame, and invisibility.

Instead of retreating, however, I leaned into the conversation and the course. For the first time, I had the language—sexism, racism, classism—along with political theories to make sense of not only my childhood experiences, but those of the individuals in and outside my community. I also realized that my being in a college classroom was a near-herculean feat, given all of the systems—the criminal legal, education, and social welfare system, among others—that worked against me and the other kids from my old neighborhoods.

I considered myself fortunate, but in no way exceptional. There were many others who should have been sitting next to me in that classroom or in different ones in other cities or towns.

epilogue

Charli and Parker

A little more than six years ago, with the help of advanced reproductive technologies, I became a single mother, by choice, to a set of twins—Charli and Parker. A few years ago, I boarded a plane from New York City to California so that they could meet my mother, their grandmother, for the first time. During our visit, my mother spoke soberingly about the difficulty of raising two children on her own. She thought that, perhaps for the first time, I could empathize with how much she struggled to give my brother and me a good life, as she was certain I too was struggling to raise my children. She said to me, "Now you know how I felt way back then. It's hard ain't it?"

While I can relate to many of the challenges that come along with juggling work and other responsibilities as a single parent, I understand that because of my education, income, and social networks and the neighborhood I live in, my experience of raising children is much different from my mother's and those of the nearly ten million women who head households and are living in poverty with no clear pathway out.

My children are also living dramatically different lives from the one I lived as a child and those of the nearly seventeen million children who live in poverty in the U.S. Thankfully, they have never had to experience hunger, home-lessness, or direct or indirect violence, and they generally have their emotional and physical needs met on a daily basis. They also attend a high-performing and well-resourced public school in our community, where I volunteer my time regularly.

In a casual conversation with one of the teachers at their school, I learned about a homeless student who was having trouble focusing and concentrating in class. He, along with his siblings and mother, lived in one of the local shelters in the city. In kindergarten, he was already far behind and needed extra support, much more than the teacher could give.

The sharp contrast between the lives of my children and that of their classmate was palpable to me. He deserved the same chances, supports, and opportunities as my children, I believed. He was already slipping through the cracks of multiple systems. The question for me, and for all of us, is, How do we work to make sure that all children have what they need to be successful and to thrive? We are being dishonest when we say that the homeless child is as well positioned for success and opportunity as the middle- and upper-middle-class child.

Over the years, since I graduated from Howard University and then graduate school, I have worked continuously to learn about and decode the many institutions and systems that govern our society. It hasn't been easy or without its own racial and class complications. I have been discriminated against, been told in different ways, through both words and actions, that I did not belong, and taken several wrong turns along the way. Many times I felt as though I were swimming upstream. From the mundane—buying my first suit for a job interview—to the significant—purchasing my first home—these experiences have all been lessons in how society works and in how people and groups are rewarded for under-standing and playing by the rules.

My mother is still often unemployed, and after I went away to college she gave birth to another daughter, Jocey, now twenty-four years old, who recently completed Job Corps. After my mother spent more than a decade as a career bus

operator, a chronic hand injury forced her to quit. After seeing an advertisement on television and feeling the need to reboot, a few years ago she decided
to obtain a certificate in medical billing. Since obtaining her certificate, she has worked only sporadically, earning no more than $8.00 per hour.

After I left Las Vegas, my brother moved back to California to live with my uncle Monk and aunt Glo. He graduated from Woodrow Wilson Classical High School in Long Beach. After graduation, he struggled to find employment and worked a series of manual labor jobs. He is now married with five children and is a professional truck driver for UPS. He and my father have a solid relationship. My father is an active participant in the lives of my brother's children.

To write this book, I conducted interviews with many of the people in it, including Rachel, my brother, my mother, my father, and Aunt Glo. I also spoke to several of my teachers and others who figured prominently in the narrative. Some declined my offer to be interviewed. Here's what happened to some of the people I wrote about:

Rachel enrolled at Virginia State University in the fall of 1993 but returned home after the first semester of her second year because she could no longer afford the tuition. When she told me that she had gone back home, I was disappointed and angry. I did not understand why she hadn't fought harder to stay. When I interviewed her for the book, she confided to me that while enrolled at Virginia State, she believed it was only a matter of time before she would have to leave. When she began to have problems paying her tuition, she saw this as a sure sign that she did not belong there. Several months after going home, she found the financial aid check that had been sent by the school to her mother stuffed in the back of the bedroom dresser drawer. When Rachel confronted her about it, her mother brushed it off and said that she thought it was a bill. Rachel attempted to complete her education at a local community college when she returned to California, but never did. Instead, she fell in love with one of the boys from our neighborhood and had two children. Soon after the birth of their second child, her boyfriend was sent to prison. Today, she is employed as a certified nurse's assistant.

As for the kids who lived in my cul-de-sac and in my neighborhood:

Ishmael won a football scholarship to Villanova University and went on to study film at UCLA. He is now a film studies professor at Villanova, focused on social justice issues. Wardell, one of my first boyfriends and the other smart guy on our block, dropped out of high school and was just released from prison on assault charges and now lives in Texas. Papa, Wardell's brother, is a truck driver at UPS, a job that my brother helped him to get. The others in my neighborhood are still there, working and getting by the best way they know how. When I come home for a visit, they greet me with huge smiles and hugs and they all say, "We're so proud of you. You made it out." It's a homecoming every time.

One of the first things I did upon my arrival at Howard University was to find Clarence Lee, the dean who had awarded me the full merit scholarship. I wanted to thank him and let him know how much I appreciated what he had done for me. When we met and I expressed my gratitude to him, he looked puzzled and acted as if what he had done was no big deal. He did not know that he had changed the entire trajectory of my life.

After my sophomore year of college, I fell out of touch with Ms. Bowman, the woman who helped me gain entrance to Howard University and who had helped so many other students attend college. When my doctoral degree from the University of Maryland, College Park, was being conferred in the spring of 2006, I attempted to contact her to invite her to the graduation ceremony. When I did, I discovered she had passed away on January 4, 2005.

Shortly after I gave birth to the twins, my grandmother Josephine came to live with me in New York City. While I worked full-time at New

York University, she provided full-time child care and support for the twins. She lived with us for a little more than a year, after which she moved back home to California to care for her sister, who had fallen ill.

My grandmother Josephine, along with my teachers, and the countless others who helped me along the way, saved my life. And for that, I am forever grateful.

acknowledgments

Many people have contributed their time, efforts, and resources to making this book possible. I am deeply indebted to my literary agent, Marie Brown, who believed in me and my writing and research from the very beginning. I also owe a debt of gratitude to my editor, Elisabeth Dyssegaard, whose thoughtfulness, patience, and gentle prodding helped me to go deeper and to tell the best story possible.

Special thanks to my sister-friends and colleagues Joy Zarembka, Marta Elena Esquilin, Roz Lee, Sonya Shields, Aishah Shahidah Simmons, LaKeysha Hallmon, M. F. James, Courtney E. Martin, DJ Lynnee Denise, and Caroline Corwell for reading early versions of the book and serving as reflections as I attempted to tell our story in the most authentic and truest way possible. Thanks to my best friends and biggest cheerleaders Gina Charbonnet, LeAndre Fields, Lisa Rast, and Shauna Brown. In this lifetime, there is no substitute for this kind of love and generosity of spirit, intellect, and time.

A special thanks to Elizah Turner whose light and support filled my days and nights with laughter and calm. I would also like to thank Anne Mosle, vice president at the Aspen Institute, along with Mekaelia Davis, Sarah Haight, Marjorie Sims, and the Inaugural Class of Ascend Fellows. Specifically, I would like to thank Mario Smalls for providing critical feedback on an early draft and a listening ear in Wye, Maryland.

I would also like to thank my East Coast family, Yvette and Noel Coleman, Bertha and Shante Nails, and Kyree Pendarvis, who welcomed me as a young twenty-something into their suburban cul-de-sac and showered me with unconditional love and support.

This book would not have been possible if it were not for my time at Spelman College in Atlanta, Georgia, where I served as a visiting professor in the Department of Comparative Women's Studies. Makeba Dixon Hill and the Spelman College Museum of Fine Arts deserve a special thanks for allowing me to present the book as a part of its Signature BLACK BOX series for artists with works in progress. I would also like to thank Michaela Angela Davis for moderating the BLACK BOX. It was the most amazing and affirming experience. Thank you to Professor Opal Moore, who listened to me over breakfast at Highland Bakery and offered early critical advice that I took to heart as I wrote. Thanks to Dana Pride Jones and Holly Smith for their unwavering support and unconditional acceptance. I also met the most amazing young women while at Spelman, including Mary Welcome, Samanta Simpson, Kendall Evans, and Maura Chanz Washington, who challenged my thinking in so many ways and kept it real with me in every single class.

Thanks to Kiristen Camper, one of the strongest and brightest young women to ever cross my path. Without you, I would not have been able to write, teach, travel, and be the best mom that I could possibly be to Charli and Parker. You are the best big sister they could have ever asked for.

Thank you to the Southern Rural Black Women's Initiative (SRBWI) for allowing me the opportunity to write about and explore the lives of Black women in the rural south. Specifically, I would like to thank Oleta Fitzgerald, Shirley Sherrod, Natalie Collier, and Shirlett Stapleton.

I would like to thank my family and all of the people, including my teachers, mentors, and friends from my old neighborhoods, who helped me to become the professor, writer, mother, and social justice advocate I am today. I also want to thank LaToya Atkins for strolling down memory lane with me and bringing forth some of the hardest memories that I wrote about in the book. Her smile and her laughter remind me of home.

Lastly, I would like to thank my mother and my grandmother Melvina Mason. Without the two of them, there is no telling where I would be.

notes

origins

1. Martin Gilens, *Why America Hates Welfare* (Chicago: University of Chicago Press, 1999).
2. Linda Faye Williams, *The Constraints of Race* (University Park: Penn State University Press, 2003).
3. Ronald Reagan, "Radio Address to the Nation on Welfare Reform," February 15, 1986.
4. David Shipler, *The Working Poor: Invisible in America* (New York: Alfred A. Knopf, 2004).

what should be done?

1. Sarah Jarvis, "Shanesha Taylor Sentenced to 18 Years Probation," *The Arizona Republic*, May 15, 2015.
2. Megan Elliott, "Who's on Welfare? Cheatsheet" (website), June 6, 2015, http://www.cheatsheet.com/personal-finance/whos-on-welfare-9-shocking-stats-about-public-assistance.html/?a=viewall.
3. Gene Falk, "The Temporary Assistance to Needy Families (TANF) Block Grant: Responses to Frequently Asked Questions,"

Congressional Research Service, July 9, 2015, https://www.fas.org/sgp/crs/misc/RL32760.pdf.

4. Liz Schott, LaDonna Pavetti, and Ife Finch, "How States Have Spent Federal and State Funds under the TANF Block Grant," Center for Budget and Policy Priorities, August 8, 2012, http://www.cbpp.org//sites/default/files /atoms/files/8-7-12tanf.pdf.

5. Ibid.

6. The tiered system family assistance program was first proposed by economist Rebecca Blank in her groundbreaking book *It Takes a Nation: A New Agenda for Fighting Poverty*. In the book, Blank discusses the function of each tier, the fluidity between tiers, and the need for highly trained and specialized workers to implement the system at the local level.

7. Ibid.

8. Title I ("Title One"), a provision of the Elementary and Secondary Education Act, passed in 1965, is a program created by the U.S. Department of Education to distribute funding to schools and school districts with a high percentage of students from low-income families. Funding is distributed first to state educational agencies (SEAs), which then allocate funds to Local Educational Agencies (LEAs), which in turn dispense funds to public schools in need. Title I also helps

children from families that have immigrated to the United States and youth from intervention programs who are neglected or at risk of abuse. The act appropriates money for educational purposes for the next five fiscal years until it is reauthorized. In addition, Title I appropriates money to the education system for prevention of dropouts and the improvement of schools.

9. Tyjen Tsai and Paola Scommegna, "U.S. Has World's Highest Incarceration Rate," Population Reference Bureau, August 2012, accessed November 28, 2015, http://www.prb.org/Publications/Articles /2012/us-incarceration.aspx.
10. U.S. Department of Justice, Bureau of Justice Statistics, "Survey of State Prison Inmates, 1991," March 1993, NCJ-136949.
11. David Lynch, "Growing Income Gap May Leave US Vulnerable," Bloomberg Business, October 13, 2011, http://www.bloomberg .com/news/articles/2011-10-13/growing- income-divide-may-increase-u-s-vulnerability -to-financial-crises; based on 2010 analysis of Internal Revenue Service tax data by economist Emmanuel Saez of the University of California, Berkeley.
12. OECD library, accessed August 2015.
13. Lawrence Mischel, "The United States Leads in Low-Wage Work and the Lowest Wages

for Low-Wage Workers." Economic Policy Institute, September 4, 2014.

14. Peter Goodman, "Cuts to Childcare Subsidy Thwart Job Seekers," *New York Times*, May 23, 2010.

15. The idea and study of connected communities was developed in 2011, while the author worked with Rashid Shabazz and Shawn Dove at the Open Society Foundations and the Campaign for Black Male Achievement.

16. Per capita income for all Blacks, which amounts to an hourly wage of $7.70.

17. Per capital income for all Whites, which amounts to an hourly wage of $30.00.

Center Point Large Print

600 Brooks Road / PO Box 1
Thorndike, ME 04986-0001 USA

(207) 568-3717

US & Canada:
1 800 929-9108
www.centerpointlargeprint.com